WHO ARE YOU
TO SAY?

WHO ARE YOU TO SAY?

ESTABLISHING PASTORAL AUTHORITY IN MATTERS OF FAITH

DALE ROSENBERGER

BrazosPress

Grand Rapids, Michigan

Published by Brazos Press
a division of Baker Publishing Group
P.O. Box 6287, Grand Rapids, MI 49516-6287
www.brazospress.com

Printed in the United States of America

Library of Congress Cataloging-in-Publication Data
Rosenberger, Dale, 1954-
    Who are you to say? : establishing pastoral authority in matters of faith / Dale
      Rosenberger.
      p. cm.
    Includes bibliographical references.
    ISBN 1-58743-114-9 (pbk.)
      1. Pastoral theology. 2. Authority–Religious aspects–Christianity. I. Title.
    BV4011.3.R67 2005
    262'.8—dc22   2005011525

For current information about all releases from Brazos Press, visit our web site: http://www.brazospress.com

To my mother, Margaret, and my father, Burton,
who taught me to love words and to love the Word.

To my daughters, Greta and Lise,
whose embrace of the same means more than I can say.

CONTENTS

Part One

On Not Going Quietly to Our Room

1

NEVER BEEN TO A PLACE
LIKE THIS BEFORE

During a camping trip to the Canadian Rockies, our family visited a glacier north of Lake Louise. Never having before seen this massive wintry formation, we first stopped at the provincial park visitors' center to learn what a glacier is and does. Apart from the geological fun facts, we noticed several conspicuous urgent warnings. One, for example, told of the German tourist who had cavorted upon the glacier just months before, only to break through and lodge deep below in a crevasse. It was only minutes before he lost consciousness and perished of hypothermia. Amazingly, this was not a one-time accident but happened with some regularity—hence the strident warnings. Warily, with small children in tow, we left the visitors' center and sidled up to read a sign at the glacier's edge.

"You have never been to a place like this before," it began. "Nothing in your experience prepares you for what lies ahead. Here all of the usual rules are suspended. Here you cannot behave as in more familiar places. Everything ahead is completely different from what you know." Seldom are signs around us as obvious as that. Still, we were then stunned to see the majority of visitors blithely trotting upon the glacier with the nonchalance of a romp through the local shopping mall. Even as all signs scream for our attention and point to the contrary, we struggle to engage our surroundings as anything other than the everyday status

11

quo. Preferring a familiar world, we do not adapt readily to either the treachery or the opportunity of new settings.

This is the situation of Christians and the challenge of the church today. As Christians we face the *terra nova* of a landscape devoid of familiar features. The world looks icily toward things Christian. The rules have changed, but we are not certain how. We face new tests and threats. The wholesale climatic and tectonic shift in things spiritual forces us to rethink Christian discipleship and congregational life.

Still, we mostly plod along on the basis of who we once were and how we have always gotten by. Accustomed to striding confidently on the firm earth of an agreeable environment in which, with a clear role and a sure welcome, we are shocked when that terrain collapses, as it does more and more. Today in the affluent West, ours is a chilly and in many ways chilling environment in which to follow Jesus Christ. But God calls the church to step out into unfamiliar surroundings confident that the iciest regions and seasons will not resist the relentless warming blow of the Holy Spirit. Rather than complain about the weather, today our most creatively faithful response is to discern together which way the Spirit blows and proceed along with it, rather than working against it or going it alone. What's more, there is the promise of great adventure, renewal, and discovery in this.

On Not Going Quietly to Our Room

One autumn back in the nineties, I accompanied an adjunct professor to her department's welcoming picnic on Colorado's sun-drenched Front Range. It was a brilliant Saturday late afternoon, with grills hissing pleasantly and a festive air as the university gathered its leadership for the beginning of yet another academic year. Striking out on my own to meet new people, I introduced myself to the two women who happened to be enjoying their meal at the same picnic table.

Although I am an introvert by nature, being a pastor has trained me in the art of reaching out to others instead of waiting for them to approach me. So I socialized, asking appropriate questions in a measured, cordial manner, being interested without being too interested, following up where it was safe, and allowing space in our conversation. Things were proceeding amiably enough as I learned about their journey to that point in time. Having revealed a bit of these women's lives and stories, the conversation then turned toward me: "So who are you? And what do you do?"

"I am pastor of a church about thirty miles away." They exchanged looks of deep distaste and inquired again in mild disbelief, as though

12

they could hardly believe it. Spontaneously and unrehearsed, looking like they had ingested syrup of ipecac, they said in unison, "Ewwww. Yucchhh." They rose in unison and found another table, where their picnic dinner presumably enjoyed better digestion.

Granted, I have known many moments when being a pastor has provided me a royal road into the lives of strangers. And for the most part, in new social settings, people regard me with indifference or quaint curiosity. They see me as a kind of anachronism, as though to say, "My, isn't that touching?" or "Isn't that something different?" Still, these strained niceties cannot blunt the point that as Christians, we live in a world that increasingly does not know what to do with us. We live in a world where our presence is rebuffed even before we get to anything like witness in our deeds or testimony with our words.

The Christendom era of the Christian faith monitoring America's common life, or being the officially sanctioned spiritual shaper of society, is past. That latter part of Christendom known as modernity, beginning in the Enlightenment, is passing also. A new era is upon us. And we haven't quite yet figured out what that would look like, or what posture God would have us assume given such profound shifts in the landscape. What lies ahead might well be more like what the church faced in its first three hundred years than in the more than 1,600 that followed. What are the new options for the church in our acidly modern and encroachingly secular society? Where can we find social leverage and lift from above in our witness to the death and resurrection of Jesus Christ in a new epoch?

A Whole New World

Recently, I read a story about Teresa Becker of Traverse City, Michigan, losing her $2,750 state financial aid because she has decided to major in theology at Ave Maria College in Ypsilanti.[1] She is suing the state for her scholarship, claiming, in effect, that if she were a cultural anthropologist studying Santería in the Caribbean or an ethnologist studying shamanism among the Aucas of Ecuador, those funds would be forthcoming. And, of course, she is right about the artificiality with which these lines get drawn. Still, I don't know whether she will win her case. America is done doing us favors. And pining for those old days to come back is the equivalent of relegating ourselves to the past.

It is part of a continuous developing story. A few years ago the Supreme Court found that we clergy could not bless the commencement gatherings of public universities with Christian invocations, even if those schools were founded by the church. Recently, I heard from a pastor near Boston whose local health board threatens to ban all church potluck suppers because of the sanitary kitchen risks ascribed to places where nonprofessionals prepare food. Tomorrow it will be a medical center insisting that in light of HIPAA protections, clergy have no right to essential patient information, even if church family is the only "family" that some aged infirmed souls have left caring for them, even if the church long ago founded many of the very hospitals now boxing us out from caring for our own people.

Brian McLaren describes what is happening in stronger terms than these:

> It's no wonder that religion was scurrying in retreat in the modern era, fleeing the exterminating gas of modern science and secularism, like cockroaches from an apartment building. Perhaps religion could survive in the hidden corners of the private sector, but in the public sector it was seen by the scientific establishment as a dirty embarrassment, unsanitary, unwelcome, gauche.[2]

As Christians we live in a time and place constantly telling us, in ways both obvious and covert, "Who are you to say anything? Why should we listen to you as opposed to anyone else? How is what you are telling us more worthy of our attention or respect than any number of other groups? What gives you a right to speak more than any other?" Or, in other words, with a more formal tilt, *Wherein derives your authority?*

Until we answer this question among ourselves—Who are we to speak up about matters of eternal destiny?—we will be consigned to margins and relegated to ineffectuality. Christianity will be sadly reduced to another "lifestyle option" of no more significance than what Oprah, Montel Williams, or Dr. Phil are all about. Bowing to the enforced shallowness of a philistine popular culture, faithfulness on our part becomes a scant possibility, being remade in God's image is unimaginable, and transformation of this world along the lines of God's reign is a receding pipe dream.

"But That's a Value Judgment"

If you don't make a secret of your faith in God, you have likely found yourself in some circumstance where as a follower of Jesus Christ you were nonplussed and backpedaling in a way that perhaps would not have transpired fifty years ago. You were flummoxed by a mind-set whose rules and assumptions you had not anticipated, almost like the trumping of "no tags back" or "no bottle caps" we bantered in childhood games and playground negotiations. This querulous orientation purported to be evenhanded, establishing a level playing field and fairness for all. But beneath that presentation, you sensed only cool, aloof distance behind its tight, wan smile toward everything at the heart of your life as a child of God and a spiritual being. Let me illustrate this scenario.

I once played in a United States Tennis Association league. One of the particularly gifted singles players on our team was the editor of the local daily newspaper in our hometown of about 70,000 people. He was a young man, new to town, and already taking that daily press in new directions, showing us the wave of the future and all that. With no small hesitation, I entered a conversation with him about our respective lines of work. I experienced trepidation here for reasons that Chris Hedges describes as a person of faith working within one of the newsrooms that are actually relatively friendly toward matters of faith, the *New York Times:*

> Newsrooms are very uncomfortable with religion. They cover religion the way they cover India, because they have to, not because there's any deep understanding or even sympathy for issues of faith. . . . The way newsrooms cover religion is covering the institutions and the leaders of those institutions. They don't want to go near those fundamental, core questions that are the real news in human lives. What is it that people think about? It's bereavement, it's love, it's sin; it's violations that we have committed or have been committed against us. This is real news."[3]

Anyway, as a local church pastor, I chatted with that local editor about the newspaper's Saturday religion page. I bit my tongue and did not describe how I truly felt about it: the crumbs the print media throws toward houses of worship so the papers can maintain the image of community- and civic-mindedness. That page—like most Saturday religion pages—represents the tokenistic reporting on religion that makes faith seem wooden and artificial. It is often edited by someone with little religious training and dotted with the occasional ad for this church or that funeral parlor. Accordingly, some clergy call it the "tombstone page" because it is such a journalistic cemetery for a force and reality so vibrant and personal as God is within our lives. Anyway, we local clergy took turns writing a "Love Thy Neighbor" column on that page, and I coordinated the effort.

"I don't think we are going to be able to continue the clergy articles," said the new editor. "After all, given the separation of church and state, it is just not right. The simple fact is what you are writing about involves value judgments." Of course, the division that Thomas Jefferson installed between church and state has little to do with the freedom of the press.

The *New York Times*, to return to the above example, has no tombstone page but regularly has front-page and feature articles on how matters of faith are changing and how deeply they influence the world we live in. They do this because, as Chris Hedges reminds us, faith figures prominently in the lives of more individuals than society allows. The number of Americans who attend worship in a given month (just less than half of us) competes nicely with those of us who attend sporting events in a given year. You would never know this from popular culture.

Faith is an all-too-invisible shaper of our common life, it has been since time immemorial, and it always will be, despite ongoing predictions of the demise of religion. Frankly, this is news in a world where it is not reported elsewhere. At one time, each Monday the Columbus daily newspaper published on its front page the Sunday sermon by Dr. Washington Gladden, a pastoral predecessor in the downtown church I served in Columbus, Ohio. It is a whole new world.

"Wait a minute. Isn't that a value judgment?" Perhaps some charge like this has been levied at you. At that moment your accuser seized upon your comment with the "Eureka!" finality of Sherlock Holmes wagging his index finger before Mr. Watson, with all of the sanctimony of Ralph Nader testifying before a congressional subcommittee, with all of the scrutiny of a dermatologist studying questionable cells around a mole.

"Be careful. Now we are dealing in value judgments." No NFL referee blowing his whistle for all he is worth could hope for the utter and complete stoppage of play that follows this declarative statement. "Out of bounds. Disregard that part of the testimony. Strike that portion from the record. Someone made a value judgment! That is a clear violation of our shared public life. Person disqualified. Comment duly expunged. Whew, and to think that almost slipped by!"

This comment and others like it are the monarch and royal family of all ethical and religious conversation stoppers. They promenade freely and with regularity. Do we distractedly step back and make room, bowing and scraping obsequiously as they glide by? But what if this emperor isn't wearing any clothes? And if that is so, shouldn't somebody—namely we ourselves—speak up?

Never mind public and secular settings, we hear the same rejoinder in the church's own classrooms, meetings, and corridors as well. The subject could be mild or volatile—how to spend money the church didn't know it had or our still barely considered, gut reactions to same-sex unions and marriages. You dare to speak out from a place where your spiritual convictions are most deeply held, out of that precious reserve of the soul that has been shaped by the most formative texts and traditions of a faith shared across millennia and continents, out of that tender personal struggle to be faithful to God in Jesus Christ across the decades you have been alive.

"Wait a minute," someone volunteers after you have given that gathering something to think about. "Isn't that just one woman's opinion? We need to be objective here." Your prayerfully considered offering, ventured as everyone else played it safe and held their cards close to their chest, compressing oral and written traditions of following Jesus across countless generations of faith, was dismissed with the ease and deftness of Errol Flynn unbuttoning the Sheriff of Nottingham. You are sent packing before the gathering has a chance to respond.

And you are left scratching your head at how something so basic as questioning the rightness or wrongness of something—in the church, of all places—is now off-limits because of an obscure methodological/philosophical "ollie-ollie-in-free." I have seen this scenario unfold. Typically, the majority silently and solemnly nods as though Christian discipleship must bow to an unwritten social compact and ply itself in some hermetically sealed corner of reality that nowhere exists.

A Level Playing Field for All, Thank You Very Much

What is wrong with this picture? In the first place, life affords us no moment when we are not making value judgments. We rise in the morning to hear the news on Fox News as opposed to National Public Radio, and we make a value judgment. We have bacon and eggs as opposed to yogurt with wheat bran, and we make a value judgment. We decide to confront our child's recent misbehavior before dropping him off at school or instead to let it slide just this one time because he has lately been distraught, and we make a value judgment.

Why all of a sudden someone should punctuate a conversation with "But that's a value judgment!" seems no less than a calculated silencing of religion given that there is no moment when we are not making value judgments. Funny how the objection springs up when distinctions are made out of a passion for God but is almost never invoked when a passion for commerce, for sports, for national issues, or for the military is carrying the day. This is not a random or guileless pattern. "But that's a value judgment" often functions as an attempt to stop a person of moral or religious conviction from speaking without having the courage to stand up and own that, and without the animus and coherence to say how and why one disagrees. This free pass is a great advantage for an increasingly religion-indifferent or religion-hostile society in expunging matters of faith from wider public discourse. Finally, it is no coincidence that these secular free passes proliferate in a day when the old Christendom free passes are being taken away from people of faith.

In the second instance, by individualizing our remarks, by saying, "But that is just *your* opinion," we are in effect being told that our Christian witness is like having a nose: everybody has one, everybody is entitled to one, but so what? This, despite the fact that at its best our Christian witness does not arise out of us individually but issues from generations of faithful working out their salvation with fear and trembling in earnest conversation with revelation, scripture, tradition, and the Holy Spirit. As Christians, we are more essentially part of a community extending across space and time than we are individual spiritual Lone Rangers.

Christian witness is more encompassing than "one person's opinion." Not only does it dig deeply into soul and sinew, but it also spans distant worlds. It includes traditions and shading of traditions that recall past millennia of disciples and anticipates future centuries of believers who shall follow us. Our temporary stewardship of this sweeping and epic panorama of abiding and mysterious faithfulness insists that we not allow the uninformed to dismiss it as one more lifestyle, opinion, or point of view. Agreeing to anything less means that faith will lose its high-ceilinged grandeur and its tenacious power to transform the world. It means that a faith that has fed the starving, housed the homeless, eradicated cruelty, and taken in the orphan and widow will wither as one more nostrum in an already overcrowded marketplace of personal boutique options.

Also, by pretending that there is a place called "objective," which is neutral of self-interest and devoid of bias, society has often subtly tilted the playing field toward rules where the self-declared "objective" play best and are most likely to win. This is not to say that under certain circumstances striving for impartiality is unworthy or that balancing competing interests is completely unachievable. Rather, those who are confident that this can easily be accomplished by invoking a word like *objective* are merely stacking the deck in favor of the invoker. Such a flip *objective* should set sirens blaring in our ears and red lights flashing in our eyes.

Funny how I am always most "objective" when I know that the "facts" as I have construed them are going to make those headed in a different direction do an about-face and end up agreeing with me. Also, "objective" has a way of draining off the one thing that our most gripping faith conversations need to be vital, engaging, and significant: passion. To invoke "objectivity" is to make the matter less personal when it is by nature something personal.

Does the church have a problem with people caring too much and being too deeply invested in the gospel? Quite the opposite, at least in

18

the wing of the church where I live and serve. To insist that our conversations of faith remain "objective" is to inoculate against passionate involvement. It is like telling Louis Armstrong he needs to be little more restrained with his trumpet if he expects us to listen to his music. It is to miss the point entirely. Sadly, we in the church often comply, living within borders narrowed from without, and then wondering why the church is boring.

Where in the World Are We?

One essential matter that publicly finds little airtime is how invisible the claims of our Christian faith are in our democratic-capitalist consumer society. Our Sunday professions of faith find remarkably little traction in the face of economic, political, cultural, and ideological forces that rule our workaday world.

This trend of disenfranchising the formerly semiofficial status of Christianity in our society, the crumbling of what we call Christendom, will not reverse itself. The church that pines for the good old days of this arrangement and expects it to magically reassemble has consigned itself to putting Humpty Dumpty back together again. For his pieces will not be coming back together. Finding ourselves now in post-Christian and postmodern America, the era of the church's complacent indifference, that is, the era of trusting our semiofficial sanction in American society to assure us our place in the larger scheme of things, is over.

In a sense, even if they seem to threaten Christianity with a less hospitable environment, these changes are probably long overdue, given the nature of national founding documents and increasingly polyglot citizenry in the West. Moreover, these changes should not be lamented, inasmuch as the Christendom arrangement seriously compromised our sovereign prophetic voice anyway. This emerging new relationship—whatever it is—could give us the chance for a more faithful voice than rubber stamping whatever the current Western empire—Spanish, British, French, or American—happens to send for the church's blessing. As mentioned before, our situation and challenge might be more like that of the church in its first three centuries rather than in the subsequent sixteen.

What we have not established is our new posture, our new foothold, and our new platform from which to speak. What remains uncertain is our new relationship with a society that insists upon bracketing our witness to the truth or to consigning it to obscurity by privatizing it. Perhaps most remarkable is how the church has acquiesced to being relegated to the sidelines without a peep. We go so quietly, deferring to the great moat between sacred and secular, a chasm the Bible would nowhere endorse. How are the grand covenantal claims of baptism so casually dismissed as together we consider what life means and where we are headed?

Spiritual authority is one official-sounding and fairly intimidating way of describing these questions. As the church, we are the living body of Jesus Christ. How can we regain the voice with which Jesus fixed the attention of the world to the hill country of Judea? How can we inspire acts like the celebrated signs and wonders on the plains of Galilee? Before his ascension Jesus promised even greater signs and wonders arising from those who follow him. Has that promise exhausted itself? If not, where is it renewed? How can God reauthorize us in a day when we have lost our warrant in the eyes of many? These essential questions are beneath many other questions that we are asking.

As Protestants and Americans, born out of revolutions against authority, we suspect "authority" as little more than looming oppression. We hardly pause over it. It barely appears on our radar. Yet because we seldom mention authority, we never cease talking about it in hidden or indirect, and also more dishonest, ways. This book aims to make that conversation more explicit, to face the issues with greater candor, and to give these considerations some direction.

The self is our default authority setting. We hear this all of the time. We invoke it ourselves. "Nobody can tell me what to do" is the final court of appeal. *Newsweek* refers to the American approach to matters of faith as "cafeteria religion." Here we pick and choose faith based upon whims rather than the formative practices and traditions of faith communities across the centuries. And this arrangement is seldom explicitly questioned, no matter how ill equipped or self-indulgent or tyrannical our unchecked selves become. We typically decry the bitter fruits this produces—daytime talk shows of wild-eyed relatives screaming at one another in the name of entertainment—while refusing to examine the soil in which such misshapen and twisted roots grow.

We Could Have Seen This Coming

Today we harvest the bitter fruit of past centuries. In 313 A.D. Constantine dreamed of restoring the glory of the ancient Roman Empire in his own day, and Christianity was the means. Remember, as we degrade ends into mere means, and elevate means into ends, the gleeful laughter of the Evil One will resound. By this one stroke, moving from the most persecuted sect of the empire to its spiritual golden child within twenty years, Christianity was both established and compromised as

20

the spiritual backdrop of an imperial status quo offering little hope to a majority of the people.

For the empire did not so much take on the soul of the church as the church took on the sinews of the empire. We became an imperial church flexing imperial muscle in the name of a crucified Messiah. William Langland's epic poem *Piers Plowman* describes this, not to single out Roman Catholics, but to call all Christians on the carpet:

> When the kindness of Constantine
> gave Holy Church endowments,
> In lands and leases, lordships and servants,
> The Romans heard an angel cry
> on high above them,
> "This day *dos ecclesiae* has drunk venom
> And all who have Peter's power
> Are poisoned forever."[4]

How was this new relationship different from what preceded Constantine's Edict of Milan in 313? Listen to these words from one who strove mightily to balance the polity of the American empire without letting it overwhelm our most essential time-honored covenant in Jesus Christ. Dr. Martin Luther King Jr. reflects upon the church then and the church since.

> There was a time when the church was very powerful. It was during that period when the early Christians rejoiced when they were deemed worthy to suffer for what they believed. In those days the church was not merely a thermometer that recorded the ideas and principles of popular opinion; it was a thermostat that transformed the mores of society. Wherever the early Christians entered a town the power structure got disturbed and immediately sought to convict them for being "disturbers of the peace" and "outside agitators." But they went on with the conviction that they were a "colony of heaven," and had to obey God rather than man. They were small in number but big in commitment. They were too God-intoxicated to be "astronomically intimidated." They brought to an end such ancient evils as infanticide and gladiatorial contest. Things are different now. The contemporary church is often a weak, ineffectual voice with an uncertain sound. It is so often the arch-supporter of the status quo. Far from being disturbed by the presence of the church, the power structure of the average community is consoled by the church's silent and often vocal sanction of things as they are.[5]

Why are we as Christians so reluctant to acknowledge and evaluate these seismic shifts, let alone respond? Perhaps it is because we, like poor cousins, have become a little too enamored of living in the prosperous household of Western civilization. It is a house where the favor that once seemed to rest upon us for being Christian has reversed itself, to put it mildly. This manor where our standing seemed favored now casts dubious glances our way. Having been sent to a crumbling corner of this affluent and expanding imperial estate, we meekly acquiesce, fearing eviction. But the extremities of obscurity and irrelevance and indulgence to which we have been consigned might as well be eviction. They might be something much worse.

So what shall we do now that we can no longer locate and feel at home in the familiar household of our upbringing? What are our options? How does God see Christian discipleship and ministry in the future? That is what this book hopes to explore.

So far we have traced how dimly aware we are of the radical and permanent shift in the church's relationship to the world. We are like the parents who are so constantly close to our children that we cannot see them dramatically changed over time, even as it is obvious to everyone else. So far we have noted that the world no longer much cares what we as Christians think and for the most part wishes that we would go away or at least keep quiet. That we persist in something so archaic as faith in a God who cannot be proved and who will not conform to the world's bidding is clearly a nuisance to the majority perspective.

So far we have located the Christian faith in a thoroughly psychological world where no authority exists apart from the floating, disembodied self. The world resents as oppressive or superstitious the clear authority of living out of places that might be described with words like obedience to God, judgment before God's throne, or God's lordship over all things. So far we have affirmed that Christian faith and practice are something more majestic and expansive and mysterious than mere private opinion or point of view. This amnesiac world will not soon understand what it means to be part of a procession of light and hope from across space and time. So far we have insisted that allowing modernity's cool, self-interested reasonableness to drain the passion out of following Christ would be, in Paul the apostle's words, to "quench the Spirit" (1 Thess. 5:19). Faith in God and participation in God's reign is life's highest passion despite a popular culture that everywhere suggests that the orgasm is humankind's only shot at self-transcendence.

While it is necessary, there is also something bleary and burdensome about this trenchant critique of where the church is in the modern world. We have talked about what is dying, but we need to move simultaneously toward what is being born. For the whole truth is that if today is a difficult day to be a follower of Jesus Christ and to be the church, it is also a day full of the promise of new horizons. "The trouble with opportunity," as the anonymous saying has it, "is that it always comes disguised as hard work." We now have the hard work of turning over ground that has remained uncultivated for a long time. We would be faithless to neglect the matchless opportunity that now opens before us, one that has not existed for centuries. We now turn toward the light of that promise of the new thing that God is doing in the world, and how that breaks through in brief glimpses.

Persistent Rumors of Transcendence

Despite the unrelieved air of anxiety this displacement in our social status can cause us as people of faith, every so often this brave new world shakes, and the vitality and durability of confessing Christ is asserted in bold and encouraging ways. Or, to put this more baldly, if the suffocating godlessness of the atheistic Soviet gulag could not kill Christianity in its seventy years of officially mocking and banning it, perhaps our faith can wreak some vengeance of grace on the more subtle Western democratic-capitalistic version of paternalistically sneering and pushing us to the margins in the name of progress and facts and Enlightenment. And this could even be an enjoyable adventure of being the salt and yeast and light that Jesus wants us to be.

Surviving world wars and global depression, despite the gathering ascendance of doubt and the considerable erosion of the church's clout within Europe during his lifetime, C. S. Lewis clearly saw and maintained the basis of such truth claims in Jesus Christ. Beyond the syncretistic back-pedaling of today's liberal mainline churches and without the nasty fulminations of conservative fundamentalist churches, Lewis strikes an enduring, quietly authoritative note.

> I have explained why I have to believe that Jesus was (and is) God. . . . I believe it on His authority. Do not be scared by the word authority. Believing things on authority only means believing them because you have been told them by someone you think trustworthy. Ninety-nine per cent of the things you believe are believed on authority.[6]

Lewis is right. We cannot claim to be Christian without submitting ourselves to claims of authority. Like him, we might learn not to be undone by this and even to celebrate it. Søren Kierkegaard wrote: "And once again, Christianity's paradoxical difference from all other doctrines, from a scientific point of view, is that it posits: authority."[7] Further, Kierkegaard writes: "People try to persuade us that objections against Christianity spring from doubt. The objections against Christianity spring from insubordination, the dislike of obedience, rebellion against all authority. As a result, people have hitherto been beating the air in their struggle against objections, because they have fought intellectually with doubt instead of fighting morally with rebellion."[8]

Many are afraid even to talk about today's spiritual crisis in authority. Either we lack the concepts and vocabulary, or we dismiss matters of authority as inherently oppressive, in a fit of political curmudgeonliness very much like the people fond of putting "Question Authority" bumper stickers on their cars. (Is it all right to question the authority of people who put "Question Authority" bumper stickers on their cars?) Karl Barth, for one, was not afraid to talk about the absolute singularity of Christian revelation in contrast to the power and beauty of the human revelations:

> But starting from Christian faith we must say of these revelations that they are lacking in a final, simply binding authority. We may traverse this world of revelations, we may be illumined here, and convinced there and overpowered somewhere else, but they do not have the power of a first and last thing. . . . All these revelations are notoriously devoid of any final, binding force. . . . The earth is full of miracles and glory. . . . But these revelations of the earth and the earthly spirit lack the authority which might bind man conclusively. Man may pass through this world without being ultimately bound.[9]

> In each really Christian utterance there is something of an absoluteness such as cannot belong to any non-Christian language. The Church is not of the opinion, it does not have views, convictions, enthusiasms. It *believes* and *confesses;* that is, it speaks and acts on the basis of the message based on God himself in Christ. And that is why all Christian teaching is a fundamental and conclusive comfort and exhortation . . ."[10]

A New Voice, Strong and Clear

God is doing something in our lifetime that God has not done in the world for centuries, even millennia. How great is that? And God is now alive, and the Holy Spirit has been loosed upon the world in ways it has not been for many generations. How exciting is that? God promises to use our lives in this unfolding drama whether we know it or not. That is also what this book hopes to explore, presuming that we will do better charting a new road map into unknown territories rather than recoiling, becoming more ingrown, and doting on the past.

The Holy Spirit is being loosed in new ways. We cannot stand on the sidelines and long for the old, familiar arrangements just because these deep convulsive waves are as painful as any new birth, not if we expect to meet the challenges of our time like the generations of Christian faithful before us. Ours is the quest to discover what God is expecting of us in this new day. We must now ask questions that the church has not needed to pause over for nearly 1,700 years. If it is a scary time, it is also an exciting time to be Christian.

What will our new voice of faith sound like in this uncertain and dismissive context? A story can help us here.[11] Not so long ago, before their simple, attractive homes for the poor numbered in the hundreds of thousands, Habitat for Humanity was a small, fledgling movement. Founder Millard Fuller ventured forth to the West Coast on behalf of Habitat for the first time, seeking financial support and imagining new affiliates dotting the landscape. He was interviewed on a San Francisco radio station, followed by a call-in question-and-answer session. To be frank, things were going poorly.

Habitat for Humanity was so new, and the concept, despite its simplicity, was so radical, that the message was not getting through. The radio interviewer kept butchering the name "Habitat for Humanity." There were few listeners, and almost no one bothered to telephone the station. Those who did wondered aloud what in God's name Fuller was talking about. What kind of social agency are you? Why do you bother with those lazy poor? How much will this cost us in taxes? What is your purpose?

Fuller is a patient interpreter of Habitat's Christian mission to all manner of seekers and questioners. He is accustomed to having to answer the same questions and say the same things over and over. But frustration was growing, and his tone took on urgency as he struggled to articulate a dream so large as God's heart and so new as to be almost without precedent.

"The name of the organization is Habitat for Humanity," Fuller asserted into the microphone, "and we build simple, decent homes for God's people in need. Our purpose? That is simple. *We aim to eliminate poverty housing from the face of the earth.* After we finish that, well, I suppose we will have to move on and find something else to do." The lights on the radio switchboard lit up like Christmas, and incredulous listeners wondered how he dared to say such a preposterous thing. Having piqued both curiosity and imagination, Fuller had them exactly where he wanted them. Muddled anonymity gave way to creeping sensation. "You can't do that," callers intoned. "That's impossible." As one conversation led into another, Fuller turned the corner and was off to the races. Habitat for Humanity will finish its 200,000th home this year.

The key to finding and then lifting our voice in this brave new world will be remaining faithful to the life and example of our Lord. It will mean broadcasting joy instead of resentment, opportunity instead of disenfranchisement, vitality instead of weariness, hope instead of discouragement, irony instead of sullenness, anticipation instead of nostalgia, truthfulness instead of sentimentality, and compassion instead of hardness of heart. For in matters of spirit, be well advised: shrill does not mean strong, intransigent does not mean prophetic, and scolding has never won the church anything but more hecklers.

Back in the sixties, as civil rights demonstrators prepared to face fire hoses, clubs, and police dogs, they would typically spend hours praying and preaching and singing in the church before taking their stand. Knowing what they would face, hope and joy were palpable in those gatherings. Before engaging a world that is indifferent at best and hostile at worst toward things Christian, we do well also to begin our deliberations in worship. For only there can we remember who we are, and whose claim upon us is Alpha and Omega. Only there is every setback and loss bracketed by the final victory Jesus Christ won over darkness and death on the cross. Only there do we discover the strength, the calm, the equanimity, the fortitude, the kindness, the determination, and the passion that are God's gifts to his people in times of great need.

Glorifying God is our first, most essential, and most formative act in remembering who we are and in revealing who God would have us become. It is where the passion and the transformation begin. If we can get praising God right, then all the rest will follow. And so it is that we now turn to Christian worship, seeking to find the way that God now opens for us in a changed world.

2

THE PLACE JUST RIGHT

M y fellow students and I were but weeks into our first year of seminary. We decided to procure scarce tickets to hear Handel's *Messiah* by the Boston Symphony at Carnegie Hall in December 1976. It was not a simple, straightforward decision, at least not for me. My head was swimming with the vast learning of an entirely new field required of me as a Yale Divinity School student. Moreover, I was still discovering why God had led me there in the first place. I wanted to stay rooted in that place, not straying far until figuring out what God was now up to with my future. Too bad life is seldom so tidy as that.

Realistically, we didn't have time to attend, what with the concert falling squarely during our first final exams. We didn't have money to go, sinking ever deeper in debt for an Ivy League education in a calling not known for its salary. We had no reason to feel like we belonged in that storied hall, as was confirmed by distinguished personages seated around us. I, for one, didn't have clothes to go, as I made do with a tired corduroy suit left over from college. We went out anyway. And sometimes, of course, that makes all of the difference.

The concert was moving along well, outdistancing the wholehearted but homespun church-choir versions of *Messiah* that dominated my memory. Early in the concert, baritone John Shirley-Quirk stepped forward for one of his solos. Holding his musical score before him like a king holding an ermine cape, he stared down the sequined and white-scarved New York audience. He glared at us like my mother would when she caught us deliberately doing things that she had time and again expressly forbidden. It was a defiant, no-illusions, no-nonsense, let's-get-to-the-bottom-of-this-and-see-who-is-truly-in-charge glare.

Then John Shirley-Quirk's mouth opened, and his sonorous voice echoed Psalm 2: "Why do the nations rage so furiously together?" He relentlessly repeated it, over and over. He sang the first word of this question in scales, only adding to the emphasis. He sang it until we felt something like shame that none of us had a decent answer for the man. He was not singing as mere singer. He inhabited the higher voice of the divine conscience, not backing off an inch, every bit equal to the task. Dead serious, not stepping out of character for a moment, Mr. Shirley-Quirk was arraigning Western civilization, or so it seemed. It was as though God was finally able to ask modernity the questions that too long had been on God's mind. And who better to ask than the Manhattan powers that be?

"Why are you so warlike? Why can't you get along? Why do you mess up what I have created? Why do you go about your daily business as though I don't exist?"

The effect was unforgettable. Clearly this man was not to be trifled with. We seminarians began to laugh. This guy was taking on the whole empire at its heart. Being like most Westerners in that we answer only to ourselves, and let no one tell us what to do, we hadn't had such a dressing-down since we had outgrown our parents. Maybe we smiled because we knew we needed it and no one was left to give it to us anymore. Looking around, not only were we amused, other listeners were strangely delighted at his nerve in putting us in our place. Now for something completely different: putting *New Yorkers* in their place! What audacity.

"Why do the people imagine a vain thing?" he rounded out the solo. "The kings of the earth cry out, and the rulers take counsel together, against the Lord and his anointed." The solo ended. Huzzahs rose from all sides. What a triumph!

Patrons likely ventured to Carnegie Hall that evening imagining they would sit in judgment of the performance relative to their knowledge of the composition, their familiarity with its arrangement and performance, their personal taste and aesthetic cultivation. But much to our surprise, something pleasing and mysterious enveloped us. For a moment, the performance sat in judgment of us.

Finding Our Assigned Roles

What happened in this turnaround? Behind this beloved oratorio, John Shirley-Quirk put on the prophetic mantle and weighed our lives in the balance. He slipped into a time-honored transcendent leverage point before a modern people who had forgotten that such a vantage point once existed or could again.

Under the guise of art, he reminded us that human life is meant to be lived before God's watchful gaze. Alas, this vacuum does not much get filled any more in the prosperous contemporary West, where we pretend to be in charge of our own lives and no one can tell us what to do. Spiritually, is there any going back?

The church of Jesus Christ sorely needs something like this basic reversal. It would renew, strengthen, and remind us why God put us on the earth. And until this happens—this reversal of performer and audience at worship—it surely cannot occur in the world. We need nothing so much as to recover our own sense as creatures, and let God be who God is: our Savior and our Judge. For confusion here is deadly serious, inviting the wrath of a God who is infinitely patient with us, but who is not fooling around; a God who wants the best for us, but will not endlessly abide our proclivity for turning the best into the worst; the God whose signature on our souls is grace, but whose judgment is no idle rumor.

Should this reversal occur in the church, it might initially shock us. It would get noticed. But soon we might smile at being relieved of running the universe. We might even enjoy yielding to and trusting One who is equal to that charge. Stark exposure to God's eternal truth in Jesus would relieve us of living the lie that we are self-made, self-sufficient, and self-sustaining masters of the universe. My guess is that we have lost track how heavily burdened we are with expending all our attention and energy toward such grandiose dead-end lies; that after an initial sense of crashing, it would refresh us to nestle into our rightful place in God's vast scheme of things. It is the assurance of the old Quaker hymn: "And when we find ourselves in the place just right, 'twill be in the valley of love and delight."

God today calls us to speak out of the transcendent revelation point that Jesus once leveraged before a generation who has forgotten that this vantage point exists. But before others will hear us, before we can convince them of living life with the Lord as their primary audience, we ourselves will first have to attempt this feat.

The strange and wondrous world of prophetic dreams can materialize only as we trust that this realm is more real than TV talk shows, three-day weekends, and mall grazing, and only as we find ways to live it into

29

existence. Having glimpsed it, we must find imaginatively inviting ways, like the artistry of John Shirley-Quirk, to project these alternative worlds into existence. Where does such an encompassing and world-shaping spiritual undertaking begin? Only in one place, in abandoning ourselves by worshipping the true and living God, an act that cuts against the grain of our pragmatic, gain-minded, businesslike selves.

But Was It Good for You?

It is strange and painfully ironic how in the name of worshipping God we put ourselves at the center of all things and make ourselves the measure of all things. Did everybody "get something" out of worship? Was I "inspired"? Were my "needs met"? we ask. On the basis of self-referential questions, we decide whether or not worshipping God was successful or "meaningful." But the point of worship is pleasing *God*. Pleasing ourselves comes in a distant second here.

From a Christian perspective, pleasing ourselves is less straight ahead and more circuitous than beginning and ending with our own pleasure. It is more indirect, as Jesus hinted: "But strive first for the kingdom of God and his righteousness, and all these things will be given to you as well" (Matt. 6:33). The pleasure that borders upon deep, abiding joy derives from pleasing God or, perhaps better, "enjoying God," as one confession has it. Quite simply, worship could be very powerful, even intensely pleasurable, if we moved ourselves out of the way and allowed God the rightful place front and center. Frankly, it is a measure of our self-absorption that something so essential to worship as this hardly occurs to us.

How often do I see God's people enter church as though they were writing a spiritual Fodor's guide. "The hymns were fairly singable, the children's message was touching, the anthem was moderately inspiring, and the sermon contained some helpful tips. I would score it a 7.5 on a scale of 1 to 10."

When I was a pastor in downtown Columbus, the morning daily newspaper had a roving religious reporter who performed this evaluative function as if he were Roger Ebert. One morning we saw George Plagenz coming. We were expecting him because we sensed he would come sniffing around the new, young senior pastor (yours truly).

We also knew how disproportionately many points he awarded for greetings and introductions, preferring as he would the "friendly churches." So the deacons and I set Plagenz up. We greeted and introduced him in every direction until we had scored thousands more points than any church in the history of the exercise. The story was nationally syndicated. People from Vermont to Arizona sent us copies. My, but weren't we wonderful?

But who was observing whom? We each saw ourselves outfoxing the other, but both were wrong. In truth, God was morosely shaking his head watching Plagenz set himself up in a role as worship observer, critic, and definitive audience. As for all of us, it was Plagenz's place to gather himself unto God's people that he might make account before God to be renewed for witness and service. Anything less than this at any time and in any place is a caricature of worship.

At the same time, to be evenhanded, God was no less disappointed to see us take our strategic measures upon seeing Plagenz. After all, it was a distraction. His visit busied us with amassing points on the religion page to attract visitors into our splendid, near-empty, downtown Gothic cathedral. But God is the one audience that matters. And settling into distractions is to consign worship to the duplicity of trying to do two things at once, and doing neither well.

Notice the assumption here. It is near-universal among Christians in consumer-driven places. People come to worship to see how effectively the ministers and musicians will accommodate timeless spiritual truths (not necessarily the gospel) to their life situation. If it isn't doesn't make sense of recently jammed garbage disposals, children fearfully obsessing over tier-one colleges, branches obstructing satellite-dish reception, and whether the breadwinner's company is facing hostile takeovers, then what good is worshipping God?

Never mind that before the weight of eternity the gospel couldn't care less about satellite dishes and SATs. While taking ourselves far too seriously we correspondingly take God far too lightly—to the point of losing sight that God is the whole point. We miss the opening to be taken up into life itself, into the Lord God. The point is we gather as people of God to accommodate our lives to the gospel, not the other way around. If we cannot grasp this and live it, then worship has lost its fulcrum, and nothing remotely like transformation can occur.

Sadly, for us God is worth worshipping only because God brings power to effect our agendas and bring about our desired results. Jesus is worth worshipping only so long as his message is profound, interesting, or illuminating, not because all power on heaven and on earth is given him as the Christ. What is this but polite blasphemy?

It would never occur to us that the agendas we pursue and the questions we ask need nothing so much as to be taken apart before the Lord's watchful gaze. God promises to refashion us in the shape of God's reign, but only if we first allow God to take us apart, such as Jesus did with his dynamite charges called parables. But such a yielding is one huge, vulnerable leap of faith, and we do not seek such utter dependence on

31

God. We have not cultivated such trust, receptivity, and patience. Our faith is more lifestyle than way of life, never mind anything approaching the very ground of our being.

The psalmist inveighed against this "vain thing" that the "people imagine": that we dictate the terms of life and faith to God; that it is God's place to build his reign of justice and grace on the foundations where we have begun; that we ask the questions and God gives the answers; that God is the performer (with a pastor, liturgist, or choir as the divine stand-ins) and the people are the audience.

My former teacher, the late Robert Clyde Johnson, describes why these tables need to be turned.

> Kierkegaard insisted that the distinctive mark of modern man is arrogance in the face of God. In his ironic way, he remarked that this has almost tempted God to feel uncertain about himself, like a king who waits anxiously to learn whether the Constitutional Assembly will make him an absolute or limited monarch. . . . Most of us are seldom openly arrogant toward God. But when Jesus redefined the dimensions of God's will for us, it immediately becomes apparent that hidden arrogance . . . is our most characteristic response to him.[1]

We consider worship so early in this treatment of spiritual authority because praising and glorifying God is the most essential thing that we Christians do. Worship outwardly demonstrates how primary the issues of spiritual authority are. For worship represents the central opportunity to come into right relationship with God and one another. Worship explicitly establishes the terms for all else that follows and implicitly sets the tone and searches our motives for doing it. As my thoughtful friend and fellow pastor Dr. Allen Hilton has written, "In worship, we bow, not before the idol of the self, but before the God who created and redeemed and sustains us. In worship, we acknowledge our status as subordinates in the universe—fearfully and wondrously made—a little lower than the angels, made in the image of God, certainly, all of these. But not God. . . . In that moment we also confess our creatureliness and our deep need for a larger and better Other. And in worship that need is answered by the compassionate voice of that Other, which rings out proclaiming forgiveness and reconciliation."[2]

Worship is the beginning point and the endpoint for the ministry of the church of Jesus Christ. Worship is our joy and our center, our life and our substance. If our practice of worship is warped, if we gather to adore God but remain stuck on ourselves, nothing can turn out well. And we might also find ourselves uncomfortable in other environments where glorifying God is the first and final agenda, places such as that eternity in heaven where God dwells. This is why we could not begin considering authority anywhere other than in worship.

And Now for Something Completely Different

This familiar but deeply flawed reversal of performer and audience is not new. Over a century ago the Danish thinker Søren Kierkegaard saw our proclivity for getting our worship relationship with God exactly backward. He described our tendency to see worship as a performance where God is prompter, the minister is performer, and the congregation is audience.[3] He did not deny that worship is a performance but affirmed that true worship is where the minister prompts, the congregation performs, and God watches it all. So the question is not how *we* feel as worship concludes. The question is how *God* feels as we close and whether that alters how we live as we go back into the world.

Bill Moyers once interviewed Julie Taymor, director of the movie *Frida*. She described a visit to Bali many years before, when she was a young artist. She once found herself alone in a secluded wood at the edge of a clearing, listening to the distant music of indigenous celebrations. Suddenly, a few dozen men came into the clearing dressed in the full splendor of warrior costumes and each carrying a spear. They started to dance, and Taymor, invisible within the thicket of trees and their shadows, observed them at length.

> And they danced to nobody. . . . They were performing for God. . . . They did not care if someone was paying for tickets, writing reviews. They did not care if an audience was watching. They did it from the inside to the outside and from the outside to the in. And that profoundly moved me then.[4]

Before we dismiss such an epiphany as thoroughgoing paganism in that they were not worshipping the one true Christian God, we might first consider how we profane Christian worship as a performance meant for consumer-onlookers instead of for God.

We have a hard time loving God in terms as absolute as Father, Son, and Holy Ghost or as Creator, Redeemer, and Sustainer. We much prefer the God who is Buddy, Consultant, and Enabler. Give us the God who is Personal Assistant or Lifestyle Guru, and we *might* make room for this God as we face intractable problems or deep crisis, at least until trouble recedes so that we can return to running the world our way again. We cycle back and forth this way with uncertainty like spoiled-child CEOs surprised to inherit all of creation like a large corporation that fell into

33

our lap. But without any polestar by which to find our bearings, we lack a real plan for the future, making it up as we go along.

Who's on First?

Funny thing . . . time was when the Christian church welcomed people who didn't come to worship expecting truth to be accommodated to their preferences and whims. No, the people who came to worship granted that the gospel was truth, and they expected they would have to accommodate themselves to it. They did not come so much to evaluate as to be evaluated before the true and living God. They did not come expecting God to make sense in their terms but came in the hope of making sense of their lives in scriptural terms.

They didn't come expecting their self-interest to reign supreme at the center of everything. Instead, they came seeking insight into God's interests, God's feelings, God's will—strange as they are—to enter into a more godly way of living. Christians even have a word for the transformation that occurs within us from living out of such a posture. The word has fallen into disuse in many mainstream churches. It is *conversion,* a good word sorely in need of a comeback.

These days our problem is that conversion runs in the wrong direction. For the world is not gaining the soul of the gospel; the church is taking on the soul of the world. We come to church to accommodate the gospel to what the world has defined as real, alive, and possible. We come to adapt the gospel to the status quo of personal utopias for how we want things. Not surprisingly, these utopias usually place the accent on our glory, not God's. This is relevance from below, and that is the altar where we worship. We fear most being called irrelevant. Suddenly, we wouldn't feel quite so young anymore. But true relevance is when the church of Jesus Christ extends itself outward to meet all people in all manner of circumstances, but on the gospel's terms, not the world's. This is how Paul, Peter, Barnabas, and the rest met, engaged, and ultimately conquered the world in the opening chapters of the book of Acts.

True relevance from above doesn't worry whether our words and deeds immediately make sense to the world. It offers an alternative sense and order from another realm and lets that good seed fall on the variety of soils as it naturally will. True relevance is more focused on changing lives in light of the gospel's stunning assertions. It offers the high-ceilinged existence of a God whose ways are higher than ours. True relevance is more about redefining the world with truth-telling and transformation than caressing it with spiritual distraction and entertainment. It will not rest with mollifying human misery but remakes lives in the shape

34

of Good Friday and Easter, where human suffering is vindicated and even triumphant.

It is only this relevance from above that engenders true conversion and can bring lasting transformation. And, paradoxically, worshipping God in the spirit and truth of letting God be our beginning point rather than making ourselves the measure of all things, of letting God dictate the terms of faith rather than deciding what the pastor should say before she or he gets there and opens the Bible, will meet our needs in unexpected ways. For here God will surface our deep core needs that we never knew existed, allowing our distracting, bogus, narcissistic needs to fall to the floor and be swept away with the leftover orders of worship.

Listen to a confessional story of personal transformation as the Reverend John McFadden, one of our strongest and brightest pastors, talks about early attempts to grasp the authority of God and the church. Listen and detect here reversals of Shirley-Quirkian proportions. This one comes from the ideological left, but it could have just as easily come from the right.

Raised nominally Roman Catholic, I lost the church completely before rediscovering it during the heady days of the anti-war movement, keeping company with Berrigan-style radical priests and earnest Quaker activists. Local churches were where we staged pot-luck suppers before climbing into buses to visit imprisoned conscientious objectors. Local churches were the buildings whose former coal bins had been converted into coffee houses, where we listened to Dylan and Guthrie with little thought for the congregations whose hospitality we enjoyed. The Minister was the poor soul who had to keep the church members upstairs happy while we pursued God's real agenda of Peace and Love in the church basement; the ministry of reconciliation expressed as shuttle diplomacy.

Remarkably, I identified sufficiently with the role of reconciler to enroll in theology school. (Having the draft board breathing down my neck provided additional incentive.) My noble goal, like that of many of my peers, was to radicalize the church into "relevance." When Rosemary Reuther was asked why she remained within a church that she clearly detested, she snapped back "Because that's where the copying machines are!" It made perfect sense to me at the time. We dutifully sat through classes in theology and church history, *but it never occurred to us that the authentic agenda of the church was far more radical than the one we sought to impose upon it.*

Within my own congregation I assumed the pastoral role for which I had been prepared. I was the great facilitator, the friendly accommodationist, the resident psychotherapist. I preached thoughtful sermons on social concerns and the quest for self-actualization. My weddings reflected the beliefs (or lack of same) held by the couple; my funerals celebrated human achievement rather than God's grace and glory. I attempted to exemplify

35

the word that most thoroughly defined what I understood to be the vocation of pastor in that time and place; I attempted to be Helpful.[5]

Do We Desire to Be the People of God?

Historically, the biblical account reminds us that God's preference and first line of approach is that we should willingly turn back to God based upon the truth of who God is and who we are. It is called repentance, and we do well on a steady diet of it, given our incapacity for keeping clear our assigned roles of Creator and creature. God has sent spokespersons called prophets, who periodically emerge, even in places like Carnegie Hall or post-Vietnam pulpits, to help us here. They grind our golden calves to dust and speak a message that no sane person would dare bring to us for fear of rejection.

The message is dangerously combustible, but when we come down to it, we can only wonder why that should be. For the message is that all God really wants is what is God's own. This is what Jesus teaches with the parable of the tenants and the vineyard (Luke 20:9–16). Jesus tells it in such a way that it compresses the history of God's relationship with Israel and culminates in what is about to happen to him.

A vineyard is planted and leased to tenants while the owner is at a distance for a time. The owner sends servants to collect the fruits of his investment, first one, then a second, finally a third. In turn, each is beaten, mocked, and chased home. The owner ups the ante, not by coming down harder upon these malcontents and ingrates, but by sending an ever more precious emissary, his son. "Surely they will see my intention in sending flesh of my flesh and will respect him," the owner reasons. But sin doesn't reason with this heart, it blindly grasps and clutches. The tenants perceive only the expedience of killing the son, heir to the vineyard, to inherit it themselves. Instead they inherit the whirlwind of the owner's wrath. Notice here that God is asking for nothing extraordinary, only what is due.

Maybe the controversy begins and the conflict emerges in that we want to have our cake and eat it too. We want to be God's own and also to elevate our rank amid what God has made. We not only want to be "like God," but also want to *be* God, as the serpent put it so delicately to Eve. Because God is holy and true, God cannot participate in such a lie. We become rebellious and self-centered, almost without noticing it. God is purity and light, wanting the best for us but unable to play along with deadly delusions. Something has to give.

So God sends prophets to remind us of these arrangements. The word of the prophets is our foremost opportunity to get back on the proper footing. Through the biblical narrative, as we turn a deaf ear to God's prophets, God has not been above sending earthquakes, plagues, great fish, blindness, and other attention-getters.

Worshipping God in Spirit and in Truth

So what would a present-day John Shirley-Quirk look like were he—or she—to arrive on Sunday morning before us at worship? How would the Carnegie Hall reversal appear within our sanctuaries? One trademark would be a messenger who places truthfulness as God construes it unflinchingly ahead of our cherished Western sentimentalities around nation, family, self, and sacrifice. Substituting such feel-good sentimentality for the way, the truth, and the life in Christ is choking the church and filling us up with empty things. But let me here offer a positive and tangible example of experiencing such a reversal.

Back in the mists of history, the man who preached at my ordination was historian and Martin Luther scholar Roland Bainton. A diminutive man, he was patron saint of Yale Divinity School. He looked for new students to spend time with over meals in the refectory. He invited groups of us up to his cottage on the Housatonic River to share simple suppers and galley proofs of his next book.

Even in his eighties, Mr. Bainton rode his bicycle up the steep hill of Prospect Street. He claimed to have the lowest gear in New Haven. His gloves never matched, because he would spot nearly new lost gloves in the gutter and adopt them like orphans. He was of a mettle and at an age where he was not shy to tell the world of its usurpation of God's role and its profane unwillingness to serve in Christlike ways. Aside from how distinguished Mr. Bainton was, he was mostly able to carry this off because he modeled exactly the opposite.

I shall never forget a sermon he preached late in the 1970s, at the height of cold war tensions. Mr. Bainton was in effect advocating a step that our president and Mr. Putin of Russia have discussed but abandoned: the elimination of nuclear weaponry. Except that advancing this notion twenty-five years ago was like swimming upstream against the current of a hopelessly polluted river.

I don't remember the text Mr. Bainton preached upon that morning. I do remember being moved at his deep and palpable pain at humankind's arrogance in flirting with the prospect of destroying what God had created. I do remember his slow, still rage at our defiance of God's authority, when we already knew it was patently wrong.

To close the sermon, this fragile, tender pacifist of a man backed away from the pulpit, eyeballed us like a bunch of schoolchildren found out of control at recess, and muttered under his breath, walking away from the pulpit, "I have no idea why God has not already wiped out the whole bloody lot of us." He sat down and it was a long moment before anyone in the chapel dared to breathe. Not one person stirred. We moderns seldom find ourselves on this holy ground.

If we had come to chapel that morning for a helpful pick-me-up, a few strategic keys to success, or a gauzy affirmation of the human spirit—all of the things George Plagenz was seeking, all of the things we are encouraged to seek in worship—we had come to the wrong place, and would have been disappointed. But it was a rare chance to move from the corruption of being co-opted by the world's sense of what is pleasing, and to be thrown into the faith-filled dilemma of what is most pleasing to God. While this is always a great personal risk, in our day the greater looming spiritual risk from every side is that something like this rarely happens anymore. Of course, it should not be the weekly diet of worship. But that it almost never happens speaks volumes about where God ranks in the pantheon of powers and principalities.

"Why do the nations rage so furiously together? Why do the people imagine a vain thing? The kings of the earth cry out, and the rulers take counsel together, against the Lord and his anointed."[6] Bainton turned the tables. We were humbled.

But rare is the local church with a pastor/scholar with the heart of a lion and the soul of a lamb who speaks eight languages like Roland Bainton, waiting in the wings to take us apart and put us back together again in God's image. Still, bringing about the desperately needed reversal between the audience and the performer in worship is finally not about academic degrees, technical expertise, and social gravitas. It is more about unflinching truthfulness, a heart for others like Jesus weeping over Jerusalem, and the willingness to become vulnerable in brave ways that no one much attempts any more because the church makes so little room for it. Most anyone whom God taps on the shoulder for this work can accomplish it. That is, God can and will raise up these prophets if the church will set aside our worldly categories of maintaining control, protecting the status quo, and not rocking the boat by instead taking the occasional risk that the Holy Spirit invites. Again, a telling example is worth more than a score of hope-filled words.

When I was in divinity school, I was a student intern for two years at the First Congregational Church of Branford, Connecticut. One year, Youth Sunday approached, bringing with it the usual mix of dread at some theological travesty and hope for something fresh in a church dating back to 1644. Back then, the man among men within the high school youth group was Drew. They adored him and he occupied a central place within their circle. But Drew was mildly mentally disabled.

38

And I was shocked to learn that his peers had chosen Drew to preach on Youth Sunday. Isn't that the wrong person in the wrong place? I wondered. How could they do this? This is unfair! How very unseemly and what a mistake!

I gathered myself into the pew with no little trepidation. The time for the sermon came, and Drew mounted the pulpit, shaking but also smiling. His peers quietly rooted him on. His sermon was written with pencil in large letters on loose-leaf paper. It was very quiet in the sanctuary, as we wondered what this moment might bring. Drew stammered a bit and had trouble getting the words out. As he tried to get his preaching legs, he fiddled a bit too much with his papers and, horror of horrors, dropped them in front of the pulpit. Everyone was silently mortified, using all of our body English in the pews for Drew to snag his papers from the air before they fell to the floor. He lunged twice and missed, mimicking my own stress dreams about preaching. Sheepishly, Drew scampered down to gather up his papers, and back up the pulpit like a furtive squirrel with winter acorns, ascending his tree again.

This sermon had become a homiletic white-knuckle run. What was next? we feared. Some were eyeballing the exits. But then Drew made one of the all-time great preaching comebacks. He said that he had a poem. He knew it wasn't a religious poem, but it meant a lot to him. Drew recited the words from the song "I'm Free," from the rock opera *Tommy,* by the Who. "I'm free. I'm free. And freedom tastes of reality." Then Drew put away his papers and told us he was free from worrying about what others might think about him. He was free to be without anxiety or fear. He was free to be glad to be alive. The only reason he was free was Jesus. He descended the pulpit into the arms of his congratulating friends, who had never doubted his gifts. After begrudging Drew that pulpit, I realized that I would never preach so eloquently. I have chewed on Drew's simple faith proclamation for three decades now. I doubt that any have lingered so long after any sermon that I have ever preached.

Notice what happened here. I was likely not the only one sitting in the pews wondering what manner of abuse the pulpit and the institution of preaching might suffer from not only a layperson, but a mere boy, and a mentally disabled one at that. What was this but the usual people as audience for the "God show"? But Drew pulled back the curtain and allowed us in for a moment to share with us how he was living his life before God. Drew had it right, and we did not. And he reminded us that despite our flaws we were all performing together for God—even in that very moment—and that is ultimately the decisive thing. The tears that congregation cried were not merely the sentimental ones for a favorite son doing well. They were humbling tears of being gently but firmly put in our place by an angel of God.

Still again, sometimes evoking this reversal in worship between performer and audience is not so much a function of worship leader as it is opportunity and circumstance. At the hour when the terrorists slammed into the World Trade Center, I was boarding a flight from Chicago to New York. After hustling a rental car and driving home all night, not much more than an hour north of where the towers fell, people were reeling to recover. A half-dozen families in our Connecticut town lost loved ones in that murderous act. We felt the world coming down around our ears.

Shortly thereafter, I sat with the head of our deacons, and we decided our strongest and best and most necessary move was to praise God and affirm heaven's goodness amid the chaos here below. When in doubt, praise God; you will never go wrong. We quickly sketched out a service of psalms, prayers, hymns, scripture, poems, prophetic readings, and a symbolic act of mourning modeled after what was spontaneously emerging down at Ground Zero in Manhattan.

From that weekday morning to that night, we went from no plans for worship to over four hundred shaken and aching souls, many of whom had never set foot in church, hanging on every word and song. Of course, this was in no way unique to where I live; something very much like this likely happened where you live. But notice what was most amazing about these all too common gatherings: how eager and glad everyone was for a locus of authority, dominion, and universality—God reconciling the world in Jesus Christ—from beyond our personal ego and self, from beyond our sentimental notions about human nature and intentions, from beyond our shallow, sketchy outlines for personal utopias.

Innately, in those moments we knew to summon a higher authority than the devices and desires of our own hearts, the politics of East and West, and the culture wars of conservative and liberal. I cannot tell you what relief I saw in those lost and groping faces to know that not everything is up to fumbling humankind, to heedless humankind, to violent humankind. But that in all circumstances we are held in the embrace of a God whose hands are steady and whose gaze misses nothing.

The Letter to the Hebrews (12:26–28a) tells of God sometimes shaking the world so that we can see what cannot be shaken. "'Yet once more I will shake not only the earth but also the heaven.' This phrase, 'yet once more,' indicates the removal of what is shaken—that is, created things—so that what cannot be shaken may remain. Therefore, since we are receiving a kingdom that cannot be shaken, let us give thanks." Perhaps it is not the assertion of God's authority that we would choose, requiring such upheaval, crisis, and loss. But God is resourceful enough to work through whatever God must to reveal and release God's dying

40

and rising truth in Jesus Christ to make us as free as Drew invited us. As the church, we might be light on our feet and ready as people are suddenly grateful to rediscover the extended nexus of ultimate related-ness awaiting us. As the liquid, fiery core of human existence repeatedly erupts through the shallow crust of polite society, we shall have more opportunities.

Authority in Doxology

All of this about reversing the roles of Creator and creature seems so basic as to be not worth saying. But in a consumer land that trades in amusement, people enter worship like approaching Carnegie Hall, to be entertained. Although it might read a little long to serve as our doxology on a weekly basis, we would do well to proclaim texts like this Easter Sunday lection that typically gets elbowed out in favor of the anticipated narrative of Jesus's resurrection. If we would sing it every week, even to pause and read it, this would remind us that the church is more than "where the copying machines are."

> God has rescued us from the power of darkness and transferred us into
>   the kingdom of his beloved Son, in whom we have redemption, the
>   forgiveness of sins.
> He is the image of the invisible God, the firstborn of all creation;
> for in him all things in heaven and on earth were created, things visible
>   and invisible, whether thrones or dominions or rulers or powers
> —all things have been created through him and for him.
> He himself is before all things, and in him all things hold together.
> He is the head of the body, the church; he is the beginning, the firstborn
>   from the dead, so that he might come to have first place in every-
>   thing.
> For in him all the fullness of God was pleased to dwell,
> and through him God was pleased to reconcile to himself all things,
> whether on earth or in heaven, by making peace through the blood of
>   his cross.
> And you who were once estranged and hostile in mind, doing evil deeds,
> he has now reconciled in his fleshly body through death, so as to pres-
>   ent you holy and blameless and irreproachable before him—pro-
>   vided that you continue securely established and steadfast in the
>   faith, without shifting from the hope promised by the gospel that
>   you heard, which has been proclaimed to every creature under
>   heaven.
>
> (Colossians 1:13–23)

41

Like the scriptural verses sung by John Shirley-Quirk during Handel's *Messiah*, and like the psalm from which they were drawn, this text was also originally a hymn. We do well to pause over words like these: "(Jesus) himself is before all things, and in him all things hold together." It is a hymn celebrating God's freedom, and the power for good that God exercises in our behalf, moving in designs that we only partly grasp, which is why bowing before them is so vital.

The point is not that we should understand God's holy purposes before responding and obeying. Where is the faith in that? The point is that these designs we only partly grasp have already fully grasped us, whether we acknowledge them or not, whether we receive their benefits or not. We know that we creatures are in right relation to the Creator when we take God's freedom even more seriously than our own freedom, when we take what God understands more seriously than what we understand. This hymn is a lyrical example of that.

Perhaps this message must be set to music, veiled in humor, cast in poetry, or otherwise cloaked with the subtleties and indirection of art in order to be heard. For we do not easily and without resistance hear that God is in charge—not the nations, their institutions, their emissaries, and all that they deem relevant. Jesus Christ and no other is heaven's divine Archimedean point, the fulcrum to the universe, in whom all things lasting begin, end, and hold together.

Discipleship: Lifestyle or Life Itself?

The first thing that must be said here is that in light of the birth and ministry, life and death, resurrection and ascension of Jesus Christ, everything human must be reviewed. And it will be found wanting. Paul was telling Colossae that what God is doing in Jesus Christ has forever changed the course of how things are. The proportions of the coming changes are not merely for the town and region, nation and empire. The proportions of these transformations are cosmic. Like the chorus we lifted that December night, it's about "King of Kings, Lord of Lords."

Serving God is not about making sense of the Christian faith in terms that appeal to the powers that be so that the church can be tolerated as culturally significant. Serving God is not about dressing up and disguising the gospel with contemporary language that squares nicely with the best available judgments of civilized Westernism. Serving God is about making sense of the nations and powers in terms that only the gospel creates. Serving God is about rewriting other ways of speaking and thinking until they begin to align with sweeping change as suggested in words like *sin*, *salvation*, *vocation*, and *witness*.

The feeling-tone of the church of Jesus Christ gathered in community, especially at worship, can indicate how we are doing. Do we gather in pews like members of the executive board of a Fortune 500 corporation or even shareholders? Or do we gather like those in Marquand Chapel at Yale Divinity School, as the chastened cocksure, awed at God's magnificence and chagrined by our defiance? Do we gather as refugees in spiritual famine hungering for a scrap of the Bread of Life? Do we tremble for the preacher in mediating the collisions of these worlds? Or do we dismiss the preacher if he or she is not as engaging as a game-show host? If we still cannot gauge the precise pitch of this feeling-tone in rightfully approaching God, consult Isaiah and witness how he approached God.

> In the year that King Uzziah died, I saw the Lord sitting on a throne, high and lofty; and the hem of his robe filled the temple.
> Seraphs were in attendance above him; each had six wings: with two they covered their faces, and with two they covered their feet, and with two they flew.
> And one called to another and said:
> "Holy, holy, holy is the LORD of hosts; the whole earth is full of his glory."
> The pivots on the thresholds shook at the voices of those who called, and the house filled with smoke. And I said: "Woe is me! I am lost, for I am a man of unclean lips, and I live among a people of unclean lips; yet my eyes have seen the King, the LORD of hosts!" Then one of the seraphs flew to me,
> holding a live coal that had been taken from the altar with a pair of tongs.
> The seraph touched my mouth with it and said: "Now that this has touched your lips, your guilt has departed and your sin is blotted out."
> Then I heard the voice of the Lord saying,
> "Whom shall I send, and who will go for us?" And I said, "Here am I; send me!"
> And he said, "Go and say to this people: 'Keep listening, but do not comprehend; keep looking, but do not understand.'
> Make the mind of this people dull, and stop their ears, and shut their eyes, so that they may not look with their eyes, and listen with their ears, and comprehend with their minds, and turn and be healed."
>
> (Isaiah 6:1–10)

Heaven and earth are full of God's glory. In doxology, in glorifying God, we discover our rightful place and our authority as witnesses to what God has done in the world. This is why we begin these considerations in worship. And as soon as we enter worship, we are invited to confess our faith, to affirm who God is and to realize who we are. We have the opportunity to articulate what we believe as Christian people. Before we delve into these cherished beliefs in chapter 4, the dreams that drive our imagination, the dreams for which we are willing to sacrifice ourselves, we clear out some personal underbrush in chapter 3. For as has been insisted so far, we live in a time and place where barriers like individualism, consumerism, and narcissism do not allow free and clear access to these faith affirmations. But one final thought to close the current deliberations.

There is a story about a visitor to the magnificent Uffizi art museum in Florence. After viewing the works, he emerged only to declare, "I don't think much of the stuff in there!" Overhearing the remark, a janitor replied, "Sir, it is not the pictures but the visitors who are on trial here." So also God calls the church gently but forthrightly to turn the tables on these times about the glorious possibility of living our lives before the true and living God. But first we must speak up and act out of the time-honored way of Christian witness. So God calls us to raise our voices about who is the Creator and who is the creature. And that is worth talking about.

If art retains authority for such reversals, then why not Christian ministry? As with Carnegie Hall and the Uffizi, this turnaround will require much faithful devotion from people and artful leadership from pastors. But the last chorus is not yet sung, and the last canvas is not yet painted in the still unfolding drama of God's redemption.

3

WE ARE NOT OUR OWN

The movie was *City Slickers*, now more than a decade old. The scene had Curly, played by Jack Palance, riding next to Mitch, actor Billy Crystal. Mitch and two New York buddies visit New Mexico to work through midlife crises by driving a herd of cattle to Colorado. Curly shakes his head at their bourgeois angst.

"You city folk! . . . You spend about fifty weeks a year getting knots in your rope," Curly uncomprehendingly observes. "And then you think two weeks up here will untie them for you." The horses pause beneath them. "Do you know what the secret of life is?" Curly asks Mitch. "No, what?" Mitch wonders. "This," Curly answers, holding up one gloved index finger. "Your finger?" Mitch asks, thrown off. "One thing," Curly answers. "Just one thing. You stick to that, and everything else don't mean [a thing]." "That's great," Mitch enthuses, "but what's the one thing?" "That's what you've got to figure out," Curly cryptically responds before riding away.[1]

It's a memorable scene not only because it's good filmmaking, but because it's an inkblot of American spirituality. Curly is the archetypal cowboy Zen master of the Old West, replete with inscrutable, brief, pregnant utterances. At the same time, you read whatever you want into his charge. What one thing does his finger represent? Getting enough protein in your diet? Scoring Pistons tickets vs. the Spurs? Getting the kids into the best schools or finding the rising mutual fund?

45

The scene grabs us because the older we get the more we realize that single-mindedness in things most essential is the ticket to live the lives we were meant to live. Flitting distractedly from one new, hot, latest thing to another can charm for a while. But over decades this enchantment wears thin. Life is unsentimental in that it refuses to smile on dead ends of wasted years and decades of chasing delusions and pipe dreams.

So forgive me if I assail the shallowness of pop spirituality in a movie that I simultaneously find funny and endearing. But does God abandon us to contrive silly, fleeting, and self-serving answers to matters so essential as living our lives well as opposed to wasting them? Does God leave something so crucial to our whims and fancies? In a word, no; as Christians we don't believe in such a God.

Rather, we hold that God reveals and invites us into the one thing that gives life fullness of purpose. We believe in revelation as a trustworthy source of ultimate truth. We also believe that going deep within ourselves to find our true selves or final destiny is like peeling the layers of the onion. If we seek an essential core where all shall be revealed, where we shall know and be known, we will be disappointed. For when we get way down within, we find nothing there. Comparing our human depths with those of the divine, my divinity school professor Paul Holmer would let the air out of theologues taking themselves too seriously by saying, "Way down deep we are all really very shallow." Even Curly.

As Christians, we are less like Mitch and Curly than we are like Jake and Elwood (John Belushi and Dan Aykroyd) in *The Blues Brothers*, punctuating our alternately sinful and antic misadventures with the dictum, "We're on a mission from God." Christianity has about it agenda and directedness rather than idle exploring and diffuse seeking that are little more than shapeless wandering.

So what is our "one thing"? It is to worship Jesus Christ and glorify God in all things. Giordano Bruno, who believed Copernicus that the sun and not the earth was at the center of things, once observed, "If the first button of one's coat is wrongly buttoned all the rest will be crooked." And so our "one thing" is also a "first thing." It is foundational to everything else. As we worship Jesus Christ in all things, our lives take on a central unifying purpose that gathers up lesser matters into a harmonious balance, giving our lives the chance to turn out well. As we do, we find ourselves living purposeful lives where others wonder and ask what makes us tick and seek for themselves centered depths in touch with the persons God created them to become. In this we glimpse authoritative Christian witness.

Our "one thing" assumes that as creatures we bear the earmarks of the Creator who fashioned us and awaits our return through the Mediator Son given for the world. Our "one thing" will not rest until all creation recognizes and celebrates these free and generous gifts of grace. It is grasping that by faith in God we can receive these precious treasures or toss them away. It is firmness in the truth that our days can be lived accepting or resisting God's firm but tender grasp on us. It is refusing to suffer any nonsense about any third way between God's way and ours. It is all of these things, and yet one thing: worshipping Jesus Christ with all that we have and are, in ways that are both obvious and hidden.

That is the one thing needful in life or in death, whether we are awake or asleep, whether we work or play (Luke 10:42). And it is not as though we have attempted this path and found it wanting. It is more that in the busyness of our "getting ahead" or in the bloatedness of our being so full of ourselves that our individual and collective imaginations never pause to creatively flesh out what such Christlikeness might amount to in the living of our days.

Only by the leap of faith of living in the sufficiency of Christ can guilt and shame over many failures melt away. Only by the leap of faith in the adequacy of God's providence can our pride, vainglory, and self-absorption be put in perspective. Only by the leap of faith in God's complete commitment to us can our own commitments come to experience God leading us in our lives, and real freedom wherever we are called.

Wrapped in a Cause Bigger than Ourselves

While I have not regularly taught our local church's confirmation class for years, and no longer personally know our confirmands as closely as I once could, the Rite of Confirmation on Pentecost Sunday remains a strangely touching service for me. I find myself tearful at the kneeling and blessing of these youth. Even more than by Christmas or Easter Sunday, I am surprisingly moved by the act.

What's that all about? I wonder, as I feel overcome. It has taken me a while to plumb these depths. It is more than sentimentality about children becoming adults. It is more than the babies whom I once baptized taking their place as full members within the body of Christ. It is more than the church replenishing and renewing itself with fresh new generations. It cuts deeper still as a source of renewal and hope.

Among the blessings we offer as we pastors and teachers lay on hands to confirm are "you are not your own; God has bought and claimed you." This revolutionary observation is rooted in Paul the apostle's centering phrase for perhaps his most distracted church: "Do you not know that . . . you are not your own?" (1 Cor. 6:19). These simple but pregnant statements deeply touch me. The more we think about it, the more we realize what a bold, deeply rebellious, and countercultural claim that is: our lives are not our own.

The suggestion here is that our lives are finally about bigger things than where we graduated from college or what blue jeans we wear, but even about the ups and downs of God's people—Jewish and Christian—over the last 4,000 years. Bringing unsuspecting youth into this cloud of witnesses is so monumental that it takes my breath away, fully aware as I am that few will experience the fullness of God's claim in ways that totally transform them and alter the world's landscape.

For at the confirming of such a faith they have been set apart, launched into the world, and permanently marked by the invisible waters of baptism. Nothing could cut more sharply and deeply against the grain of our culture. Nothing could launch us on a trajectory more sharply divergent from what we see on television. Nothing could set us up more for a collision with what scripture calls "powers and principalities."

We are not champions of our own destinies and unmoved movers of the world around us. As Christians, we hold that history moves purposefully under God's direction toward a fulfillment, an end, or a telos of which we now have only brief glimpses. We are the children of God's purpose, and each of us is given a small but crucial part in heaven's unfolding drama of redemption. Even more than lighting out on our own into brave new trails of personal discovery, our principal task is finding our own specific place in God's encompassing plan of redemption.

As Christians, we dwell in a different, more purposeful universe. Jesus did wish us the serenity of letting the day's troubles suffice for that day. But he bid us rest from anxiety within this grander overarching framework of God's ultimate triumph. It changes everything, most especially how we discern right and wrong. These are no longer a function of controlling mutual self-interest (utilitarianism), or an extension of the self-evident nature of created things (natural law), or the personal volition of human units alone in a vast, empty universe (existentialism). Right and wrong issue out of a much larger context across space and time, and are rooted in the nature of God, and coming to know ourselves as made in God's image, and taking our marching orders from God.

If you were to sit down and read all four Gospels without stopping, I predict that your single biggest surprise among those pages would be the degree of emphasis granted the *eschaton*, the culmination of time, the consummation of history. Jesus gave us this glimpse beyond not to create a deterministic universe where we can sit back idly and await preprogrammed results. The intended effect was not quietism, passivity, and resignation to the status quo. Just the opposite: the reason he lifted the veil obscuring this ultimate triumph was to create urgency, to stoke our passion, and to quicken our hunger and thirst for righteousness here and now, knowing that the smallest efforts now shall loom infinitely larger at the fulfillment of history.

Jesus spoke on and on about this already/not yet kingdom that his Father would consummate as an alternative order, to trust its unshakable and abiding reality, and to embolden us to live it into existence with lives that at every point bear its imprint. For discerning and adventurous souls, our lives as Christian people have not only structure but agenda, an agenda that will not quit.

If this is where life is eventually headed, we ask, then why does our world so little resemble it? The truth is that our faith must be tested by all manner of countervailing evidence, struggle, suffering, and even death. For God wants to make sure no one hops aboard this train who does not want to arrive at its destination, and that no one would happen aboard by mistake. So this train does not carry the triumphalistic, but the chastened. Instead of trumpeting ourselves, we pour our passion and celebration into Sunday morning, glorifying the God who has won this great victory and given it to us as a gift. Living on this side of Easter, knowing that Christ conquers, makes all of the difference, in life and in death.

A People with an Agenda

My first work out of seminary took me to the fetid underbelly of the American dream. As a research assistant with Yale University and Connecticut Mental Health, I spent my first summer interviewing those closest to the heroin addicts on the rough side of New Haven, Connecticut. These secondary interviews were with individuals who were often also addicts themselves. I interviewed them to check the reliability of the heroin addicts' primary self-report.

We quickly learned that absolutely no one was close to the addicts in any real sense. Essential to getting into such deep trouble as heroin addiction was effectively isolating yourself from others who genuinely knew and cared for you. The only "family" the users knew was the network of contacts on the street, where concern went no deeper than procuring enough dope for everyone. I recall reporting my findings to a group of psychiatrists, psychologists, and research associates. They were curious not only about the results, but also about how I had procured publishable data after a few short months.

One researcher asked a flurry of questions: How did you get them to speak to you? What if they were lying? How did you survive moving through dangerous parts of town without being menaced, robbed, or attacked? Indeed I moved through buildings where there were "shooting galleries," tawdry rented rooms that informally made themselves available for groups of addicts who were intravenously injecting themselves en masse. It reminded me of delivering baked goods in the heart of the Detroit ghetto, where I used the same technique.

"Find a clipboard. Stick papers on it," I told her. "Then take that clipboard, walk briskly at full stride, and if anybody looks at you cross-eyed, stare back like you might close down the whole neighborhood. But never, ever attempt such a thing without a clipboard." To be sure, the biggest part of this was youthful, foolish bravado. But yet another part is a genuine ingredient of what makes for authority.

So few people have anything like a deep and abiding direction in their lives that when someone appears who is possessed of anything like clear purposefulness, it clears a way and pulls others along. This is what Curly did with Mitch and his two endearing but lost friends. So many wandering souls today are lost in the guise of "seeking" and "questing," dabbling in native American religion or crystals, that our firm agenda, clear goals, and compelling destination as Christian people bring with them an honest chance for something like respect. What remains true today of society in general was only more true of the sad souls lost in the labyrinth of intravenous drug abuse in the late seventies.

What we believe about where life is headed speaks volumes about what we do and how we live now. So much of the boredom, loneliness, and "flatness" in our affluent, opportunity-laden society is the feeling that life is no more than a grim, one-blasted-thing-after-another series of events randomly impacting us for good or ill. The feeling here is that intentionality in the universe is asleep at the wheel, if in fact it ever drove anything, and that no hand is guiding the tiller of history.

So many resign themselves to the arbitrary fate of making it on their own rather than embrace the higher destiny that Jesus announced and inaugurated in God's reign. They worship regularly and intensely at places like slot machines and lotteries. They find their belonging and community in soap operas or reality TV shows or procuring enough heroin for everyone around them. Such as these are without an end point, a purpose and final result to pull them forward.

If we Christians are anything, we are a people with an agenda. And if anything is unique about our agenda, it is that it transcends "looking out for number one." This is tantamount to a revolt against a time and place where everyone is painfully aggrieved and insistent about getting their due. It is that our destiny as individuals is caught up in our fate with God's people and all people. Ever since the resurrection, we believe that history moves inexorably toward its consummation. Battles will be lost, yes, but the war is already won. Christian joy, even in the face of evil, suffering, and death, is hopefully trusting in that end point more than in any human assurance or promise. Christian ministry is living out this gospel while offering it to those who have not heard it, or only dimly know it.

Søren Kierkegaard describes what has been true of every Christian in every age. Each of us is "called by a revelation to go out in the world, to proclaim the Word, to act and to suffer, to a life of uninterrupted activity as the Lord's messenger."[2]

What is the goal for which we long and labor? It is making our home in God. It is living such that we find ourselves taken into the heart of Jesus Christ (rather than formulaically quizzing everyone if they "have Jesus in their heart"). It is the reconciliation of sisters and brothers of all places and races, even of heaven and earth. This is our "end," our telos. Our greatest thrill in following Jesus is to know the story ends well, even if we don't yet grasp how we will get there. The struggle and opportunity of Christian vocation is finding our own personal part in proclaiming and enlivening this glorious destiny awaiting God's own.

Sadly, it is as though we have forgotten this one central, essential calling. No body other than the church can remind the world of this soul-grounding, essential truth that our lives first and finally belong to God. And that God intends our lives for specific applications within the context of God's larger, blessed, encompassing purposes. No body other than the church can help us discover our unique God-given gifts for key specific redemptive purposes (as opposed to lifting ourselves above the masses by scoring big on *American Idol*). No other body can quicken us in our gifts' intended destiny, calling them out of themselves and into paths of service, witness, and praise that are literally the chance of a lifetime.

How do we find our individual place in God's greater scheme of things? It is not easy. It asks abiding faithfulness and deep discernment of us. Our marching orders from God do not come to us like the list of chores for the house that our parents left while away for the weekend. Kierkegaard observed it is as though we are handed an envelope that we cannot open. Inside is our assignment from God. We must find ways to discern the contents while unable to tear open the envelope. In other words, this process we wish were more straightforward and explicit requires prayer, self-examination, patience, and openness to the insights of others who know God and can recognize our gifts. However demanding, the discernment of our individual vocations before God is within our reach.

To get inside that envelope, many churches today do more with spiritual gift inventories, helping the laity find their vocational wheelhouse. These tests help us see how God endows us with our own unique set of spiritual gifts. They represent an exercise of insight and empowerment,

51

of discernment and diagnosis, and of authorizing and commissioning. They amount to a searching dialogue of individuals within the Christian communities where God placed us, rooted in shared assumptions and values. This unexplored frontier is a growing edge as the church looks to win hearts and minds in a new day, as serving God alongside one another comes to mean more than sharing donuts during coffee hour.

One promising area to begin such discernment around Christian vocation is with the arrival of new members within the church. This is probably the best, first foothold for spiritual gift inventories. So often we lament how individuals and families come eagerly through our front door only to wander away into the mists through our back door. This happens because the church has inadequately helped these members find their role within the greater scheme of things and to find their niche within a local church. Like the fish unaware that it swims in water, so often we are unaware of the places where we glide effortlessly forward within our proper element. We tend to discount our personal gifts or assume that everyone is as gifted as we are where we are. Not so. Helping people sort through this will most certainly help individual pilgrims and fortify the corporate body of Christ, getting the best people into the right stations as the church mobilizes for witness.

Playing to Our Strength

Let's face it, the contemporary image of the church in America, not exactly aglow for many decades now, has taken a nosedive in recent decades. Not coincidentally, this freefall has been in direct proportion to how much power and prosperity America amasses as a world empire. Even without scandals of priests and televangelists undercutting our authority, what we are about as the church strikes people as unimpressive. Steeples that once dominated city skylines anachronistically shrink into the shadows of soaring glass banks, office towers, and apartment high-rises.

Moreover, our rituals strike the unchurched as arcane, our various systems of organization seem choked, and the delivery of our message does not exactly inspire the imaginations of twenty-somethings, whose grip upon the wondrous is dominated by three-second sequences involving special effects.

As a twenty-two-year-old announcing that I was headed toward seminary, I was met with groans and the rolling of eyes, often by Christian friends and family. You could be a lawyer or a professor, they insisted. Why do you want to do *that?* Today the influx of gifted young people into a seminary/pastoral leadership track has slowed to a mere trickle.

For some time now we have been losing the war for the imagination of the hearts and minds who will shape the future of the prosperous West. Will the Christian church in North America become another museum piece, a historical artifact of affluence, a lofty memory of departed grandparents, as it has in most of Europe?

For the past fifty years, many church leaders have responded to this "crisis in relevance" by seeking to reground the Christian church in more appealing cultural trends, hoping that people would flock back, noticing that we were finally dealing with sexier matters. We have responded to the crisis of relevance by worshipping at the altar of what the world deems relevant. This is about as winsomely convincing as a middle-aged joker like me trying to win over my teenage daughters by wearing gold-plated pendants and talking like Snoop Dogg. Not only would they be unimpressed, they would wonder if I had lost my marbles, and they would flee in the opposite direction. Where has the church lurched awkwardly and uncertainly in these years? Walk with me on an oversimplified tour.

In the 1950s, depth psychology was still au courant, and the church tilted toward a therapeutic model. Spiritual struggles were understood as unresolved childhood conflicts. Biblical figures like Moses or Paul were analyzed through the characteristic defense mechanisms, and their messages were deeply qualified by these insights. Adult Christian education classes became thinly veiled group therapy sessions or psychodramas. Spirituality became the numinous recesses of human consciousness. Gifted pastors exited unglamorous local church parish leadership toward new frontiers of pastoral care and counseling. The social sciences held the prospect of revealing the real meaning of our sacred texts and rituals. So psychological relevance took us inward, and words like *ego* and *projection* and *transference* displaced words like *sin* and *evangelism* and *salvation*.

In the 1960s the crosscurrents of race, war, and urban unrest dominated society and consequently the church. So the church embraced an activism-in-the-streets model of faithfulness. Sacred music, at least for coming-of-age baby boomers, imitated the prophetic poetic reflections of folk-music coffeehouses. Our mission frontier shifted from the Congo to urban American halfway houses and soup kitchens. As John McFadden observed, gathering in churches to worship God was suddenly qualified by more pressing and pivotal world issues, and often found wanting. Preaching was deemed archaic at best, extinct at worst. The real and exciting ministers wore work shirts, strummed guitars, and championed social causes or issues of race, war, and anti-imperialism with quixotic charm. Fifteen years later many of them found themselves working as investment bankers. So the quest for relevance through activism took us into the streets and larger social movements as the epicenter where God's kingdom was stirring.

In the 1970s the quest to become fully actualized, self-fulfilled, authentic creatures was at the forefront. In some ways this was a populist, grassroots, self-nurturing follow-up to our 1950s interiority. The church located its constituents on Abraham Maslow's hierarchy of needs to chart its beginning and end points. Never mind that Maslow was openly contemptuous toward matters of faith. We listened to each other's feelings and did our level best to validate them. Sunday school classes became "rap sessions." All of the resources that had been previously committed to the Vietnam War were suddenly marshaled toward the wholeness of individuals and humankind. The key was beginning with our stated needs, and then working forward and upward. So the quest for a more holistic relevance took us deeper within ourselves and our idea of what it means to be human beings.

In the 1980s, relational sentimentality waned, and the raw currency of outright ambition resurged. After the economic and political setbacks of the preceding decade, America was ready to assume its rightful place as the king of the hill without apology or shame. Orgies of nationalism and capitalism resulted.

The church took its triumphalistic cue; megachurches rose where thousands and thousands worshipped, often in places unremarkable or nonexistent before. Managerial and technical formulas for reaching those outside the church—getting all of the stripes and signs right in the parking lot—were emphasized without fretting too much over how the content of our faith was being neglected, forgotten, and jettisoned. Even the churches historically less focused upon spiritual seekers mimicked the megachurches, setting up workshops and institutes to train others in the formulas they masterfully executed. So relevance became knowing how to take care of business, meet the needs of the religious consumer, and build a formidable institution whose wallop included lots of human and financial assets.

From the 1990s through today, we have focused on information and technology, thinking this social spasm can save the church, maybe rescue us from obscurity, or at least keep us from falling behind as our surrounding American empire surged to the top of the world's heap. Every denomination and now most every local church has its own Web site to disseminate who it is and what it is about, sometimes actually even mentioning Jesus and the gospel. Information has abounded, but ultimate belonging—hitherto the strong suit of the church and still a yawning void within Western society—has lagged considerably.

Contemporary worship, some of which generated out of the megachurch experience, took on a new buzz. Even churches that weren't doing contemporary worship felt as though they should. With hymns attractively and accessibly projected by computers, and an airbrushed theology for surmounting the vagaries of modern life, the church borrowed liberally from the shopping mall, the soft-rock concert, and the spirituality/self-help section of the local bookstore. The consumerist impulse of scratching where people itch can make satisfied spiritual customers who bear little fruit in the world. And it raises as many questions as it answers about the place of the Christian church in the present and in the future in a time of swift change. Is relevance enough if it means no more than keeping abreast with the soaring American empire as a world-shaping cultural, political, and economic powerhouse? Or does that mean that something serious has been lost along the way?

The painful part about the church's prospects for lending some direction and leadership to modernity's trackless chaos is that we have replicated the world's confusion inside the church. Instead of bringing our modern virtues up before God to see how they stack up before his relentless gaze, we size God up inasmuch as God conforms to our capricious, dubious modern standards that are obsolete in a few years. If the time-honored God in Jesus Christ proclaimed by the church does not fare well on these unquestioned criteria, our God is rejected as irrelevant.

The church then fashions a brave new god from politically palatable scraps of historic faith (for the sake of legitimacy) mixed with a glitzy conglomeration of hot causes (for the sake of relevance). As Eberhard Jungel asserts, "Philosophy perishes when it has become anthropology." So does theology. Faith cannot sustain itself with gods that fail to transcend a world whose final answers do not lie within itself. These gods are too small.

Can't Find Our Way Home

In truth, despite the critical mood in the foregoing section, much has been learned and gained in the church from each of the epochs, here vastly oversimplified. And clearly the church cannot exist hermetically sealed in a vacuum apart from the movements and crosscurrents of society at large. Frankly, the church cannot know who it is apart from the world, apart from existing over against the world's powers. We are like kites that rise against the wind.

But in another era of incredible change, Paul wrote to the heart of another empire, Rome, bidding those Christians not to be conformed to the age, but to be transformed by the renewal of their minds, by what is good, acceptable, and perfect (Rom. 12:1ff). He wrote this with the intention that, having been transformed in the pattern of Christ, the church would go forth to serve God as an agent of transformation in a world that cannot see the power that lies in the weakness of the cross. And so they did until they stood that Roman Empire on its head.

We are not our own. Neither are we the world's. Rather we belong to God. It is one thing to mark the Zeitgeist of a place and time, the spirit of the age, to play off its symbols, customs, and institutions, and to feed off its momentum, turning them back toward God's purposes, making careful distinctions as we go. Jesus did as much in his Sermon on the Mount. "You have heard it said . . . but I say to you," is the logic by which it moves. Paul did as much in his sermon at the Areopagus: "Athenians, I see how extremely religious you are in every way. For as I went through the city and looked carefully at the objects of your worship, I found among them an altar with the inscription, 'To an unknown god'" (Acts 17:20).

Still, it is something else for the church to be owned and operated by the Zeitgeist of a place and time. While the heady relevance of such a ride can enchant, this move fritters away our transcendent charge to be molders of a higher consensus, surrendering to being shaped by things below. It forfeits that cherished and convicting transcendent leverage point sketched out in the previous chapter, where letting everything that follows from pleasing God matter more than pleasing ourselves. Rather than commanding authority for the good and the holy, our captivity to worldly logics surrenders the church's witness as a shaper of society. How can the church resist the tendrils that would pull it into the world's clammy hold? How can it retain the authority of its transcendent leverage point? We cannot retain our integrity if by going out to meet the world we end up falling in.

The personal endgame of church historian and dean of Princeton Seminary James Nichols, is instructive here. His daughter wrote about Nichols facing the onset of Alzheimer's disease, how he accepted it and nobly pressed on, how lustrous his Christian witness remained.[3] Her father the professor did not have the "self-conscious self most of us haul through life," a self tortured by the self-analysis of always wondering whether our needs are getting met and whether we are getting our due from life.

A key to Nichols's perspective was the passage from Calvin's *Institutes* that we considered earlier with regard to confirmation. It hung in Nichols's office at Princeton and was included in a colleague's eulogy to him: "We are not our own: let not reason nor our will, therefore, sway our plans and deeds. We are not our own; let us therefore not set it as our goal to seek what is expedient for us according to the flesh. We are not our own: insofar as we can, let us therefore forget ourselves and all that is ours. Conversely, we are God's: let us therefore live for him and die for him."

In a time when the church is having trouble remembering who we are, stricken with corporate Alzheimer's, unable to remember *whose* we are, we might gaze a while at the plaque on Nichols's wall. For despite being stricken by the historian's most devastating disease—terminal forgetting—he managed not to lose his dignity, his integrity, or his soul in living out his life before God. At our current rate of forgetting who we are, and to whom we owe everything, we cannot say the same.

Theologian and Congregational minister P. T. Forsyth once observed, "If within us we find nothing over us, we succumb to what is around us."[4] Before we belong to God, we do not belong to ourselves, or to our contrived needs, or to a culture of success ("what works"), or to relevance as the world defines it. Losing track of this basic truth, we risk losing our soul in the affluent ease of depending upon ourselves and our own answers because we can now afford to, at the expense of depending on God. Here is how one church dug its heels into this slippery slope, made a stand, and reversed its ground.

Counter to the Culture

Consider these words from a contemporary hymn sung at an Anglican church in the Midlands of England. This church, dating back to the 1100s, was nearly dead. But it came back to life through firm, committed, Christ-centered pastoral leadership and a Sunday evening contemporary service where young families came together seeking an alternative to the grim, declining, postimperial British pop culture around them.

Even as its poetry leaves something to be desired, this hymn singles out the true and living God among idols. So much of being the church today in the post-Christian West is a matter of willingness to confess, "We are not like other people and institutions," and then being willing to name those differences.

Even as the church is again resurgent and on a firm footing, yes, they are still a remnant people, and newcomers are not stampeding to Sunday evening worship at St. Peter's Ipsley. Still, they do share something vital and powerful in that they belong to God and to one another as a living community in a way they refuse to belong to the latest BBC special on which Hollywood celebrity is being detoxed where.

> Counter to the culture, going against the flow,
> Finding new direction, your kingdom is upside down,
> Your kingdom is upside down, your kingdom is upside down.

Justice, peace, and righteousness, the politics of your government,
Where the poor are blessed and the strong are weak,
Earth is inherited by the meek.

In resistance to the spirit-of-the-age,
Live a lifestyle that can be sustained;
Undermine the idols of technology and science,
The need for the latest gadget or appliance.

I'm falling on my knees, offering all of me.
Jesus, you're all this heart is living for.
Broken, I run to you, for your arms are open wide;
I am weary, but I know your touch restores my life.[5]

We do not live in thrall to the latest exploits of Elizabeth Hurley and Hugh Grant; we honor the saints. We do not seize on how brand names sanctify human life; we look for how God dignifies people the rest of the world forgets, in places like Paraguay or south Chicago. We do not live in thrall to the latest and next big thing; we know that the cross of Jesus Christ is the only thing big enough to ignite the kind of revolution for good that we and the world yearn for.

We do well to look to the vitality of splinter movements in Europe, where for centuries pockets of Christians have resisted being co-opted into alien political and economic values. For they, like Jews everywhere in the world over the past millennia, have much to teach us in a day when Christians in America are new to neutralizing the acids of late modernity.

Several years ago a pastor friend with a Hungarian Reformed background shared the then-untold story about a Hungarian Reformed pastor in Romania. Laszlo Tokes was pastor in Timisoara of a small Reformed church in Transylvania. His predecessor had been a card-carrying ecclesial apparatchik and collaborator, even wearing the red star of Communism on his clerical robes. But Tokes was unafraid to preach the Christian gospel with uncompromising boldness and clarity. It wasn't long before this church numbering no more than a few dozen had grown into the thousands, attracting everyone from university students to the elderly. One doesn't have to speak all that much truth in a context of pure lies before something like a sensation results.

The Communist authorities—infiltrators from within and goons from without—were not amused. Policemen, armed with machine guns, were stationed around this congregation to intimidate on Sunday mornings. Church members were subject to harassment. One night Tokes's wife came home to find her husband being beaten. They took away his ration book so that he couldn't buy basic goods like food or fuel. The state-controlled church reassigned him to an obscure country parish. Tokes refused to go and called upon his people to help him resist. On December 15, 1989, the local Communists came to arrest him and send him into exile.

The word had spread among the parishioners that their pastor was about to be seized. They formed a human wall around the church. What's more, they put their own children at the front of their human wall, sure that the troops wouldn't hurt innocent children. The people stayed all night, through the next day, and into the next night. Demonstrations broke out. Members from other churches joined in as their spontaneous confession of faith shaded imperceptibly into political protest.

As the Communist Party powers grew infuriated, the security forces finally opened fire on the people. Hundreds were killed and wounded. The murdered were buried in a mass grave. Of course, evidence of the massacre was hushed up. Even in this cynical and oppressive Eastern bloc where innocent people were regularly stifled and squashed, the populace could hardly believe that security police would open fire upon a gathering of church people and their children. When they unearthed the mass grave and the heinous act was undeniable, it sparked the first of the revolutions that ended up with the overturn of the Soviet Union and its satellites. The dominoes of Communist advance that NATO had so feared throughout the cold war fell backward and took down with them a house of cards. And it all began with a pastor and his church.[6]

Enduring Battles in a War That Has Been Won

We are not our own. We belong to God. We are not the masters of our fate. Life moves toward its appointed *telos* at a time and place of God's deciding. And the final outcome of our lives and this world's destiny is not ours to call. That is bad news if we thought that we were the best part of the world and were going to save it. But it is good news if we confess our part in the world's discord and soberly understand that we alone cannot ransom this prisoner-world. But we know the One who can and would proclaim Jesus's name in all circumstances.

Our hope resides in this One who moves on the stage of universal history with the alacrity and confidence of having undertaken measures equal to our need, as though God owns it all, because he surely does. God moves with sure-handed proficiency and adequacy although God is clearly on his own timetable. God is carrying a clipboard and is in full stride for those with eyes of faith to see.

"He came and told both you who were far from God and we who were near that the war was over," Paul wrote (Eph. 2:17). We live in the in-between time when the enmity between heaven and earth is ended but the peace is not yet fully established. This is like olden days, when soldiers would keep fighting their wars long after a formal peace had been struck.

The Battle of New Orleans is a case in point. This so-called needless battle was fought on January 8, 1815. The British sent 8,000 men to capture the city of New Orleans. Despite there being several possible routes to the city, the British army chose to march straight at the entrenchments dug by General Andrew Jackson. American artillery and sharpshooters killed and wounded about 1,500 British troops, including their leader, the general Sir Edward Pakenham. The Americans lost very few.

It is called "the needless battle" because a treaty of peace had been signed at Ghent, Belgium, some fifteen days before. So things used to be. The enemy would be defeated and concede. A treaty of peace would be drafted and signed, bringing the war to an end. But time would elapse—weeks, sometimes months—before the couriers would arrive on the outermost frontiers of the fighting with the good news that the war was finally ended. In the meantime, battles would continue in their bloody way. Every hour was still crisis-laden, as though nothing had changed. Peace was established, but the fighting could not cease. And for all involved, everything remained a matter of life and death.

So things are still. The reign of Christ has been established. But this good news must be carried into the trenches of suffering, defeat, and despair. Jesus has won the peace for us on the cross, the charter of human salvation. But he awaits valiant foot soldiers willing to deliver the message into the teeth of conflict at front lines where the battle remains fierce, where a life-and-death struggle wages still between reconciled foes. This is our telos. We do not lack agenda or purpose.

Trusting that God has put all of this into place for us, even in the face of needless loss, ample discouragement, and haunting grief, is the "one thing needful" that Jesus revealed to Martha (Luke 12:42). It is the one thing that Curly could have meant unwittingly, wagging his finger before Mitch. It is the one and only thing that we need to know in the face of life and death. We are not our own. Rather we are God's. For our story and our end point are greater than we are, left to ourselves, thanks be to God. Even if our private dreams are paltry, God's dreams are singular and substantial, compelling, and true. The gap between our dreams and God's dream, and how we might participate in the salvation of the vast dream of God's reign, is what we consider next.

4

GOD'S DREAM AND OUR DREAMS

America churns out dreams like Detroit manufactures automobiles. They practically roll off an assembly line. Our nation is a dream factory like no other place on earth. And when we dream, it is in the multihued Technicolor of personal choice and individual fulfillment, with strokes of triumphalism mixed in. (Witness the celebrities who annually make the "Most Admired List.") Over time these colors can run and fade as we discover that our allegiances are misplaced, that the celebrities who command our attention are not what human life was meant to become. It comes as a surprise to learn that God's blessing does not shine with the glare of media spotlights, but on less traveled places and less obvious stories. In the prayerful dialogue between Christ and his people, we can sort out these deep allegiances and loyalties, and that is what this chapter is about.

A World without Bearings

A pastor tells of her halting attempts to navigate the rocky shoals of marital discord with a couple. The husband, whom we will call Nick, approached his pastor and disclosed a disturbing scenario. Not only was his wife, Melinda, withdrawing from their marriage, she was also growing inappropriately close to another at work. Nick confessed his part in these troubles. Abuse of alcohol had led to his insensitivity toward and neglect of Melinda. He feared that he had squelched a fragile flame of marital trust and tenderness. And so Nick approached his pastor prepared to do his part, motivated to reclaim his marriage and eager to make amends.

Both Nick and Melinda held responsible positions outside the home. They had two grade school children, Lana and Jeremy. They were both active and concerned parents. They were fairly new members at Central Community Church. The couple had many church friends, and Melinda's sister, Denise, was a church leader.

Melinda was adrift. She, like many working women of recent times, was showing signs of a sad rite of passage that had been devouring working men since the 1950s and 1960s: the midlife crisis. After so much sacrifice, what did it all mean? After focusing on the needs of others, what about my own needs? After working a job that maybe did or did not make any difference, what was it all worth? After all the unavoidable hurt that accumulates in a marriage, where is there any power for forgiveness? What about my happiness? And who will look out for me if I do not?

Melinda agreed to meet with the pastor and Nick for only one session. Remote and evasive, she was obviously merely going through the motions. Clearly, another gravitational pull was exerting itself. Not long after, Nick learned just how involved his wife was with a coworker. They had moved beyond kindred spirits to soul mates, and a level of physical intimacy was coming into play. Melinda referred to this coworker as her "friend." She saw no reason why she should pull back and put distance between them. The "forsaking all others" part of her marriage vows was lost upon her. Nick tried to be calm and patient, but the panic of losing her did not bring out the best in him.

While Melinda would no longer meet with the pastor, Nick continued to do so for support and guidance. The pastor counseled that at a time when Melinda could not see what she was doing, she needed others to help her find clarity before it was too late. She couldn't hear it from her husband or pastor. Melinda needed an intervention no less than Nick had before in facing his alcohol problem. What about Melinda's sister, Denise, a church leader? Or someone else? Instead Melinda heard from others: do sincerely whatever you need to be happy. Whatever you want most, that is what you deserve. Only you can know what is right and best for you. The stalemate continued.

Months later, Nick glumly sat in the pastor's study. Melinda had asked for a divorce. The marriage was ending. Nick asked for prayer. The pastor asked if she might pray publicly for them now that it was decided. It was that church's custom to mention personal struggles and joys in the Sunday pastoral prayer. Nick said yes, and thanked her.

That Sunday, along with other concerns, the pastor prayed for "Nick and Melinda in a time of change." The response from the pews was immediate. Some asked what was going on. Without elaborating, the pastor indicated they were struggling and deserved support. In a church that barely functioned as community and rarely came together (symbolically, all twelve board members lived in different zip codes), the church suddenly became as one, at least to this couple.

The effect was dramatic. With people asking how they could help, without prying, no longer was the couple alone in their struggle. Melinda's ties to her coworker were placed in the context of the vows of marriage, the well-being of a family, and life lived before God. Against this backdrop, her decision became a no-brainer. It didn't happen easily, but Melinda steadily withdrew from her liaison before more damage was done.

Through the faith community rallying, unwittingly, around them, Melinda's perspective shifted. She was unhappy about it, but she did go back to work within her marriage. Room for forgiveness was somehow found when it didn't exist before. Feeling as though prayers had been answered, Nick was grateful and wanted to make the most of having another chance.

Curiously, Melinda and Denise blamed the pastor for her eight-word public prayer in behalf the couple. They found it deeply unfair that Melinda had to resolve this situation other than in complete secrecy. When queried, the pastor pointed out that Melinda had asked for a divorce and Nick requested prayer. Both of them were getting exactly what they wanted. Divorce, like marriage, is by nature a public act, not a private one. And the truth was that Nick needed help, even if Melinda desired her secrecy.

Denise met with the pastor to air her grievances. She felt her sister had been slighted. The pastor had let them down. The pastor calmly answered that if being disliked was the cost of salvaging a marriage, she would gladly pay it. "You can despise me if you like," the pastor told her. "But you might be grateful." The pastor told Denise that *she* had let her sister down by providing little spiritual leadership. Melinda needed more from her than, "Do sincerely whatever you feel you must."

In the end, the couple stayed together in a marriage as imperfect as most. They remained active in the church and for a while led the youth program. Years later, they did divorce. However, Denise quickly departed, complaining that the pastor talked too much about Jesus. This veteran lay leader professed an interest in many "spiritual" things, but not Jesus.

As someone who has walked this blighted, barren path of divorce, I find the faithful response of the church deeply instructive, even humbling. Truthfully, it would have been painful for me if every one of my

1,300 members sat down to challenge me as their pastor to search out the issues of my marriage falling apart. At the same time, if no one had approached me and asked, "Are you absolutely certain that it must be this way? Is there no other way? Have you exhausted every other possibility?" that would have been more painful still. For it would have meant that we were not a community in any deep and significant sense. It would have meant that we were asleep at the wheel of our shared covenantal life. For as one marriage goes, so all feel the stress or the support, and so all rise and fall.

In the case of the church that I serve, some twenty-five or so members did approach me and asked hard, searching questions. A few did so in angry and strident ways, and that was perfectly understandable and acceptable. Others did so in calmer and more reasoned tones. Still others simply wept with me and cared for my family. Their palpable grief showed that life is not supposed to be this way, and marriages are not supposed to end. The point is that lifelong holy public vows are not to be taken lightly, not to be trifled with. We are not cubicles of privacy. We are interconnected and accountable to one another before God.

Choosers? Or Chosen?

These reflections reveal some of the forces buffeting us and what is at stake in the struggle of life. "When we defend the family," G. K. Chesterton wrote, "we do not mean it is always a peaceful family; when we maintain the thesis of marriage, we do not mean it is always a happy marriage. *We mean that it is the theatre of the spiritual drama, the place where things happen, especially things that matter.*"[1] Indeed, marriage is a microcosm of final allegiances, a stage where many spiritual battles between the gospel and the powers are played out.

Have you ever noticed how we are capable of imagining ourselves most free just at the moment when we are most deeply enslaved? In this we are all Melinda. The consumerist West has a painfully tragic flirtation with freedom. We confuse freedom as we idolize it. And then we resent any needed corrective to this confusion as an intrusion upon what people must be left to fix by themselves. This is called "being true to ourselves."

What Oswald Chambers writes on our public and private selves is instructive here:

> There is no such thing as a private life, or a place to hide in this world, for a man or woman who is intimately aware of and shares in the sufferings of Jesus Christ. God divides the private life of His saints and makes it a

64

highway for the world on one hand and for Himself on the other. . . . We are not sanctified for ourselves. We are called into intimacy with the gospel, and things happen that appear to have nothing to do with us.[2]

America and the affluent West teach that the essence of freedom is unfettered power to choose. The more choices there are, the more freedom there is. America cuts its teeth on this creed. And once the field of choices focuses and narrows, the natural consequence of moving through life, freedom feels lost. People then panic because they are "missing out on life." Is it any wonder that "midlife crises" loom so large for so many? In effect, these sham crises are programmed into our common life by how we mislead each other on personhood, freedom, and dignity.

No friend of the church, much less a theologian, comedian George Carlin observed that most of our choices are about things that mean little (costume earrings in accessory stores). He insists that we have little choice in things that matter most (whether or not we go to war). Carlin is right. Who among us chose our DNA? Who among us chose our mentors and teachers to bring out the best out in us? Who among us chose to be born in an era when childhood immunizations are common? Who chose the families into which we were born, and the households where children heard books read aloud?

Carlin suggests an inverse relationship here. The more important something is, the less choice we have. But multiplying options on long-distance providers and Internet servers creates an illusion of freedom, of boundless options, of zero boundaries, of unlimited access, as advertising campaigns everywhere scream these days.

As Christians, we bring a different perspective on choice. More essential than anything we have chosen is the world-changing reality that *God has definitively chosen us* through Jesus's birth and life, his death and resurrection. This is prior to us and not of our doing. We could have never imagined such a boon to our sagging fortunes.

"You did not choose me but I chose you. And I appointed you to go and bear fruit, fruit that will last, so that the Father will give you whatever you ask him in my name. I am giving you these commands so that you may love one another" (John 15:16–17). I always read these words to new church members as we receive them. At first blush, they might sound "limiting." Ultimately, however, they are words of comfort, of good news, and of situating life within its proper context. For what we cannot do for ourselves, God has graciously done for us. Whatever battles we must enter, we engage them knowing the longer and greater war has been won. For the most important choice—God's on our behalf—has already been made.

The tragedy of prosperous people who have lost all sense of dependence upon God is our reflexive rejection of the best thing that could have happened. Why this rebuff of God's gracious initiative? We reject God's response to what ails us *because it was not of our personal choosing. And if we didn't choose it for ourselves, it cannot be right. It cannot be right because it can never be fully "ours."* Because God's gracious response to our despair was not of our deciding and only unwittingly of our "execution."

Along the same lines of putting individual choice ahead of divine initiative, many Christians note the time of salvation from the moment of "accepting Jesus as personal Lord and Savior." Why this moment instead of when the Son saw fit to die ignominiously for us on Calvary? Simple. Because we rate our choices as more important than God's. When asked when I was "saved," I respond, "Two thousand years ago on a hill outside Jerusalem." Then I make a point to ask, "When were *you* saved?"

Nothing offends more than grace. For nothing is more out of our hands or beyond our control. Our much-vaunted choice gives us the illusion of power, the image of control. Our motto is John Milton's: better to reign in hell than to serve in heaven. But we are not the masters of our destiny, the shapers of the future. We can accept or reject God's gifts of grace, like any good gift. But we cannot replicate or substitute anything vaguely like it. This will never change. Humankind proposes, God disposes. These are the terms of life. We can rage against it, but good luck. None of our stammering and yammering will ever change it.

"You did not choose me, but I chose you. I appointed you to go and bear fruit." These words do not soothe our democratic sensibilities. We can rework our church by-laws and constitutions all we want, but we cannot alter the charter of our salvation, which does not originate within us or depend upon us. And little scandalizes many Christians more than realizing that God's reign is not a democracy of equal partners. It is not one God, one person, one vote. God has cast the only vote that matters. And it happened without any meeting, other than the gathering outside of Pilate's *praetorium,* whose representatives chose the less dangerous Barabbas over the spiritual revolutionary Jesus. God's reign is not a democracy, but a Christocracy. Those of us from democracies regularly stumble over that in our walk of discipleship.

"Being free to" is but one part of the Christian vision of freedom. We are also aware of how essential "being free from" worshipping false gods is. Unwitting idolatry is a wasted life of abject enslavement and pointless servitude. These gods are legion around us, from Nike to Nextel, from Bloomberg to BMW. In the final analysis, these gods don't really have any power, because they are not the true God. Their ads seem to offer the best of life, but living in thrall to them leads to the culture of death.

For us "being free to" is deeply qualified by "being free from" and "being free for." For us freedom is not a guaranteed right. It is not inherently bestowed as our right by our human nature. Rather, it is a costly gift purchased with precious blood. It issues not out of how we see ourselves, or our place at the top of the food chain, but out of God's nature. Freedom has little to do with the control that revels in choosing. Freedom arises out of the encounter with the true and living God. Freedom begins in Jesus's loving sacrifice to seek the best for us and for the world before seeking for himself.

Where Submission Is Not a Dirty Word

To stick with our marriage metaphor, in matters of authority and freedom, I am reminded of fresh-faced couples who approach me, hoping that I will preside at their wedding service. When we plan that service, I give them a brochure suggesting biblical texts having to do with marriage, and ask which they would select as most fitting.

Nestled among the more rhapsodic biblical texts are some that never get selected. Texts like Ephesians 5:22–28 and Colossians 3:18–19. Texts where Paul the Apostle enjoins wives to subject themselves to husbands, and husbands are commanded to love wives with Jesus's submissive love. If one word makes the hair on back of our neck stand up, it is *submit*. Westerners submit to nobody. For us to submit is to be dominated and to forfeit liberty. To submit is to lose the dignity of shaping our own lives according to our own tastes. Yet according to this measure, that makes Britney Spears or Deion Sanders—the poster children for submitting to none but the self—the quintessential free persons. In view of that, are we so impressed with what we call freedom? Perhaps within our daily constraints, the romance of such a freedom seems more promising than how it is lived out.

For Christians, submission is not ugly, but beautiful. It is our ultimate end. In song after song, the psalmist longs to bring his will into accord with Yahweh's. The effect verges on ecstatic. Paul meant nothing less harmonious as he urged wives to submit to husbands, and only a little less pointedly, husbands to submit to wives.

For Christians, submission to God in Jesus Christ and being subject to one another in mutual accountability is not tyranny. It is how God dwells at the heart of our covenantal community. It is the living stuff of faith. Letting ourselves get caught up in collective dreams beyond our own falls hard on our ears, having been told that it is up to us by ourselves to decide what life means and let our dreams rule.

All of this hints at a great mystery. For as we conform to God's will, what to most might seem like abject servitude transforms us in wondrous, unexpected ways. Things are revealed to us and within us that would otherwise never appear. We awaken to new realities and possibilities. Our vainglorious dreams are subsumed under greater, more redeeming dreams. We become something better than would be otherwise possible left to our own decisions and devices. Freedom is becoming the people God meant us to be, singly and together. Freedom is doing what God created us to do. Freedom, it might seem, is found in unexpected places.

Strange Dreams: When Conforming Becomes Transforming

My confirmation of faith at age thirteen was the result of two years' study, prayer, and church involvement. All fifteen of us deserved our reputation as "the worst confirmation class" the pastors ever had. Years later, I still feel guilt about the senior pastor's heart attack. For we were unruly and inattentive, obtuse and defiant. We made it clear that we were there only because of our parents. For us the class was a joke. We were benevolently dragged, sighing and moaning, toward citizenship in God's kingdom.

As Confirmation Sunday approached, Pastor Edwin T. Clemens smiled a smile of mild retributive justice. The church had only the vaguest idea how much trouble we had been. But as we stood before the entire congregation on Confirmation Sunday, nothing could be hidden. If we were unprepared or belligerent, as we had been not infrequently in class, it would be evident to all. As we had caught flak from our parents for rumors of our uncooperativeness, we denied it and blamed it on the misbehavior of classmates. But no such cop-outs on Confirmation Sunday.

Our Lutheran tradition meant a Confirmation Sunday format where weighty Augsberg-like doctrinal questions were to be put to us and we immediately answer with memorized deep, coherent, and considered answers. We were completely intimidated. Late in the year, we met after class and met the challenge head on.

What was our response? While no budding theologues, we did know the score. Our only chance of throwing off our deserved reputation was to learn these assigned responses dead solid perfect and smile radiantly in our white robes. No whining. No excuses. No exceptions. We administered considerable peer pressure to these ends. We even stooped to helping friends to learn catechetical responses.

Confirmation Sunday arrived and our plan unfolded seamlessly. We were such wise angels for being so young! Only once did a confirmand

even hesitate. The congregation concluded we were misunderstood and needed a chance. We were but rascals who at bottom truly loved God. The clergy scratched their heads.

Turning the tables on the ministers and redeeming our reputation was less of a thrill than we expected. Children are masters at extricating themselves from the trouble they create. It is at best an adolescent thrill. Instead, another unexpected satisfaction arose. Despite ourselves, we unwittingly mastered much of the core teaching of what it means to follow Jesus, phrases that were burned into our souls. Having already seen our confirmation responses illustrated by innumerable examples within that congregation, it took deeper root in us than we would have supposed. We became better than we deserved by standing on our own feet where we had been sleepwalking. We had taken matters in hand and risen to the occasion. We had become young men and women. This was real freedom.

If this transformed us—and it did me—it happened because we first conformed. All of this was possible because at the peak of America's iconoclastic defiance (1968), at the apex of our own personal rebellion (age thirteen), we had conformed to a will and story higher than our own. Submitting to the authority of a community better and holier than we were authorized us to become who God intended us to be.

Our Dreams and God's Dream

If anything is sacrosanct in America, it is the consistent message of parents to youth that they are obligated to become whatever their little hearts desire. What is more American than the little "you can become anything you want!" talk with our children, even when what we want isn't worth much. As a result, my own boomer generation retreated into countercultural utopian communes only to quickly stagger back into the mainstream when we ran out of money, direction, and ideals.

Today, after fleeting adolescent flirtations with becoming marine biologists in order to save the dolphins, youth flock to the MBA/investment banker/corporate executive track. "You teach me that my obligation is to serve myself by fulfilling my dreams in what I choose to do? That's simple. The answer is: 'Show me the money!'"

The first problem with letting our meager dreams drive our life's direction is that we so lack imagination. We lack awareness of the full range of options for what wonders and miracles might transpire in the world. Our dreams may sound impressive, but they are usually too small. It is only our exalted part in them—the money, the fame, the success, and the power—that makes them seem grand. When our dreams do become great, it is only because a community of transcendent ideals and character has somewhere grabbed us and had its way with us.

For example, it never would have occurred to a Yugoslavian girl that she could alter the world's willingness to love our neighbor by caring for the dying in the streets of Calcutta. That is monumental. It took the Christian community of the church in all of its compassion and loving-kindness to suggest such a thing could happen. The church made Mother Teresa.

It never would have occurred to a Swiss pastor that the Christian West was dangerously misguided in accommodating matters of spirit to the world in the name of progress, ignoring gulags and holocausts right under the nose of our bank accounts. That is beyond human scale. Then World War I hit, laying threadbare our sad illusions of inexorable human improvement and relentless progress. It took the Christian community of the church, with its deep reflection and stubborn witness across time and space, to give Karl Barth this awareness. Then he began writing and talking, paddling against the seemingly omnipotent public opinion, resisting the Nazis while conservatives and liberals were selling out, reminding us to start with the sovereign God rather than with ourselves.

It never would have occurred to a lanky Alabama lad that he might spearhead efforts to eliminate poverty housing in the world by rallying the rich and poor together to build simple homes with no-interest loans. That is prodigious. It took the Christian community of the church, hungering and thirsting for righteousness, to advance such an impossibly ambitious proposition. Then Millard Fuller initiated his crusade, and Habitat for Humanity began building homes for those who dwelt in shacks, building homes by the hundreds of thousands.

America is a dream factory like no other place on earth. It is too bad that the dreams we buy and sell are so absorbed with ourselves and individual greatness. This is why our dreams are so small. As the Evil One has divided us up, he has conquered. The good news is God has a bigger dream, and that dream has been revealed. The New Testament advances this dream. A remarkably large portion of the Gospels announces and describes the establishment of the kingdom of God.

This kingdom or reign of God is nothing other than God's dream for all of the earth. It represents a deep longing for right relationship as primeval as Eden. It takes into account everything dark and forbidding that has happened since then. God's dream represents the consummation of 4,000 years of God trying to win us back and create a lasting peace. It is as personal as every one of us in our uniqueness; it leaves no one behind. It brings power to make right what we cannot correct. It is a still unfolding drama of redemption. And we each have a key role that no other can occupy.

We are constantly more susceptible to selling this out than we realize. For example, a pastor in Illinois arrived new to his congregation. When Advent neared, the secretary asked him about their themed approach to Christmas that year. Of course, the Christmas season is when we need to be most careful with our dreams, given how the surrounding society has co-opted them. The pastor asked her to repeat the question. "How will we 'do' Christmas? Last year the theme was snowflakes. The year before it was candlelight. The year before that, sleigh rides." A pause. "Our theme this year will be the birth of Jesus Christ," he countered. "And we will probably be repeating that again for the next few years." We can substitute lesser dreams for the dream of God without even realizing it.

More than anything, what keeps us from finding our place in the dream of God's reign is the American prejudice that it is all up to us to decide what our lives mean. It is all up to us to figure out what we are to do with our lives. It is all up to us to author and shape and live out our personal dream. We cannot participate in God's dream until our personal dreams of glory recede into God's larger, more encompassing dream. If we cannot relinquish our personal dreams in favor of this vast holy dream, we are captive. We are captive to the unspoken tyranny of the self. America is a dream factory. Whoever shapes our dreams has power over us.

When Dreams Collide

Where do dreams—human and divine—gather and collide more forcefully than around weddings? When I began my ministry, I saw weddings as a means of grace to introduce newcomers to the gospel and to invite them into life within Christian community.

So if couples expressed even the vaguest interest in these matters, I was their man. I would "do" the wedding. The problem is that couples will say most anything to obtain access to the church for its backdrop to stage wedding fantasies entertained since childhood. Then having staged the Ken-and-Barbie dream extravaganza, polite respect would shift to rueful disregard. After a few years of this, I realized what I was doing wrong. These couples were expecting something from the church, and getting it. We were expecting nothing from these couples, and we also were getting it. Something was clearly wrong.

I counseled with leading lay leaders about this state of affairs. We decided to focus on couples already part of a Christian church (needing to be married in our locality) or couples willing to unite with a church. It didn't have to be our church (avoiding religious imperialism), but they had to indicate their intentions to unite with their new church to their new pastor. This guarded the church from abuse and kept me from ending up feeling like a cult prostitute, servicing the American empire by providing a whimsical backdrop for its dreams—a picture-perfect church wedding. I applied the policy even-handedly, even for the grown children of the local church I served. After all, the wedding liturgy everywhere presumed couples living in Christian community. Why not express this up front as an expectation?

Among the inquiring wedding calls I received was one from a daughter of our congregation, living in California. This young woman had been something of a wild child, but she was now settling down and making a life. We had a pleasant conversation and she was excited about life with her fiancé. She asked me what she needed to do to be married in her home church. Aside from the meetings to counsel and to plan the wedding, all that we asked was that they attend to the spiritual foundation of their marriage by finding a local church where they might worship and serve God, creating a context for living out the vows they would make. Only this one thing needed attention before we could plan the wedding.

At this point our visit became less animated. She pointed out that her husband didn't have a church background; that they might well be moving in the not-too-distant future; that they were leading busy lives and needed Sundays to rest. I responded that she didn't want merely a church wedding, but a marriage with Jesus Christ as covenant partner. And this was all but impossible separated from others seeking the same goal.

She promised to think about it, but I never heard from her again. Basically, they were married in a church that asked nothing of them. This was hard on her, but much harder on her parents, who were among the strongest Christians in that church. I had worked closely with her father as the chief lay officer of the church. They worshiped every Sunday they were in town. They were stalwart friends of my predecessor and yet fully opened their arms and respected me as a callow thirty-year-old "senior minister." They guided and comforted me in trying circumstances. He had supported me completely when we were forced to dismiss staff. They were generous in every way. We dined in each other's homes and laughed at each other's jokes. And I could feel how sorely disappointed they were with me.

Her parents could have driven me out of that church with a wave of their hands. But instead they bowed to what we were attempting without completely grasping it. Weeks later, rather than avoid this ache, I called the father to ask how things were. "I'm all right. But you might speak with her mother. She is still broken up." Not only did they receive my pastoral care, they supported me as I stumbled along, and continued like nothing happened. Their rare demonstration of loyalty to Christ's church still stands as a bright light. The faith of people who would submit to the church's spiritual authority as bigger than themselves is humbling indeed.

What do we do when cloying personal dreams clash with the unsentimental claims of God's dream? Does the church have the authority to expect anything of those in its pews? Or are they religious sellers, where the customer is always right? Do clergy have only responsibility to do as we are told and no authority in such matters? And if we do have authority here, how can we wield it in faithful instead of self-serving ways?

Where We Are Right Now

Increasingly, without having yet articulated it, we are realizing that this land of personal affluence and global influence is not what we were yearning for. And it is even further removed from the biblical vision of our destiny. We hear echoes of that as persons in places of power step down to pursue callings as artists. As couples making money hand over fist exit the fast lane, retire early, and simplify. As youths swarm World Trade Organization conferences and plead, "How much is enough?"

Local churches have as many guiding dreams for their raison d'être as there are rides at Disney World. Sometimes those dreams have to do with the spirit of being productive and useful Americans. Sometimes the dream of a church is a center to train our children in what is good and edifying and to protect them from what is wrong and destructive. Sometimes these guiding dreams have a civic-minded ethos of like-minded people helping one another to get ahead. Sometimes the dream is lobbying legislatures and working the channels of the state—from the ideological right or left—to create a more perfect union. Sometimes it is becoming an arts center that emphasizes themes of "spirituality."

Sometimes—most amazing of all—churches aspire to follow in the way Jesus walks before us and to become the living body of Christ, the light of God in a darkened world, showing how cruciform striving rises up into resurrected living. As a pastor, I am most surprised by how few Christians and how few churches are interested in the last of these many options.

Don't mistake my meaning. Nothing is wrong with loving your homeland and your place in it. Nothing is wrong with giving our children a solid moral foundation of virtue. Nothing is wrong with helping one another to get ahead in a tough world. Nothing is wrong with inviting government to support the cause of Christ or letting the arts narrate the stories and images of faith with creative expression.

The problem arises when any one of these usurps the first importance of worshipping Jesus Christ in all things. The problem is taking the primacy of Jesus for granted by saying that he already comes first when clearly he does not. The problem is our reticence to live out his exalted place in our lives as demonstrated through basic practices like regular observance of the sacraments, reading God's Word and seeing our lives in new ways, offering hospitality to the needy and strangers, keeping the Sabbath in specific ways that free us, praying our way through crises as though everything depends on God, practicing sacrificial giving in the form of the tithe, observing the seasons of the Christian calendar, and constantly challenging one another to let Jesus rise among us in new ways and to let all other distractions fall to the floor.

Today people of faith are becoming more aware that we cannot serve two or three masters. We are asking to whom we finally belong. Which claims upon us are binding, and which are negotiable? Where do we take our bearings? Under which reign are we finally citizens? We answer that every time we take our children to the soccer tournament instead of to the confirmation retreat; every time we book the luxury cruise and toss whatever income we have left over toward God's purposes; every time we feather our own downy nests at the expense of faceless workers losing jobs; every time we shop for a more agreeable church as issues like these surface. Such tensions lurk beneath our glossy, polite surfaces.

This haunted landscape—rich in things, but poor in soul—might seem fertile ground for the proclamation of the death and resurrection of Jesus Christ as an alternative to the wealthy, successful, and civilized despair around us. And the good news now is precisely that.

As the church, we are the living body of Jesus Christ today. How can we regain the voice with which Jesus fixed the attention of the world to the hill country of Judea? How can we inspire acts like the signs and wonders celebrated upon the plains of Galilee? Before his ascension Jesus promised greater signs and wonders arising from those who follow him. How can God authorize us for faithful witness in a day when we have lost our warrant in the eyes of many? These essential questions underlie the indifference and inertia that we find in the pews of churches.

With secular society pushing the church away, with the steady advance of insulating our various Western homelands from God, the church now has the chance to offer a new life in God's realm under the reign of Christ in a way that offers something completely different and full of hope. Indeed the opportunity now exists for the gospel of Jesus Christ to come alive among us in a manner that has not been possible for many centuries. While being a Christian is currently tough, with the breakdown of long-established ties, I would not exchange this day for any other.

I have seen the church spontaneously rise up into the charge of its lofty destiny in ways that have personally touched and sustained me, and I suspect so has the reader. We do well to pause over these moments and not neglect them to see what they suggest as possible for the future. For example, I remember, not long into serving that difficult downtown church mentioned earlier, finding myself seriously ill from having eaten a bad oyster. I was very sick, sleeping fourteen hours per day, and highly contagious. My wife was pregnant with our second child and working a demanding internship to finish her terminal degree. Her mother was dying, she was sole parent to our two-year-old, and had moved to our new community less than a year before. On the church front, just before taking ill, I had led the way in hiring a promising new associate pastor who was clearly not yet equal to being that, never mind covering for both of us in my absence.

That local church pulled together to care for our family when my wife alone could not. They brought us meals every night, picked up prescriptions, and ran other errands for us. People constantly asked what more could they do for us. We had just come through a draining three-year interim ministry, and that church filled in around the associate pastor to get us through these weeks and make certain that what needed to get done was getting done. They hid from me their crisis in leadership until I was strong enough to hear the news and do something about it. It was a remarkable lesson in how, when it needs to do so, the church can become much more than it has been or usually is.

Likewise, I have seen the church respond in ways that have touched the world and made a difference. For example, as "crack" was first reaching epidemic proportions in large cities back in the eighties, an African-American pastor called me. His church was in the Twelfth Precinct of Columbus, at the epicenter of the new drug problem, and his people were panicked about what this would mean for their lives, their homes, and their families. We knew it wouldn't be a wholly adequate response to this new demonic wrinkle in drug abuse, but we decided upon a symbolic response to take back this neighborhood from this new threat and to announce that we would not meekly surrender.

As churches we would band together to march upon and pray over the crack houses, the new foothold for crack in Columbus. On Sunday morning I announced to our downtown interracial church the plea from our sister church and reported that I would march with them that Friday night. Would anybody care to accompany me? That Friday about fifty of us joined the African-American churches in the Twelfth Precinct. As in the civil rights days, we first spent considerable time in prayer, song, encouragement, and testimony. As a fellow downtown pastor, I found a microphone thrust before me and preached my first sermon without a text. What did Jesus tell his followers? Don't worry about the words you will be asked to speak; they will be given you when it counts the most. In that moment, Jesus's promise held true.

The police guarding us from a distance were quietly stunned at how we at once peaceably and forcibly came together, grateful for not having to be the only force resisting this new menace. We marched with candles in hand on several crack houses, forming a circle of light, singing songs and praying prayers, directly addressing those inside, lingering long enough to assert our presence. I shall not forget the users fleeing the back door upon our approach, the furtive looks from behind window curtains—like roaches scattering when the light comes on in a seedy room—the palpable sense of fear and panic among those causing so much fear to the vast majority of hardworking and law-abiding neighbors. From that time until I left the city, I regularly did citizen ride-alongs with police officers in the Twelfth Precinct, not wanting this real threat to our neighbors to get too far away from me.

How did John put this at the opening of his Gospel? "The light shines in the darkness, and the darkness did not overcome it" (John 1:5). Sometimes we simply have to visibly live this and outwardly say it, and the threats we face will themselves tremble. Again, it was a remarkable lesson in how the church can become much more than it has been or usually is in a time of crisis.

Backbone without Arrogance

Speaking of dreams, the dreamiest book in the New Testament connects who we are (worshippers of God in Jesus Christ) with what we do (ministry and mission) like nowhere else. The following is one of the visions that close out the Revelation to St John.

Then the angel showed me the river of the water of life, bright as crystal, flowing from the throne of God and of the Lamb, through the middle of the street of the city. On either side of the river is the tree of life with its twelve kinds of fruit, producing its fruit each month; and the leaves of the tree are for the healing of the nations. Nothing accursed will be found there any more. But the throne of God and of the Lamb will be in it, and his servants will worship him; they will see his face, and his name will be on their foreheads. And there will be no more night; they need no light of lamp or sun, for the Lord God will be their light, and they will reign forever and ever. And he said to me, "These words are trustworthy and true, for

76

the Lord, the God of the spirits of the prophets, has sent his angel to show his servants what must soon take place." (Revelation 22:1–6)

Notice what transpires here. As the river of the water of life flows through the streets of the heavenly Jerusalem, it waters the roots of trees whose fruit will be unfailing in feeding us and whose leaves will be used for the healing of the nations. What are the origins of that river? It flows from the holy temple where the saints and cherubim and seraphim are all ecstatic in their worship of the Lord.

The connection between who we are and what we do is necessary and essential. Without it, we confuse things primary with things secondary and tertiary, and we will end up worshipping ourselves in a variety of guises rather than the one true God.

Today the most creative—and unasked—questions for the church are: Where can we assert the cross at the center of that temple ahead of foreign priorities that have edged God to the margins of our lives? How can we reintroduce the sovereignty of God's choices in places where the practicalities of "getting by" have crept in and rule how things get done? Must discipleship always bow to family vacations, fashion magazines, sports teams, declarations of the State Department, and policies of public schools? How can the Holy Spirit speak to such parties with a voice they have not recently heard? The churches that find their way into these questions, and follow Jesus Christ with deep and coherent replies, are those that will lead God's people into the next millennium.

5

POWER OR AUTHORITY?

L. Gregory Jones, Dean of Duke Divinity School, tells a tale of two T-shirts.[1] Son Nathan called his parents from a summer academic program to which his high school had nominated him. He was outraged. "Mom and Dad, you won't believe what they put on the official T-shirt we bought. I won't even wear it!" On the front of the shirt it said, "Accept nothing," and on the back, "Question everything."

"Those sayings are just wrong," Nathan insisted. "They're not what I believe." As a person of faith, it would seem to be enough to be the parent of such a child, but there is more. The summer before, Nathan had attended a youth academy for Christian formation. And that had been a wonderful, spiritually empowering experience that allowed him to claim the Christian faith in a new way. Never mind the stellar roster of Christian scholars and theologians he had devoured.

More tellingly, he had also brought home a T-shirt that became his favorite to wear to high school. Black with bold white letters, on the front it read, "loser." On the back, it quoted Jesus: "Whoever loses his life for my sake will find it." Wearing such a T-shirt to high school is much more deeply and creatively radical than any of the Students for a Democratic Society antics or Weather Underground posturing I saw in my high school days. Not surprisingly, Nathan had adopted this deeply countercultural stance by looking to Jesus.

Look to Him and Be Radiant

"You call me Teacher and Lord, and you say well, for so I am" (John 13:13). For the most part, Jesus is low-profile in terms of ascribing authority to himself. Jesus's authority as Son of God is something that he never insists upon and certainly not something he would ever argue with others. For the most part, the Gospels record the people responding not to Jesus's claims of authority, but to his acts of authority: Jesus taught with authority (Luke 4:32), he commands evil spirits with authority (Mark 1:27), he has authority to forgive sins (Matt. 9:6), for example.

For Jesus, ascribing full authority to him as Lord and Master is a matter of encountering, knowing, and living the truth. For Jesus, let us not forget, authority is inextricably linked with truthfulness. Once the veil is lifted and the scales fall from our eyes by what God reveals in the Son, it is only natural that we affirm Jesus for who he is, only natural that our lives overflow with praise and service, only natural that we seek after the full human stature he showed us by our own simple obedience. We emphasize early and often in this pivotal chapter: true authority does not compel or force or even insist on acknowledgement. But when such an authoritative truth as the life, death, and resurrection of Jesus Christ is lifted up, it cannot help but draw all persons unto itself.

Jesus never demands, "You *will* submit to me." Divine love (or any love, for that matter) ceases to be love as it forces the beloved to respond with love and adoration. Jesus leaves up to us the discernment of the ultimate claim upon our lives. Interestingly, Jesus was harder on those who imagined that they could minimize or sidestep the faith dilemma of this hard decision about his place in the ultimate scheme of things than those who denied him altogether. Jesus came to bring the sword of throwing us into this kind of faith dilemma.

We are perfectly free to choose, as we like to remind ourselves. We are so free, in fact, that we can attack and persecute Jesus, as his home synagogue did. We can spit in his face, mock and deride him. Or we can put him to death, as the demented proxies of humankind accomplished. Jesus could have called down legions of angels from heaven to enforce his authority, as he reminded his follower in Gethsemane, when he bid him to put his sword away after taking off the ear of a temple guard. Jesus never called down his authority in this way.

But once Jesus's life is recreated in us through the judgment and grace wrought upon the cross, we cannot help but recognize Jesus's absolute authority over us. Jesus stooped to the grimy depths of humankind to conquer, and conquer he did, as the resurrection evidences and affirms. The upshot is a complete and effective dominion, in which I acknowledge, "You are worthy, our Lord . . ." (Rev. 4:11). And yet, I must offer it freely, my extreme gratitude for his redeeming acts seeking to match the magnitude of the grace I have received.

If our Lord only insisted upon our obedience, he would become simply one more taskmaster and forfeit any real authority. Instead he invites obedience without demanding it. Or better, his presence commands authority without demanding it. For he knows that as we see him for who he is, we must fall to our knees. Then he is easily Lord of our life, and living in adoration of him becomes our fullness of living.

Authority and obedience have a bad name in the world, mostly because of the abusive ways in which worldly power has been wielded. John Buchanan of the *Christian Century* writes,

> These days, an exercise in word association would probably elicit *abusive,* *oppressive,* and *misused* before hitting upon any benign terms to go with *authority.* We instinctively tend to regard authority as something that constrains people, not as something that empowers them. But clearly authority does both—and it empowers precisely because it constrains.[2]

Young Nathan Jones reminds me that the level of my growth in grace is revealed by the way I look at obedience. We should have a much higher view of the word *obedience,* rescuing it from the world's mire of somehow being diminished or dishonored by it.

Can't Anybody out There Play This Game?

I have served as a senior minister of multiple-staff churches for two decades now, since age thirty. Over certain periods I have struggled mightily to distinguish how the fact of our being Christian as staff and lay leaders made the slightest difference in our being together. Coming into church leadership, what I hoped would be an interpersonal oasis of Christian solidarity has too often ended less convivial than a random gathering of passersby at an interstate truck stop.

In launching my ministry at local churches, I have met with coworkers and explained how I saw myself as leader and overseer of their work. As their supervisor, I have watched other clergy and staff smile and nod, never ask questions or volunteer their own initiatives about our shared challenge, only to use my own views on the ministry against me behind my back. In other words, despite my shortcomings or maybe because of them, I have felt royally set up in what should have been close and cooperative Christian working relationships.

In particular, I remember a minister of Christian education. She refused my supervision, because, she claimed, no person should have to answer to or be "under" another. And any hint of hierarchy on earth below or heaven above was inherently oppressive and unchristian. (Never mind that Peter, James, and John as well as others like Judas and Mary Magdalene enjoyed closer proximity to Jesus, and also more intense scrutiny before him.) Sadly, the work of this gifted woman suffered most in her inability to be accountable to anyone but herself. She ended up leaving the ministry because of a lack of direction and focus, lost somewhere on the trackless plains before the forever receding horizon of her "needs," resentments, and perceived slights. Moreover, in her next line of work, a different profession within the public sector, she was asked to leave.

The point here is that there is much spoken and unspoken resistance to working out matters of authority in a church staff setting. I have sat at staff meetings effectively unable to convey that serving Christ's church is a greater honor than working at the Bureau of Motor Vehicles. We had no more passion, no more joy, no more commitment, no more a sense of shared hope and adventure than this in our daily routine. How could such a grand calling—and *everyone* on a church staff is called—digress into punching a time card and getting along by going along?

I have led church staffs where the drama of who said what, how thus-and-such took it, and who was lining up with whom reigned supreme. A petty soap opera crept in and displaced the foundational drama of God reconciling the world in Jesus Christ. It was the sad ecclesial equivalent of smarmy reality TV shows, with the self-absorbed smallishness of innuendo and backbiting delighting our inner philistine. In the church, this waste of energy and time squanders most any chance that God might have had for transformative ministry through us.

Our authority as pastors and church leaders is in direct proportion to our willingness to serve in ways like Jesus, even if only God and not humankind recognizes it. Father Henri Nouwen wrote:

> Compassion must become the core and even the nature of authority. When the Christian leader is a man of God for the future generation, he can be so only insofar as he is able to make the compassion of God with man—which is visible in Jesus—credible in his own world.[3]

How much we are servants, how little of the time we pastors get to be "bosses," and how emotionally and spiritually demanding this is could be the biggest surprise for students coming out of seminary. Mark Schwehn says this better than I ever could:

> For Christianity, the quest for truth is bound up inextricably with discipleship, and therefore the shape of power is for them always cruciform. . . .

So long as Christians remember that, for disciples, power is not dominion, but obedience, faithfulness, and suffering servanthood, they can rightly claim an integral connection between truth and power.[4]

What Schwehn calls rightfully constituted power is here denominated as true authority.

Blessedly, in recent years the more ragged staff relationships have become the exception (I tolerate them less). And I have also been blessed by working relationships where the sense of trust, partnership, compassion, and mutual submission as Christian servants has carried the day. Admittedly, this is hard to find, and staff relationships are never without bumps. But God looms larger, we loom smaller, and more gets accomplished when servants of God come into right relationship with one another.

It *Can* Happen Here

On the positive side, the church staff working relationships blessed by God and charmed by the Holy Spirit have carried the day in recent years. One such relationship was with a pastor in a church to which I was eventually called as senior minister. Already the associate on staff, she had also applied for the position. The head of the search committee had strung her along, not wanting to alienate her, but never taking her candidacy seriously. When I met with the staff during the interview process, she and I exchanged warning shots across each other's bows. This conflict was intentionally set up by the search committee's chair, he later confided to me. It was his own *Lord of the Flies* experiment of putting between us something that we couldn't both have and then seeing how we would "handle" each other. Miraculously, we quickly recovered from this initial act of sabotage.

By the grace of God, we found enough common ground to make a go of it, together serving that local church. Within days of my arrival, she was fending off a divorce. I was still a bit raw coming off a rocky relationship with a church staff (just described above) where I had been roughed up. My senior pastor predecessor remained in the community and was trying to play us off each other behind the scenes. She and I were of a different generation than the power core of the church, which my predecessor further helped to feel disenfranchised. Of course, this sounds completely untenable, and a recipe for disaster. I suppose it should have been.

Such elements do not typically suggest the makings of a rare and holy friendship where both parties would put themselves sufficiently aside to let Jesus reign. But upon reversing our painful start, and sidestepping other personal hurts, from the beginning we pledged ourselves to both kneel before Christ. And what we declared to one another, by the grace of God we also backed up with our words and deeds. As moments inevitably came when we failed to live up to such a lofty aspiration, we called each other on it and forgave each other. This is always a rare and beautiful thing.

Trust, respect, humor, loyalty, sensitivity, and frankness were our building blocks. Companionship, prayer, confidence, and laughter were the concrete holding them together. Together as pastors we both grew more than we could have apart. And the church grew as well, not just in numbers, but in depth of faith, range of witness, and scope of compassion. The key to this productive working relationship was holding ourselves accountable to God first, despite the natural resistance of our sinfulness. No equalizer is more powerful than both parties on bended knee before God. That is the beginning of genuine authority.

Theologically and generationally, we faced a church that came hard at us from several sides. Putting on the whole armor of Christ, standing back to back, and allowing no one to get in between us, we repulsed divisive threats. Things began to turn. She deployed herself more toward veteran members and I toward new members. She played more of a reconciler/peacemaker role, while I stood ground theologically in other areas that had been sorely compromised. God did unexpected and wonderful things.

Benchmarks were established in our common life by which that congregation still measures itself. To a surprising degree, the church was living off our leadership, like a family depending on parents for stability and direction, come what may. When tested by irrationality and pettiness, we reminded each other, "*We* have to be the grown-ups." She was better at not returning evil with evil than I was, but by the end of our tenure together, she had taught me much about reconciliation. In turn, she had become stronger and more indomitable in those areas of faith and ministry where compromise is anathema.

As our time serving together was winding down, I once insisted that she, and not I, make a difficult pastoral call to confront someone. She laughed out loud and remarked that it was the first time I had actually pulled rank and issued an order. It was true. In terms of articulating the church's theological vision, I had mostly played lead, and she had mostly played accompaniment, but not always, and almost never by fiat, mandate, or decree.

At the same time, in pursuing that vision, often blindsided by flak, there were moments when long negotiations about a course of action would have been a stupid luxury. She laid out the issues and told me exactly what needed to be addressed, the necessary steps for follow-up, and I followed down her directives. And I felt that same liberty and trust to address her in a similarly straightforward way when I saw something that required her immediate response and attention.

Needless to say, maintaining personal boundaries between us as man and woman was essential. As Buchanan observed, authority is like the Hoover Dam: it can empower only because it also constrains. Still, we collaborated in all things. And after our crabby Spencer Tracy/Katharine Hepburn beginning, we realized that we were well suited as working partners, and that God was working through our unity. As I said earlier, I have known church staff relationships when they have not served God, and also when they have. But I have learned much more from the latter, confounding the rule of thumb that we always learn more from our mistakes.

If we pastors feel the need to exercise our authority for its own sake, then it is worldly power that we exercise, and we have probably already lost our spiritual authority. But if we bring true authority, the clout of that leadership is not so much brought to bear in a capacity to compel, command, and order. We can hardly notice where credit and account-ability for one person begins and the other ends.

At the same time, let us be clear. If there are worthy shepherds but no true followers able to respond by recognizing and following true leadership—like Jesus's being chased out of his home synagogue at Nazareth—true pastoral authority loses its capacity to make a difference and transform. A shepherd cannot lead a pack of hyenas.

True spiritual authority issues from an elusive but not unreachable place that is a combination of conviction, compassion, authenticity, sacrifice, and godliness. Above all else, it is feeling passion where Jesus Christ felt passion and finding ways to share it. Frankly, that trumps everything else. It may take time, even years, for people to fully sense this and respond accordingly. But finally, whether they say so or not, our people can tell. We are known by our fruits.

Rebels without a Cause

As mentioned earlier, our Western secular popular culture is natu-rally suspicious of authority. The rebel—any rebel—has become our quintessential self-image. And there is both good and bad in this. It is good that we have proven fairly resistant to ancient forms of tyranny foisted upon us by unquestioned institutions. It is bad that in refusing to acknowledge good and rightful authority because of deep-seated fear, we are blind to subtle contemporary forms of tyranny—like isolating and corrosive individualism—which creep in, enslave, and make life much less than God meant it to be. Today such destructive forces are often protected as "freedom."

It is hard for us to imagine a common use of the word *authority* that is not pejorative and burdened with negative connotations. This is not wholly irrational. Frankly, history teems with so many episodes where authority was wielded in such authoritarian ways we might imagine there is no difference. When we think of authority, we picture raw, acquisitive power seizing and controlling the unwitting, as worldly empires have employed it since time immemorial until it was wrested from their grasp by another, fiercer empire. Ultimately, this is a matter of coercion and force, violence and killing, which are all linked with authority in our way of seeing the world.

Phrases like "spiritual authority" are barely out of our mouths before they conjure painful fears about black marks on our history in the form of abuses like the Spanish Inquisition, the Salem witch trials, or the Crusades. Born out of a revolution against medieval authority, the simple truth is that Western democracies increasingly do not like authority. At camps like the one Nathan Jones attended, authority is set up like a straw man and pelted with overripe fruit. We cannot imagine why authority is important or worth talking about.

Rather than striving to constitute authority in ways that are healthy and foundational for all that follows, in ways that allow for leadership and direction in a world where professional wrestling is high drama, we focus upon building hedges around it, putting in place checks and balances that will keep it from becoming monstrous. While accountability is always important, this reining in betrays our prejudice that authority is a necessary evil that is barely to be tolerated rather than a locus of direction and vision for a people who have lost their way. Is it any wonder that so few want to be pastors, or, for that matter, presidents, anymore? Douglas John Hall, Canadian theologian and scholar, has written,

> Standing at the portal of the third millennium, the Christian movement as a whole, and mainstream Protestantism especially, cries out for leadership. Never in its history has Christianity been so confused about itself, its message, its mission. When clerical authority is genuine, it is nothing more or less than a humble response to this need—not, therefore, to the need of clergy to achieve status.[5]

The problem with remaining distant, oblivious, or suspicious toward the shape of authority is that in this vacuum the human self has elevated itself to that throne and created a tyranny and captivity that we only begin to recognize, as chapter 3 began to explore. The problem with ignoring these matters is that those of us who imagine that we are free and clear of the well-documented historic abuses of authority are probably those most subject to them. We have all observed—in others and most painfully in ourselves—that the moment when we are most deluded is precisely when we see ourselves as free of all self-deception.

There are other problems with keeping our heads in the sand here. Miroslav Volf has observed that where no space is cleared for rightful authority, our lives become choked and overwhelmed with rules—big rules and small rules, rules that frame our interactions and rules that tangle the fine fabric of our personal lives.[6] This is the price of our socially sanctioned tyranny of the self, where a narrow sense of freedom rules the day—freedom from the church, freedom from God, from the state, from conventional morality, from nosy neighbors. This is the price where freedom from everything and everybody beyond ourselves is the absolute and ultimate good.

And then we wonder why churches spend years writing and rewriting documents like our by-laws or personnel policies, expending endless energy for what is almost always a fairly small return, and why these documents assume a centrality and a sanctity in our common life disproportionate to their limited role, while our churches are largely ignorant of and oblivious to the Word of God, which gives life itself instead of merely order. "Question authority!" scream bumper stickers. "Challenge everything," invites the slogan for video games. "Live highly regimented lives" is the much lamented upshot. Because we have slain the dragon of medieval-style tyranny, and because we submit to no one, even when deference to another can show a still more excellent way, we end up being nibbled to death by regulatory ducks. In this we are penny-wise and pound-foolish. We do not often consider the price of our generally aversive attitude toward authority. It hasn't occurred to us that we live such heavily regulated lives in part because, lumping authority with all things authoritarian, we give such scant attention to how authority looks, acts, and talks when it is right.

In the early 1990s Coach Mike Krzyzewski and the Duke University Blue Devils won two national championships in NCAA basketball. More than this, they won in a dignified and enviable manner, without players being suspended by the university, cited by tabloid headlines, or arraigned in courts of law. This is rare in a day when the destructive antics of adults seep downward into what should be the purer amateur spirit of college and high school athletics. How did this come about? Did the coach write a massive codex of team rules, shadow every player to make certain they toed his line, and enforce these comprehensive and exhaustive regulations with an iron fist? Just the opposite.

Having already carved out his authority as leader by his record and treatment of others, Coach K asked his captains to meet with the team at the beginning of the year. He didn't attend this meeting. Together the players considered the many things they needed to do and how they needed to behave to reach their ultimate goal, a national championship. The players wrote and enforced the rules in service to their common goal. In view of their shared goal, the players owned and obeyed these standards, not as oppressive imposition from without or above, but as their one shot at the freedom of becoming those players and men they wanted with every iota of their being to become. I like to think this happened not only because Krzyzewski is a Christian, but also because he believes in God's reign (and the NCAA championship, hopefully in that order) as the end point from which we take our bearings and distinguish right from wrong. And if we start from the endpoint and work backward, great things will happen. Theological scholars call this teleological ethics.

This illustrates not only the importance of having an end point, a destiny, and a final vision of what life is supposed to be and where it is supposed to go as we travel life's path (the point of our discussion of teleological living and Christian ethics in chapter 3). It also shows how authority can function as a blessing rather than only a curse, how it gives freedom in constraining us rather than merely stifling our humanity.

We instinctively regard authority as something that constrains people, not as something that empowers us. But authority's power to empower, or to authorize what is creative and good and godly, lies precisely within its power to constrain. "If you want freedom," writes Miroslav Volf, "freedom from rules, freedom to be your best self, freedom to enjoy both God and neighbor—then you will want the divine law inscribed on your heart. Everything else is slavery, more or less!"[7]

As One Unafraid of Authority

As comfortable as Jesus was both exercising and confronting authority, he will not let us get away with balking at, dismissing, and avoiding this great neglected issue of our time. The Gospels repeatedly describe Jesus as one who taught "having authority, and not as the scribes" (Mark 1:22) In our preference for rules and regulations over authority, with their endless process and infinite appeals, in some ways we seem to have chosen the scribes over Jesus Christ.

Because Jesus had faced down dauntingly self-aggrandizing temptations in his larger-than-life charge from the Father in the wilderness before starting his ministry, he was comfortable with authority, whether confronting its abuses or properly exercising it.

> A dispute also arose among them as to which one of them was to be regarded as the greatest. But he said to them, "The kings of the Gentiles lord it over them; and those in authority over them are called benefactors. But not so with you; rather the greatest among you must become like the youngest, and the leader like one who serves. For who is greater, the one who is at the table or the one who serves? Is it not the one at the table? But I am among you as one who serves." (Luke 22:24–27)

What we see in scenes like this is the world stood on its head as authority is reconstituted in ways that the visions of heaven comprehend but will forever leave this earth scratching its head. Throughout his life, facing his death, Jesus never lost track of which way was up and which was down. If we avoid matters of authority, and are therefore also vision-impaired, we need only look to him for our starting markers.

Jesus did not employ focus groups or bow to consumer demand. He did not consult with polls to carve out a constituency. He did not search out and then defer to public consensus. Jesus commanded attention because he molded consensus. His authority derived from neither institutional standing (he had none) nor from degrees and diplomas (he learned in the streets and temple courtyard) nor his embeddedness in the prevailing establishment (he was outside looking in). Jesus's authority was conferred by God and quickly recognized by the people because everywhere apparent within it was the rightly ordered purpose of ministering first to God's but no less to our best interests. That will always speak volumes.

When Jesus revealed the wisdom of a way greater than we were capable of conceiving, much less inventing, when he spoke more explicitly of a salvation through a cross rather than the usual conquest and subjugation, followers began to fall away. Jesus remained undeterred, and his authority undiminished, despite the waning of mass hysteria around him. He could maintain his standing without embellishing his status in the world's eyes, because his authority was rooted in his solidarity with the will of the Father. We should not neglect that the intersection of Jesus's oneness with the Father was finally in the way of the cross, which only the two of them understood at the time.

> When many of his disciples heard it, they said, "This teaching is difficult; who can accept it?" But Jesus, being aware that his disciples were complaining about it, said to them, "Does this offend you? Then what if you were to see the Son of Man ascending to where he was before? It is the spirit that gives life; the flesh is useless. The words that I have spoken to

you are spirit and life. But among you there are some who do not believe." For Jesus knew from the first who were the ones that did not believe, and who was the one that would betray him. And he said, "For this reason I have told you that no one can come to me unless it is granted by the Father." Because of this many of his disciples turned back and no longer went about with him. So Jesus asked the twelve, "Do you also wish to go away?" Simon Peter answered him, "Lord, to whom can we go? You have the words of eternal life. We have come to believe and know that you are the Holy One of God." (John 6:60–69)

In a day when the church cries out for leadership, when never in its history has the Christian church been so confused about itself, its message, and its mission, such steady and unshakable bearings are worth noting amid our stormy seas.

Worldly Power and Spiritual Authority

In reverent awe, born of hard-earned experience as a skilled pastor, the Reverend John McFadden describes how the difference between worldly power and spiritual authority was revealed to him in the life of the church. The context was his working relationship with his Wisconsin Conference minister (our low-church equivalent of a bishop) in the United Church of Christ. John penned these words at the occasion of the Reverend Fred Trost's retirement and publicly feted him with these warm pearls of insight.

It was the Budget Committee. Fred greeted everyone warmly, prayed earnestly, and outlined the difficult issues associated with balancing a budget in a year where funds were tight. Then, in a cordial but firm tone of voice, he identified the items in the proposed budget that were not open to discussion or debate!

Having been trained in Puritan self-control, I succeeded in choking back my outrage. Who does this man think he is? What is the point in serving on a committee of the Conference if the Conference Minister makes unilateral decisions? The word "arrogant" was one of the more printable I assigned to him, and I determined to maintain a certain distance. I am certain that for the next year or two he saw me as cool and aloof. The Great Facilitator had met Herr Pastor Trost, and the distance between the two appeared to be unbridgeable.

I can now look back and chuckle at how badly I misunderstood Fred and his motives in that early encounter. What I then perceived as arrogance I now appreciate as conviction; what I then heard as "this cannot be debated!" I now know was "let us debate this with real passion!" I was so deeply schooled in the ways of power that I failed to recognize genuine authority when I encountered it.

Fred Trost stands first among the mentors who have taught me that the integrity of the pastoral vocation grows from daring to claim the spiritual authority vested in us by the church. True spiritual authority begins only when we reject the sinful temptation to embrace the ways of power. Power is self-centered and self-serving; its clarion cry is "my will be done!" Power is measured in dollars, in clout, in control. It is brokered by fear and intimidation. Its goal is always to win and, in winning, to create losers. Power builds fiefdoms and empires. Power always believes in its own wisdom, its own strength, its own purpose. Power answers to nothing beyond itself, not even to God.

Authority is temporarily entrusted to our stewardship by that which is greater than we are and to which we are accountable. Spiritual authority must answer to scripture, to tradition, and to the living community of the church, from which it never stands apart or above. Spiritual authority grows from the humility born of knowing we are creatures, utterly beholden to our Creator. As such, we can never possess absolute certainty that our thoughts are wise, our actions righteous, so the authority invested in us must often be discharged in fear and trembling.

Yet, paradoxically, spiritual authority also grows from the confidence born of knowing that where our wisdom and righteousness end, God's begin, and that through the actions of the Holy Spirit these frail, earthen vessels may convey deeper truth and work greater deeds than our own limited abilities would permit. Spiritual authority acts most boldly when it first prays most humbly; it speaks with the greatest strength when it first listens most carefully. Spiritual authority seeks to empty itself of the conceit of possessing its own wisdom, so that it may say not "my will be done," but "Thy will be done."

True spiritual authority may reside in either a Great Facilitator or a Herr Pastor. It often leads us to a place somewhere between the two. When a Great Facilitator understands the truth of spiritual authority, he or she seeks to help the saints discern the prompting of the Holy Spirit in their discussion and debate. The goal is not to build consensus or resolve an issue by taking a vote. Rather, it is to discover together how the living Spirit is working and speaking through the gathered community of the church.

When a Herr Pastor understands the truth of spiritual authority, that person spends years in coming to know the saints of the church deeply, grieving with them in times of pain and loss, celebrating with them in their joys and new beginnings, until the pastor can no longer say with certainty where his or her own life ends and the life of the congregation begins. When the line between "I" and "we" becomes sufficiently blurred, Herr Pastor can speak with a clear, authoritative voice that is no longer tainted by the presumption of personal power.

Both the Great Facilitator and Herr Pastor must return frequently to the sources of their spiritual authority. They must study God's word in

Holy Scripture, preferably in fellowship with other Christians. They must pray, both in the stillness of their own hearts and in settings of Christian community. They must read the thoughts of saints who preceded them, so they can dialogue with the wisdom of the ages. They must worship God frequently, so that they never forget who they are, and whose they are. They must immerse themselves in Christian theology until it becomes second nature to experience the world through God's eyes, rather than their own.[8]

Blinded by the Light

McFadden is right. We do confuse authority with power, and then we throw out the baby with the bathwater. Unschooled in and unwilling to pause over the differences that John so lucidly sketches, we bunch the two as one, eschew the former, and fall unwittingly to the latter. So we do well to pause here.

Power is becoming my own authority unto myself, my own law unto myself, and answering to no other. Power accepts no judgments other than what works best for me and for all who stand with me. Usually these power moves get veiled by good manners and savoir faire, respectable social standing and institutional credibility. But make no mistake, power works by domination, coercion, and control. Its methods are manipulation, exploitation, and intimidation. Power trades on the fears of others, even as it is invisibly driven by the despair of its own gnawing fear. Like Herod sending for the magi, then bidding them to abet his evil, power senses that it is finally nobody. Power must finally fear another One greater who is excluded from its schemes and whose say is ultimate.

Because it is always on tenuous spiritual ground, power necessarily and obsessively looks to vindicate itself. As it does, it has blind spots the size of Montana. These pathetic, grandiose attempts issue forth in making additional conquests, in striking ludicrous postures, or in pompous extravagance in praise of oneself. We see the wretched excess of power in immortality projects that ultimately mock themselves in the high rises of Donald Trump and columns of Nicolae Ceausescu, the records of Pete Rose and the shrine of V. I. Lenin. We see it as Saddam Hussein's larger-than-life statues topple, and he tells us, yes, he was a very firm, but always a fair ruler. Power unconvincingly asserts itself in loud vainglory because its efforts to control must always necessarily be incomplete. It must protest and shout so loudly because it is ultimately so weak.

We also *confuse authority with authoritarianism.* That is, we cannot imagine how leadership or service could be exercised except in ways of worldly power. Therefore, even to submit to the One who created us becomes a kind of failure, as opposed to the glad surrender of finding our rightful place in God's greater plan as life finally reaches back toward its source up toward its destiny.

Here we brush up against autonomy, the sense that the only real freedom and goodness we can hope to gain as humans is in submitting to none but the self. Authoritarian power demands autonomy, meaning not so much freedom as becoming a law unto oneself (in Greek, *autos* means self, *nomos* means law), an immortal power needing only oneself, not needing God or neighbor. As we insist upon autonomy (too often an unalloyed good in my Congregational tradition), we glimpse this same trend within ourselves that we see in tyrants. For as the hair on the back of our neck stands up every time we hear that word *submit*—even if it is submitting to a parent, a mentor, or even our God—we see ourselves as self-generated and not wholly dependent at every moment on the grace of God.

To understand and destroy our wrongheadedness on autonomy we must realize the difference between human will and laws, and divine will and laws. As Miroslav Volf points out, the former is external to our being. The ordering of human ways is at best finding a way to get along with one another. At the same time, God's will and ways, aside from being an expression of the divine being, map what it means to live human lives and to be human beings. In harmony with God's will, we fulfill our calling as persons. This is why we can delight in God's law, like the psalmist likening it to honey (Ps. 19), but still feel dragged down by human rules and regulations.

In the time of Moses, God's will was given on tablets. In the time of Jesus, the law of the Messiah's new order is written on hearts of flesh. In the time to come, God's will and ways are so much a part of the ground of our existence that our greatest pleasure will be doing what God's will commands.

Finally, we *confuse authority with arrogance,* as McFadden confided in his first impressions of Fred Trost. And it is not a matter of submitting merely to another person, but even to our Creator and Redeemer. "Why does God need your praise?" those uninitiated to worship ask. "Why do you feel that you must do this every Sunday? Must you spend so much time and effort slaking the divine ego? Is this God so insecure as that, so needful of being exalted and putting people in their place?"

Such questions would all be excellent if God were merely a very large or very grand human being. But what this fails to see—until entering into whole-souled praise of God—is God's grandeur, God's mercy, God's grace, and God's love in making us. God is all in all, and we are but specks of stardust. Krister Stendahl once sighed that the older he became, the less excited he became about himself, and the more excited he was about God. That is so very wise.

I remember sitting in the front row of Manhattan's excellent JVC Jazz Festival. We awaited the band that had the night's top billing. But another duet, a Dominican pianist and a Spanish guitarist, unexpectedly took our breath away. Serendipitously, the music was magical, powerful, sensitive, and of a complete unity. The place exploded in applause and convulsed with delight at letting the artists know they had been heard, and that the incomparable sound was not unnoticed. After such scintillating music, if we had not responded—in praise—it would have been deeply painful. Frankly, we applauded more out of our need to respond than out of their need to hear us. That urbane crowd did not esteem themselves too low nor did they value the artists too high. No, it was just right.

Worshipping and consequently serving God is very much along these lines. As Christians, we put God first, before all other delights waiting to be enjoyed. Adoring praise and devoted service celebrates what mere compliments alone cannot convey, and when we are in touch with it, we know we are most alive, we know that we have brushed up against what is most essential in living.

In the final analysis, we can recognize this world's power and the ends it achieves by its willingness to manipulate, intimidate, threaten, menace, coerce, and even kill for what it believes in. In much the same way, we can recognize heaven's authority in Jesus's willingness to forgive, heal, invite, nurture, sacrifice, and even die for what God believes in, namely, us. These two can appear much the same, but appearances are deceiving. For power and authority begin in different places and ultimately transport us to different places. That is never so apparent as when they meet face to face, as in this Gospel text.

> As soon as it was morning, the chief priests held a consultation with the elders and scribes and the whole council. They bound Jesus, led him away, and handed him over to Pilate. Pilate asked him, "Are you the King of the Jews?" He answered him, "You say so." Then the chief priests accused him of many things. Pilate asked him again, "Have you no answer? See how many charges they bring against you." But Jesus made no further reply, so that Pilate was amazed. Now at the festival he used to release a prisoner for them, anyone for whom they asked. Now a man called Barabbas was in prison with the rebels who had committed murder during the insurrection. So the crowd came and began to ask Pilate to do for them according to his custom. Then he answered them, "Do you want me to release for you the King of the Jews?" For he realized that it was out of

jealousy that the chief priests had handed him over. But the chief priests stirred up the crowd to have him release Barabbas for them instead. Pilate spoke to them again, "Then what do you wish me to do with the man you call the King of the Jews?" They shouted back, "Crucify him!" Pilate asked them, "Why, what evil has he done?" But they shouted all the more, "Crucify him!" So Pilate, wishing to satisfy the crowd, released Barabbas for them; and after flogging Jesus, he handed him over to be crucified. (Mark 15:1–15)

Authorized to Live

Spiritual authority is about how human life is redeemed and restored to its original designs and proportions. It is about abandoning our deceptions of being self-generating and self-sustaining as we come into communion with the Author and Restorer of all things. It is about taking our lead from this God and the leaders with a sense of where God in Jesus Christ is at work in the world today and where God is headed. It is about our willingness to imaginatively follow as disciples in such well-worn paths before leading much more than it is about blazing any brave new trails on our own.

Spiritual authority is not about the power to coerce or dominate. It is about the chance for a true and abiding response to the question "What shall I do now?" when we are finally done running this way and that. It is about being authorized to live as God intends rather than as Adonis-like billboards invite. It is about finding a purpose and a compass for our lives larger than ourselves as individuals, and yet as personal and specific as our unique gifts. As Alice Camille writes, "The voice of true authority does not crush us. It lifts us up into the delight of being the person we are in our sweetest dreams."[9]

Spiritual authority is about living the life God meant for us to live rather than trading this birthright for a mess of pottage. It is about finding ourselves in a living and breathing community as opposed to the lonely isolation that most experience as normal. As Presbyterian pastor Donald W. McCullough writes about human life being pressed to the ultimacy of asking the most essential questions,

> To have a life worth living, we have to ask ourselves hard questions: Whom do I trust? For whom do I care? For what will I sacrifice? Such questions reveal the trajectory of love. They lay bare the foundations of meaning and integrity; they illuminate the deepest, most elusive spiritual mysteries inhabiting the human heart. The good life depends upon our laying claim to these deep, mysterious reaches of our own compassionate souls.[10]

This cannot happen in the morass of life lived by trial and error, without the clear sense of purpose and direction that rightful authority gives life.

Spiritual authority is about coming alive to a bold, confident, yet humble walk that serves and glorifies the one true God. In a world choking on the vainglory of self-worship, worshipping God in Jesus Christ represents our only real chance for a revolution of true freedom and goodness today. The rest is imitation or illusion. Glorifying God is our only chance to be changed and transformed and to make an enduring difference in the world. In our Christian sense, this is what spiritual authority is.

Raising the Questions, Seeking the Answers

In the first half of this book, we have described on what alien ground the church finds itself today. Something fundamental in our relationship with the world for the past seventeen centuries has been altered, and we have been slow to realize this, much less to creatively respond to the pressures of secular marginalization. This is the biggest challenge the church has faced since the Reformation.

We have considered praise of God as the first and foremost place to come into right relationship with God and one another. Only worship can counter the narcissism that is not only the most telling sin of our time, but is even socially acceptable and fashionable. Worship holds promise to tame our arrogance in the face of God and help us find our place in the advancing reign of God, and with this our life purpose.

As the baptized, we understand that life is not ours to do with as we please. Life is a gift from God, and our story is caught up in the pilgrimage of God's people over millennia. We are not our own; we are God's. We can know what our lives mean only as we grasp to what end point God directs history, and deploy ourselves accordingly. This gives life urgency and agenda to replace our trackless wandering. This gives us a shot at the dignity and nobility in a higher purpose and greater significance than we could have invented for ourselves.

To see how we can live out of God's agenda even before our own, we hold up our incomplete dreams against God's advancing dream, which Jesus called the kingdom of God. Created free to choose whatever we want, we paradoxically submit our wills to God's will as expressed in this holy dream. And in obedient service here, we find real freedom. This is what it means to be disciples, to live out of God's understanding of what it means to be human even before our own.

The first half of the book has described the current crisis in authority for the church. We Westerners generally resent authority and prefer the tyranny of living enslaved to our own shallow ideas of what being human means. Jesus was not so squeamish about authority, commanding it and freely exercising it. We can appreciate spiritual authority as we realize how different it is from raw worldly power. Acting this out is never unambiguous within the life of the church, but avoiding issues of authority out of ignorance has been costlier to the church.

In the second half of the book, we look to specific loci for regaining our voice and lifting our witness in ways that might compel others to live their lives, *coram deo,* before God. Jesus Christ is our beginning point in this endeavor, and so we have edged up to and around him again and again in this chapter. Then we consider Jesus's living body in the world, the church. Next, we move the message from on high in the form of God's Word, and then how that Word takes sacramental shape as we actively live it out in the world. Finally, we consider pastoral ministry and the stewardship of leaders around these sacred mysteries.

PART TWO

WHERE COMPELLING CHRISTIANITY BEGINS AND ENDS

6

WHO DO YOU SAY THAT I AM?:
JESUS CHRIST

I n retrospect, German theologian Eberhard Jungel described his
mother's concerned astonishment and his father's evident disap-
proval at his decision to study theology in East Germany before
the Berlin Wall came down. Why would our boy do this, knowing full
well that such an act would overshadow any chance he had to get ahead
amid the choking socialism of the German Democratic Republic? they
wondered. This was not a particularly pious household. Yes, his mother
taught the children their prayers, but religion was never discussed. Jungel's father had only ridicule for the Christian faith. So then, why did
young Eberhard willingly choose the shame and censure of identifying
with so retrograde an institution as the Christian church?

The answer is simple, Jungel answered. He realized that the Christian
church was the only place in a Stalinist society where one could speak
the truth about the world around him and not be penalized. The church
was the only place where candor was tolerated, even welcomed. "What
a liberating experience," he declared, "in the face of ideological-political
pressures that dominated school! Friends were arrested, I myself was
interrogated more than once—only because we dared to say what we
thought. . . . At least this much is clear: on the basis of these experiences in which I encountered the church as an institution of truth and,

for that reason, also an institution of freedom, I decided to become . . . a theologian."[1]

Jungel reminds us that wherever a society is predicated upon lies, Jesus and his body might stand as an outpost of truth. And this is at the heart of our authority as a Christian people, and is universally true, not just in the Eastern bloc. For regardless of where we are situated—left or right, East or West—our position is really not so different from Jungel's. Are we in the West more free than he was, living in East Germany? Outwardly, in our comings and goings, certainly, yes. But inwardly, as regards matters of spirit, the bondage of the West is considerable. Do you remember the East Berliners launching a shopping orgy into the West after the Wall came down? It is reminiscent of our Friday after Thanksgiving, Black Friday, as it is called. What is this but a movement from one form of captivity to another, from Communist repression to our more familiar Western glitzy, consumptive capitalist version, where we are rich in things, poor in soul?

When it comes down to it, our vaunted freedom often amounts to little more than an abject tyranny to the phony needs, the fabricated desires, and the easy half-truths of the unsatiated self. Western popular culture is a frenzied, impotent herd driven first this way and then that. What does it add up to? We find ourselves numbed and deadened by the disconnectedness of such a life, and then call it "freedom."

As Christians, we cannot call such bolting back-and-forth "freedom" and keep a straight face. In truth, we live with our own ideological-political pressures that are less obvious, but no less formidable than those Jungel faced. The pressures that test us are undeniably different, but equally oppressive. If we are honest with ourselves, we realize that we are no less captive to powers and principalities, but far less likely to recognize it.

Since reading Jungel, I have asked myself, What would we have to do as the Western church to be found so faithful? How can we become messengers of truth instead of one more institution glad-handing the world's deceptions and silently enjoying its benefits? Where is God calling us to forsake the comfort and status of our own ideological captivities to humbly but boldly confront the world with the gospel of the cross?

Frankly, because I'm a coward by nature, I would rather not face such questions. But in three Gospels, we hear how Jesus prompted this very confrontation on the road to Caesarea Philippi. "Who do the crowds say that I am?" Jesus asked disciples out of the blue. Embarrassed glances were first exchanged. Then varied responses were ventured out of the awkward silence: some say you are Dr. Phil. Others claim you are Jay Leno. Still others say Christina Aguilera or Brad Pitt or Stephen Hawking or Lebron James. "But who do you say that I am?" Jesus pressed

100

them more directly. "The Christ of God," Peter burst out, his legendary impulsiveness putting him in good stead for a change (Luke 9:18–20).

"Who do you say that I am?" When Jesus asks this question, it strips us of ideological captivities and lays us bare. On the religious left, his question slays our sacred cows, for it is not about sensitivity, inclusiveness, and the affirmation of our common humanness. It strikes point-blank between the eyes. It divides and separates, singling us out, asking for our most basic allegiance where we flit between opinions that shift with the evening news. It smokes out our lukewarmness, our mildness toward God, our tendency to consider our "religious life" as just another compartment alongside our "family life," "work life," and "recreational and leisure life." Also, there can be no pale talk about Jesus as merely some wise teacher, no hedging our bets like saying that Jesus is every bit as wise as Emerson or Gandhi or Socrates.

Again, Douglas John Hall cuts through the gauzy layers in which we wrap Jesus and his call to discipleship, like some crèche figurine packed away eleven months per year:

> The New Testament affirms that Jesus "taught with authority." . . . Doesn't the preaching of the gospel (gospel!) challenge our pseudo-democratic deference to consensus? Neither Jesus nor the prophets expected—or got—consensus. Does not "the foolishness of preaching" demand of us that we take courage, venture out of the shell of our real or assumed modesty, and "speak with authority"? Not an authority that expects to be heard because it is part of the authority structure of the Establishment (it isn't any more!) and not one's own authority as the possessor of degrees and diplomas (for all their necessity they count for little in the scheme of things); but an authority being bestowed upon us for the express purpose of this ministry, and confirmed as such by the church.[2]

"Who do you say that I am?" For the religious right, Jesus's question defies our pretense of mastery and certitude in matters as unfathomable as judgment. Here he dares us to venture beyond that comfort zone where we feel in control and to articulate the unutterable. Here we are irretrievably led into holy mystery, where we must abandon our pretenses of being under control. Confronted like this, look what becomes unacceptable: glib talk of "accepting Jesus and taking him into my heart," rhetoric making Jesus our lapdog on a sequined leash, saving whomever we decide he should lick on the hand, a "pet" master who does our bidding, remaking others in our image of what being saved looks like. Just who is the Chooser here, and who are the Chosen? As we said earlier, Jesus, to be sure, would insist it is his place to accept *us* and take *us* into his heart. Just who is the Redeemer here, Jesus asks, and who are the redeemed?

101

So we can forget all about the politically correct and the smug status quo in the face of Jesus's direct and personal inquiry. For his question defies tidy categories and stock ways of understanding. In that tremulous moment Jesus's challenge to his disciples was our human collision with divine truth. In asking that question Jesus was weaning his followers from the cult of personality, the aura of celebrity, and the glib superficiality we describe as charisma. Here Jesus strips us of all familiar truths that we naturally construe by various logics of the world: from the therapeutic encounter, from the legal rhetoric of rights, from the shopping-mall spree, and from the Pentagon spokesperson. Jesus deliberately split his message away from all foregoing messengers to place new truth at the center of this world's life: the truth of the cross.

We Should Have Seen This Coming

Jesus was still in diapers when the aged Simeon gathered him into his arms and blessed God for what he perceived now happening in the world. As the baby gurgled, Simeon turned to Joseph and Mary and soberly forecast, "This child is destined for the falling and the rising of many in Israel, and to be a sign that will be opposed so that the inner thoughts of many will be revealed—and a sword will pierce your own soul too" (Luke 2:34–35). Compare this with our annual evergreen-trimmed, egg-nog-lubricated cooing and clucking over the baby Jesus in the church at Christmas. The contrast—that we strike one note, but not the other—should give us pause. For you and I are among those who shall experience this falling and rising that Simeon predicted. And Christmas is a time when we would rather not hear such talk, thank you very much.

We all like Jesus as a child, cute and safe, utterly embraceable on our own terms. But we get upset when he comes to us as a full-grown man, no longer cuddly, challenging us to decide what matters most, pressing us as to where our final allegiances lie, the Jesus whose beginning point is the God whose ways are not our ways. We resent that he comes from such a different place than where we are, so large and threatening in nature.

We will take the baby Jesus (our version, not Simeon's) over the man Jesus any day of the week. For the grown-up Jesus compels us to review and reshape dubious values that have become foundational to everything we say and do. We quickly forget that the Jesus of the Gospels was a babe for a few fleeting verses, but the Gospels were written to proclaim his full stature as Son of God and Savior of the world. Of course, the whole point of Christmas wasn't that Jesus remained a baby. It is that the baby became a grown-up man. And this man Jesus insists that we live before God's watchful gaze and never cease questioning our motives and how we translate them into action. He demands that we renounce forms of power, greed, and self-serving that we hold dear.

We want our embrace of Jesus to be like our unalloyed attraction to a matinee idol. That is why we prefer him as baby. That is why we ever make him meek and mild, soft and accommodating, a sentimental romantic hero. That is why we neglect the flight into Egypt, a portent of Jesus the adult. But our embrace—if embrace Jesus we do—must necessarily have this deep hesitation mixed in. This cannot be a relationship without ambivalence, just as all of our most important relationships—with dear friends, parents, spouses, and our children—are not without ambivalence. "I have not come to bring peace, but a sword," Jesus warned (Matt. 10:34).

In Hebrews (4:12) we hear that the truth of Jesus was "sharper than any two-edged sword, piercing until it divides soul from spirit, joints from marrow; it is able to judge the thoughts and intentions of the heart." Indeed, Jesus was born into this world for this: to grow into full manhood and speak the truth, to *become* himself the measure of truth. And the truth that was Jesus never did conform well to hearers' whims and prejudices. Jesus was not one to remain content with a status quo that only led people to despair. Jesus was not one who got along by going along, who quietly paddled along with the current. He came to show us an entirely new way.

In encounters like that in Caesarea Philippi, Jesus began to describe his ministry in terms of dying to himself, giving his will over to that of the Father, and sacrificing himself for the sake of many. He described discipleship in terms of his followers doing the same. At this juncture in John's Gospel, it was at a synagogue in Capernaum, just as Jesus's popularity was peaking, that he began speaking of dying to ourselves in order to become most completely alive to God's reign. The disciples, Jesus's closest followers, responded, "This teaching is difficult; who can accept it?" (John 6:60). Then follows one of the most underrated verses in the Bible. It is a simple, throwaway sentence that says volumes about how we instinctively respond to God's admittedly unlikely plan for human salvation: "Because of this many of his disciples turned back and no longer went about with him" (John 6:66).

A certain Reverend W. E. Orchard tells what this scene might look like today. He and his wife were visiting another church as worshippers one Sunday. They had heard about this celebrated church and how its pastor passed his days in a buzz of excited and adoring people. The Orchards wanted to attend in person and see what the big deal was. As they settled into the pews, it became obvious. As they looked around they saw a frivolous congregation evincing no visible interest in worshipping God. Everything was on the horizontal plane of human bonhomie with nothing of the verticality of letting themselves be interrupted with God's revelatory interventions. Yes, there was a buzz about the place. But was this of God? Or was it merely the excitement of like-minded people confirming who they already were, how they already intended to live, and sacralizing it all in a tidy package called God's will?

Without being told, the Reverend Mr. Orchard noticed his wife's contempt at what she saw. Graciously, he commented, "It is all very well that this should upset you, dear. But I could not fill this church." The woman's sure reply came swiftly. "No," she said, "but you could empty it in no time." She meant that as a compliment.

Eugene Peterson helps us grasp the meaning of Mrs. Orchard's remark:

> The congregation is not about us. It is about God. The operating biblical metaphor regarding worship is sacrifice. But this is not the American way. The major American innovation in the congregation is to turn it into a consumer enterprise. Americans have developed a culture of acquisition, an economy that is dependent on wanting and requiring more. We have a huge advertising industry designed to stir up appetites we didn't even know that we had. We are insatiable. It didn't take long for some of our colleagues to develop consumer congregations. If we have a nation of consumers, obviously the quickest and most effective way to get them into our churches is to identify what they want and offer it to them. Satisfy their fantasies, promise them the moon, recast the gospel in consumer terms—entertainment, satisfaction, excitement and adventure, problem-solving, whatever. We are the world's champion consumers, so why shouldn't we have state-of-the-art consumer churches?[3]

In imperial America, where bigger is better and biggest is best, it wouldn't ordinarily occur to us that having fewer and more deeply committed people could perhaps be more godly worship. But it was after all the temple that Jesus drove the money changers out of.

This is true because the gospel of Jesus Christ is ultimately the gospel of the cross. It must be the gospel of the cross, because that is the only way to the resurrection. And the gospel of the cross, once it is recognized as such and no longer concealed, will never attract the masses. Yes, we must always simultaneously lift up the joy on the other side of the cross, and this joy is both the first and final word. But the high cost of such a salvation has always repulsed humankind at one level. For in this gospel and its salvation, we are revealed as the self-seeking sinners that we are. We are reminded that we cannot make it as our own little gods and must instead depend upon the one true God. And we deeply resent this intrusion. How dare God! Perhaps this is why the Spanish philosopher-theologian Miguel de Unamuno ends his most famous book, *The Tragic Sense of Life*, with the words, "And may God deny you peace but give you glory!"[4]

We should have seen this coming. The prophet Malachi (3:2–3) foresaw it: "But who can endure the day of his coming, and who can stand when he appears? For he is like a refiner's fire and like fullers' soap; he will sit as a refiner and purifier of silver, and he will purify the descendants of Levi and refine them like gold and silver, until they present offerings to the LORD in righteousness."

For Such a Time as This, for Such a Moment as Now

Alan Wolfe, sociologist at Boston College, talks about how the expectations and the appetites of people have shifted beneath the church over the past few generations. As a sociologist, he is accustomed to speaking in terms of roles. Religion has moved from an *ascribed* role, Wolfe maintains, to an *achieved* role. An ascribed role is one you are born with; an achieved role is one you choose and work with. The implications of this are greater than first meets the eye. Wolfe outlined his thinking in a book that he, with good reason, wanted to entitle *The Taming of American Religion.* His publisher overruled him into the milder, *The Transformation of American Religion: How We Actually Live Our Faith.*[5]

Wolfe suggests that matters of faith were not long ago considered vast and momentous, bigger than our personal predilections and beyond our individual agency. Today, being religious has become a lifestyle enclave that we rummage through in order to find the most personally advantageous package. An interview with *Homiletics* magazine indicates that this trend is less than encouraging.

> Wolfe: "(F)or more and more Americans now, religion is something that—at a certain point in your life—you decide that you're going to feel invested in and empowered by, that you're going to recommend to others, but you can't necessarily enforce it on others, even your children, as much as you might like to. This is the single biggest change . . .
> *Homiletics:* "If a church doesn't empower us, we switch churches or religions. We've become a nation of switchers, as you call them, or a nation of free agents, and our pastors, priests, rabbis and imams know that."
> Wolfe: "I use the phrase 'balance of power,' that is, the way the balance of power has shifted in the relationship between the clergy and the congregation. The authority in many ways once lay with the clergy. They had a message, and their job was to preach the message, and the congregation was expected to sit there and absorb the message. In

many ways the power has shifted from the clergy to the congregation. The congregation now says to the clergy, 'You give us a message that we want to hear or we're going elsewhere.' That's what free agency is. We see it all the time in sports, and it certainly leads to better contracts, but whether it leads to team loyalty is another manner."[6]

It raises the question once again: is it more important that God has chosen us? Or is it more essential that we might choose God? While the emphasis in theology has always been upon the former, these days the pendulum of popular opinion gathers momentum toward the latter, and this throws spiritual authority out of kilter. Do we like Jesus so long as he will please us, the quaint baby of that charmed and burnished memory of cherished Christmas past? Do we go elsewhere as the grown Jesus rises up into a man of full prophetic stature, who brooks no nonsense and takes no idol hostages, unsentimentally urging us toward painful transformation that will purify us like a refiner's fire?

The real test of following Jesus is not following him up to Caesarea Philippi or to the synagogue in Capernaum. Plenty are willing to go the first half with Jesus. The real test of following him is traveling with him beyond the watershed of the cross, when it is our own rising and falling that are suddenly at stake, when it is the tip of Simeon's sword that is touching our heart. Can we remain steadfast by the One who shook some loose and to whom others stuck fast? We seldom talk about this, but everything depends on it, so far as the integrity of the witness of Christ's church goes.

Not Indulgent of Idols

Who do we say that Jesus is? Who does God say that we are? As Jesus here presses hard for God's truth above every other truth, to receive him as King of Kings above every other hero, he challenges the fleeting ideologies and idols to which we are captive. He pushes us here because only in the painful but immutable truth of the cross are we free. But the truth of the cross isn't the world's truth. The truth of Christ crucified and resurrected represents a troubling and radical alternative to the status quo, business-as-usual, always-eager-to-please posture of getting along by going along. To be free in the truth of Jesus, first we relinquish those captivities that Jungel so perceived and rejected, whether from East or West, left or right.

In truth, the church has locked itself into a tired harangue between conservatism and liberalism. The angrier this quarrel has become, the more emaciated the church has grown. We have seized upon the world's quarrels, imported them into the church, dressed up these ideologies as theologies, and become so deeply divided that the Evil One must be giddy with delight.

We have allowed a word alien to God's Word to define the terms for the most vexing issues of our time and then been surprised when there is nothing remotely transcendent about our witness to the world. We have looked to preserving life as we know it (again, "lifestyle" is our term for this sacred cow) at the expense of entering into and practicing in a whole-souled way the sacraments that define us. Should we wonder why people despair of the church as liberator and protector of all that is holy and look elsewhere for "a still more excellent way" (1 Cor. 12:31)?

Let us trace how this proceeds on a sample live-wire issue that the church has seriously mishandled: abortion. Much like the world surrounding us, the debate within the church alternates between pro-lifers on one side who squawk about "fetal rights" and pro-choicers on the other who rant about "reproductive rights." Rather than introducing something new and holy to the fruitless quarrels, instead of transforming these futile disputes, we have bought whole hog into these confused terms and become confused ourselves.

If we can agree on one thing, it is that this exchange has taken us exactly nowhere. It is morally bankrupt and spiritually exhausted. It generates wasted heat and very little light. The nasty shouting matches and ever-mounting violent acts illustrate that both camps are terminally infected with self-interest. And, to be fair, it works in equally useless ways from both ideological camps.

How has this happened? Instead of speaking out of our own unique truth—that God is in Jesus Christ reconciling the world to himself—we have spoken for worldly truths, such as rights. Do we not know that the language of rights is the language of the democratic nation-state? Training a people to at every point insist upon their own rights will not make us more virtuous or Christlike, but only more self-interested and self-assertive, expecting that our mutual selfishness will serve as a check and balance on individual selfishness. This is not a pretty sight: fighting selfishness with more selfishness.

All parties here tenaciously protect the lifestyle where they already dwell and wrap it up in morally inflected ideological righteousness. It leaves a bad taste in our mouth, as well it should. This scene has about it what C. S. Lewis once called the "ruthless, sleepless, unsmiling concentration upon self, which is the mark of Hell."[7]

Indeed it is fraught with consequence to put our ultimate trust in democratic institutions such as "rights." Let us be reminded that Pilate put the question of Jesus's crucifixion to a vote, a popular referendum, outside his *praetorium*. With the sanction of that spontaneous town

107

meeting Pilate whipped up, his superficial sympathy for the odd Galilean vanished. Those straw votes cleared the way to Golgotha. Public opinion overwhelmed this jaded man who vacillated before true man and true God: what is truth?

Rights are the device by which Western governments define and establish justice. Scripture hardly mentions rights, and then only the rights of the defenseless, the widow, the orphan, and the sojourner—in short, the rights of socially vulnerable others. The Bible does not lift up rights in a way that sets up a gravitational field, ever pulling all things back toward our never-quite-satisfied centripetal selves. Rather, it assails such a constellation as human pride, putting self ahead of God's greater plan for good. On the whole, scripture does not depend upon rights to establish a justice higher than the tug-of-war of human wills. Can we see the One who selflessly died on a cross stomping his foot, insisting on his rights before the Father? What would that look like? Our Christian faith has other methods than the secular state's, no matter how enlightened or prosperous that nation-state.

For Christians, life is not our right to exercise in ways that aggrandizes our position in the world. Life is a gift. Life is a gift of God and belongs wholly to God, despite any appearances to the contrary. And whenever people receive gifts, the study of anthropology teaches, obligations spread in all directions and compel the response of the beneficiaries. This is universally true everywhere in the world. For us, life is a gift of grace that begs for nothing so much as our eager and generous response, an answer in the image of God's saving initiative over us, as we deal with our neighbor, until those waves travel throughout the world.

Maybe instead of fueling the rancorous tug-of-war over rights, we Christians might start articulating responsibilities that come with the gift of life. What are our obligations to mothers- and fathers-to-be who are themselves children? How would God have us pour ourselves out to those children whom tests show will be born less than perfectly formed? What are our obligations to parents who can't handle or otherwise refuse children? What are our obligations to the unborn? Not: what are our rights here? Rather: what does God expect of us in these circumstances, having placed frail and tender gifts of life—embryonic, newborn, and parental life—within the humble stewardship of Christian community?

Why respond out of such worldly stories at the expense of our own neglected and unfinished drama of redemption? Why respond out of our shallows when we might respond from the depths of holy mystery? Should we expect our folk to bother coming to worship when we are merely regurgitating the best available judgments of intelligentsia, whether the editorial page of the *New York Times* or the columns of the *National Review*? For that, most would just as soon stay home and watch the staged exchanges of CNN's *Crossfire*.

Divided We Fall

The liberal-modernist churches excel at identifying pagan ideological captivities of churches on the right: the sentimental idolatry of the domestic family, the triumphalistic sanction of U.S. militarism, uncritical trust of technology and progress, sanctification of economic individualism, carte blanche blessing of capitalism with its concomitant materialisms as no less than divine providence. In fact, the liberal-modernist churches border upon obsessive in exposing conservative churches, viewing and often describing this other wing of the church as the enemy.

Similarly, the conservative-fundamentalist churches critique the churches on the left: self-fulfillment displacing confession, therapy displacing repentance, a blithe neglect of the scriptural narrative, an underwhelming affirmation of Jesus as the Christ, a "you do your thing, and I'll do mine" sense of moral rigor, substituting pseudoliberation causes for the reign of God, an "open-mindedness" to all things whereby our brains sometimes fall out.

Each side might be proud of exposing the other's captivities were each not in such deep denial about its own. Both liberals and conservatives act as though the other has sold out while they have not. With sudden amnesia, we forget to ask, Who is Jesus Christ? in the midst of deeply vexing, worldly issues. We can only remember who we are as we recover the language and the practices of our faith. Otherwise, we shall never cut through the language of the democratic state, the debased notions of progress, the therapeutic mindset, the consumerist frenzy, and the cult of the celebrity. Quite simply, the bride-of-Christ church that marries the spirit of the age—whether left or right side—is sure to be a widow in the age to come. Ask the Russian Orthodox Church, which became too closely wedded to the czar, about this.

When the debates of Christian theology digress into the left side of this versus the right side of that, we have sold our birthright for a mess of pottage. This is anything but bold and prophetic, as both sides preen and posture. Rather it is a smug deal by which both sides inoculate themselves with such a mild case of Christianity—letting the world do most of our thinking for us even before we get to Jesus—that we have shut ourselves off from the deep and transformative revolution that is the reign of God upon this earth.

How can we stand over and against fleeting trends to proclaim Christ if we have first fallen captive to their logic and language? It is not that these worldly stories and ways of thinking are without merit. It is simply that they are not *our* truth. People look to us for something different, something of God—such as a world reborn by a cross and glimpsed in a stranger outside an empty tomb—even if we should expect them to deride and reject us as we proclaim it.

Shall we always permit these "ideological-political pressures"—to borrow Jungel's phrase—to pose the question, establish the agenda, and limit the answers? If so, our distinctive witness to America promises little that is significant. How sad this is in a day when the West desperately needs to hear the message that God has called the church to deliver.

Now into the third millennium, the challenge of the church is to speak out of our own peculiar truth of Jesus as the Christ rather than either politically correct or conventionally acceptable answers. Because we have done so poorly here, we have not died to ourselves and come alive to God in the way of the cross and the empty tomb. Rather, we have died a death of worldly blandness and insipidness. There is little remotely majestic or transcendent about our witness to the world. We occupy a purgatory of uncertainty, where we haven't a clue who we are and what we stand for as people of God.

It is on precisely this front that the leader churches will usher us into a new era above the fray of ideological battering. Such churches will steadfastly maintain and creatively interpret above all other truths that God was in Jesus Christ. He will be the way, the truth, and the life before whose throne all other ways, truths, and lives shall be understood. Such churches will insist that the people linger over the peculiar man Jesus long enough to be thrown into the moral and spiritual dilemma where the people of God become necessary and vibrant, a genuine alternative to the self-interested clusters of popular culture. This is forever and at all times the opportunity of Christ's church, if only we have the willingness and the courage to venture forth in this faith. We can do this better than anyone. Moreover, only we can do it.

The Right Stands in the Right Places

I once served a congregation where a United States senator and his family were members. Not that they were active during my tenure there; I could barely get them to return my telephone calls. But before my time, when the family was growing and the children were small, they did sometimes darken our doorways. This family-centered idolatry of "dipping our children in religion," so they won't get DUIs or pregnant as teens, and then bailing out as the youngsters grow up is familiar to the churches of the affluent West. On top of using the church in ways like

110

this, the exiting family, once the children are old enough, often blames the church, saying "Things there aren't the same anymore" or "The new pastor didn't care about us."

A pastoral predecessor in that congregation related the story of when the senator's child was a member of his confirmation class. Of course, even back then holding together a confirmation class was a little bit like setting up the infrastructure for nuclear fusion: it is a matter of holding together highly disparate elements forever threatening to fall apart, hoping that a trickle of usable power will somehow, somewhere result from the process. Levels of commitment from the families involved are typically so varied that completing this spiritual pilgrimage with adolescents is a real trick.

As Confirmation Sunday approached, the pastor enlisted the families' support and emphasized their shared focus: get them to rehearsal on time, make sure your child knows his or her part, everybody is expected bright-eyed and bushy-tailed. On Confirmation Sunday, every confirmand in this large class was on time and neatly in place. One family, however, did not show up at all. It was the family that the pastor sensed might blow off the day, the family of the U.S. senator. The confirmation morning at church unfolded splendidly, but the pastor quietly steamed at being so casually brushed off by the powers and principalities. He sensed that the absent family was not only in town, but likely lounging around home, perhaps picking at brunch.

After morning services the pastor made a beeline to the senator's house and knocked on the door. Unsmiling and unamused, without any ingratiating or deferential hello at the door, without even being invited into their house, he strode in and found things there much as he had expected. Imposing himself upon their lazy Sunday morning, he opened his briefcase, extracted the confirmation liturgy, told everyone where to stand, and went through the rite without asking anyone's permission. After that child of God and the church was confirmed, he put the liturgy back in his briefcase and walked out the door. It is the only forcible confirmation of faith that I have ever heard of. And the senator and his wife didn't dare venture back one word to that confronting pastor.

How can church leaders be equipped to respond in bold, strong ways like this? We certainly will have to go on a diet free of the sentimentality to which we seem so addicted. This means telling the whole truth in the church. Not just the sweet baby Jesus in the manger, but also the terrible slaughter of innocents. Not just the hundredth anniversary celebration of the church, but also the time they ran off the preacher against the war in Vietnam. Not just the Jesus who stopped the stoning of the adulterous woman, but also the Jesus who told her to go and sin no more. Sometimes we imagine that the only word the church should

111

speak is approbation and affirmation. We want to be liked. We want to be popular. We want to be successful in a time and place where success means everything. "Keep it upbeat, affirm the people, give them what they are looking for. Throw in a little pop psychology and self-help."

We end up finding ourselves in a church like the Reverend and Mrs. Orchard, a church rich in things, but poor in soul, a church that preens itself, looking only to those things that can be seen at the expense of those things that cannot be seen. "For what can be seen is temporary, but what cannot be seen is eternal" (2 Cor. 4:18).

As God's people we are not a support group, but rather followers of Jesus Christ. And this means that we don't sanctify and bless every need just because it is sincerely felt. We must tell of broken covenants and renewed covenants. We must proclaim God's holy rhythms of sin and sacrifice, repentance and forgiveness. And we must tell of the Lord God who speaks a word of judgment before we can even begin to hear God's word of grace. For as we are always ready to understand, but never willing to expose clever, self-serving lies, then ministry of the church is not only corrupted. It becomes impossible. We are already too seriously accommodated to this world—whether conservative or liberal, Wall Street or Washington—to bring a redemptive presence. Pleasing humankind rather than God, we become sentimentalists. Once our churches have an appeal to the Eberhard Jungels of the West, then we shall know that we are getting somewhere and beginning to make a difference.

Faith begins not as we blaze brave new worlds of discovery. Faith begins as we hear a lonely figure ask a plaintive question on the dusty road to a place that we have never been. "Who do you say that I am?" If we answer with Peter—you are the Christ—then we are also going to have to trust God that his Son is enough for the world, despite the ideological-political pressures so eager to sidetrack and supersede what he died for.

The problem isn't that we haven't heard about Jesus. The problem is that we know him in ways so severely reduced that we take him for granted and approach him as a pretext for what we were already inclined to do anyway. "*Ecce homo*," proclaims Pontius Pilate, referring to the scourged man who stands before him, clad in purple and wearing a crown of thorns. "Behold the man!" (John 19:5 KJV). But this is not a man that Pilate feels he must deal seriously with, as though life and death—his own—hinges upon it. Like the senator so nominal about the church, Pilate doesn't realize that he is on trial, not Jesus. For him Jesus is merely a curious man he must regrettably dispose of in an expedient manner.

The upshot is a ubiquitous Jesus who stretches 3,000 miles wide but is only two inches deep. And the popular celebration of this Jesus goes something like this: "Church bad, American individualism good. Religion bad, spirituality good. Christianity oppressive, other religions lighthearted."[8] When did our encounter with the Son of Man become a matter of opinion rather than conviction, a matter of preference rather than God's commissioning? It is hard to see how Jesus left that much wiggle room for us when he addressed Peter, and thereby all of us: "Who do you say that I am?"

Can we resist the temptation to conform ourselves to slicker messiahs and lesser truths? Are we willing to abandon the comfort and advantage of living in thrall to user-friendly gods? Do we have the courage and conviction to live cruciform lives? Much is at stake. Lives and even civilizations hang in the balance. God watches and awaits our response.

Is There a Savior in the House?

Who can rescue us from ourselves, coming to church to worship the true and living God, only to make God captive to our decidedly earth-bound human categories and concepts? There is only one. John the Baptizer, the very height of the prophetic line, declared that he was not worthy to untie the thong of his sandal. Jesus is not a man like other men. Perhaps a Hindu fable borrowed for our own purposes can help us understand how Jesus was a man set apart.

Ramakrishna, the Hindu saint of the eighteenth century, tells the story of a motherless tiger cub who was adopted by goats and brought up by them. The goats took in this lost tiger as their own, and he seemed to be fully one of them. They taught the cub to speak like a goat, to move like a goat, to eat like a goat, and in general to believe in all things that he was a goat. Then one day a real tiger came along and things changed. All of the goats scattered in fear except for the ersatz goat. This young tiger was left haplessly alone to confront the massive predator—afraid yet unafraid.

The confused cub bleated awkwardly and continued nibbling nervously at the grass. The grown tiger could not fathm the cub's silly charade. Frustrated and embarrassed, the dominant tiger had seen enough. He carried this "goat" in black stripes and lush tawny fur to a water pool. The senior tiger forced his junior to see their reflections side by side and figure out the lie that he was living. When this failed, the grown tiger offered him his first piece of raw meat. At first the cub recoiled from the startling taste. But as he felt it warm his blood, he began to eat more and more, and the truth gradually became clear to him. Lashing his tail and digging his claws into the ground, the young beast surveyed the landscape and felt a swagger he had not known before. Eyeballing his environs, the squirrels and birds vanished within the canopy of foliage. For the first time the whole jungle trembled at the sound of his exultant roar.

So also One has come to us to remind us who we are and that our destiny lies with him in a fate laid down for us before we were born. So warms our blood when we eat of his shared flesh. "In the juvescence of the year," T. S. Eliot wrote, "came Christ the Tiger."[9] And this Messiah would not recoil but would insist that we live out our birthright according to the designs laid down at our creation. I realize that this runs afoul of the images of Jesus Christ that we lift up every year with crayons in our vacation bible schools. And this certainly would not be to commend a predatory or violent Jesus, anything but that. But this fable names a side of Jesus we must recognize and affirm, like Simeon balancing out our sweet baby Jesus images of Christmas.

Rather than defend the gospel on the world's terms, setting ourselves up for failure by the very terms of the exchange, we might consider loosing Jesus and his gospel through our risk and sacrifice, and seeing what happens. Certainly church would no longer be staid and boring. Without wanting to posit any "golden age" of Christianity, that is how Jesus's apostles and first followers overturned the Roman Empire.

Along with the fable's and T. S. Eliot's image of Christ the Tiger, we would do well to see the iconography of Jesus Christ in the Eastern Orthodox churches. His posture is purposeful; his expression has arc-weld intensity; his eyes are burning embers; his jaw is set as one who will not be denied; his gaze is that of one who will searchingly and relentlessly root out every last bit of "goat" within us. He has come to us for this formidable task, and nothing less. You can see it in his face. Perhaps this alternative portraiture is a needed corrective to the syrupy-sweet Jesus portrayed in the Sunday school pictures where Jesus could as well be endorsing a brand of hand cream as saving the world from its destructive violence.

We should understand that the reason Jesus cuts against the grain of what already is, is not because he had a flamboyant or histrionic need to be different. He was not about drawing attention to himself because he had a personal need to be at the center of things. "Tell no one what you have seen . . . ," he told his followers more than once, actually suppressing the truth of his identity.

Jesus rubs against the fur of well-groomed empires, because as the Good News is heard, believed, and lived out, it makes us truly different. It makes us strangers in the eyes of the status quo. It flies in the face of conventional common sense. It cannot rest easy in what seems practical and efficient in the moment. And following Jesus here, the people of God can seem like a wrench thrown into the accustomed manner of doing business. For if one thing is certain about the close of the Gospels, it is

114

this: Jesus was not crucified for offering familiar and prudent answers that already made sense to everyone. And he was not resurrected to send us back to them.

Jesus once told off his own mother at a wedding. He described as a dog a Syrophoenician woman he later helped. He disparaged Peter as being in the grip of Satan for being too solicitous as the moment of truth approached. He answered the brave and empathetic tears of women as he shouldered the cross saying, "Daughters of Jerusalem, weep for yourselves" (Luke 23:28). He wasn't being mean or petty or ill-tempered. No, it was something else. It was something that both those earliest disciples and we contemporary followers only dimly understand.

Yes, it is true that there is much that is beautiful, enchanting, and lovely in this world. But despite the tenderness and charm of this world, it remains fundamentally hostile to the truth. It tolerates the truth only in the smallest doses, which is why Jesus's active ministry lasted all of three years. The ways of the world are dead set against the ways of God as they were most fully embodied in Jesus Christ and his final return to Jerusalem. Jesus paid a terrible price for unequivocally proclaiming and standing firm in the truth of God. He paid it not only by dying on the cross but in a thousand little deaths every day. Should it then surprise us that his interactions with others were so challenging, so formidable, and so unsentimental?

Sometimes when we have the flu, must endure a capricious boss, or scrape paint from the eaves of our homes, we describe those unpleasant circumstances as "the cross that we must bear." But we moderns do well to realize that not all struggle and suffering is of the cross. The cross of Jesus Christ does not first stand for general human pain and suffering as our common lot. No, the cross symbolizes what happens when we take God's account of what is real more seriously than the version we are fed by marketers, celebrities, politicians, TV therapists, and all of the rest. This is why Jesus told Peter that he was "setting your mind not on divine things but human things" when Peter insisted he would let no harm befall Jesus.

As we forsake the worldly gospels in order to live the good news of Jesus Christ in defiance of these powers that be, that is the moment when we participate in the power of the cross. And as we travel that path, we can be sure that it will be noticed. We would be surprised how little of God's truth in the cross we have to speak or live to draw the ire and rejection of the world. That is why the cross is demanding, difficult, and confrontational, not because Jesus and his followers should take pleasure in sticking it into the eyes of our detractors.

The cross of Jesus Christ means that he was more intent upon pleasing God than on pleasing himself or his constituency, more radically willing to obey God than to project a winning image or placate our whims to snowball a fan-based following. But consider this: if Jesus first plays up

115

to us, he not only spurns the Father, but he will also eventually leave us feeling indulged and patronized. If he obeys the Father, he is right in the only relationship that ultimately matters, and the glow of this is so bright and warming that the whole world can forever bask in its power and joy.

So as Jesus wins the world but abandons God, he loses both ways. But as he loses according to the world's calculations, and wins the reconciliation of earth to heaven, his victory is vouchsafed eternal in the heavens, and it becomes our victory as well. By pleasing God the Father first and last, he was delivering the divine pleasure over to us. And he was giving over for all time the immense and lasting delight of God's all-conquering love. All victories that have ever been won will be arranged around this victory. All other victories that will ever be won will be measured by this victory. This is why all four Gospels are written from Good Friday and Easter backward, looking back across the whole of Jesus's life through the lens of the crucifixion and resurrection. This is why when all is said and done, no matter which direction we live—toward the past or into the future—we are an Easter people.

Writing about the dominion of Jesus Christ over the world and over our lives individually, consider these words from professor Alice Camille:

> If Christ is our king, the stakes are high. The usual controlling bodies—media, public opinion, the quest for security, the lifestyle of acquisitions—have no sovereignty over us. The authority of Christ is not just another voice; it is the only voice to which we need to respond. And Christianity is not just more homework, a dungeon-like oppression to suffer; it is the only authority that liberates those who subject themselves to it. Not to embrace Christ the King is to continue to bow before the countless sovereigns of the world and to light the sacrifices at too many altars. Not to listen to Christ is to face the schizophrenia of voices beckoning, demanding, cajoling our obedience, all the while spinning their web of half-truths.[10]

We close this chapter essentially where we began, with a story about the church behind the lines of a hostile empire living out a narrative other than God in Jesus Christ reconciling the world to himself. Walter Ulbricht, former leader of East Germany, once had a conversation with Swiss theologian Karl Barth about the new society being built in his communist country.[11] Ulbricht boasted that the Communist Party would teach the Ten Commandments in the schools. He looked forward to the day when the Decalogue would provide the moral foundation for that new society.

Barth listened politely and said, "I have only one question, Mr. Minister: will you also be teaching the First Commandment?" *I am the Lord your God; you shall have no other gods before me.* That is what Jesus meant to ask Peter and all of us with his query: "Who do you say that I am?" That is the question we are answering in the living of our lives.

7

STUMBLING INTO THE KINGDOM: THE CHURCH

W hat do art museums want?" began a *New York Times* article by Roberta Smith a few years ago. "(They are) driven by the desire to be financially successful, wildly popular or socially relevant. . . . (They are) mounting exhibitions that are terminally afflicted by what looks like a certifiable fear of art. . . . They often behave less and less like museums—that is, places where the goal is the . . . experience of art objects. . . . They represent the failure, for one reason or another, simply to let art be art, to honor its specialness and mysteries, and allow it to work its effect. One gets the feeling that for many people in charge of museums and exhibitions these days, art is not enough. . . . In general, questions of cultural or historic relevance [take] precedence over issues of aesthetic[s]." Smith answers her own question: "They want to be anything but art museums."[1]

The affluent Western church might listen closely to this soul-searching self-examination of a venerable institution whose identity is at stake and whose future is at risk amid the consumerist acids of contemporary culture. What do churches want? What does God want for the church? These questions precisely are our questions. In the course of our lifetime, it has become unclear what churches want and who the church is. Indeed it seems that in too many cases we want to be anything and everything but the church. Much of what we do evinces a certifiable fear of Jesus, crucified and resurrected. This is remarkable in that this is something the church had not been unclear about for many centuries.

Eager to impress the world rather than fulfill our mission before God, wistfully longing for megachurches or ahead-of-the-curve social agencies, external measures such as swollen budgets or the trend-stampeding of the masses or social cachet increasingly drive the church. In a celebrity-mad culture, it is as though many local parishes themselves long to become celebrity churches. And our day care, youth programs, and adult classes, to cite the most visible examples, testify to a certifiable reluctance about God. We read the Bible as though it is supposed to be more about us than about God. We call ourselves "spiritual" because we liked *The DaVinci Code* and have discussion groups about it.

But like middle-schoolers shrinking from the dance floor, we are too embarrassed to proclaim Christ's reign and too awkward to unabashedly glorify God. For neither of those acts would answer the question that more impresses and obsesses us: what is in it for me? Somehow it is no longer enough to allow the sacred gospel mysteries entrusted us to do their work through the witness of our word and deed. We are talking about a deep identity crisis here.

One gets the feeling that for many involved the God of the cross is not enough. Questions of immediate relevance take precedence over the longer view of enacting the reign of God, actually living as though God's promises in Jesus are more real than the world's promises, and letting the power of the Holy Spirit ineluctably unfold by what results. Too often we want to be anything but the church of Jesus Christ.

A Spiritual Failure of Nerve

I became senior pastor of a historic midwestern downtown church in the mid-eighties. (Ironically, it was set immediately next door to that city's lovely art museum, which was in the process of remaking itself.) Some wondrous things were being done there by way of ministry as I arrived, owing no part to my own leadership.

This was the epoch of the genocidal Pol Pot, when millions perished and thousands of Cambodians became refugees, some fleeing to the United States. A pocket of Cambodians settled in the downtown where I was called. Looking to our majestic neo-Gothic church and seeing sanctuary, they approached our church governing body and asked for help in adapting to a new environment. Our church council, in the tradition of religious bureaucracies like the Sanhedrin in Jesus's time, was overwhelmed by this opportunity and issued a flat no. We would like to help you, was their response to these broken, hopeful people, but your needs are too great. We lack the resources. We would like to do something, but this would be way over our heads. We fear getting sued for making promises we can't keep. We are sorry, but goodbye, and God bless you.

Then something miraculous happened. These earnest and desperate Cambodians kept coming anyway, knocking on our doors, and asking for our help. Never having heard of it, they lived out the parable of the insistent widow who wouldn't let the supercilious judge alone. Their need was so great and their awareness of our being poised to assist them so compelling that they kept coming and entreating us. God bless them, their need was so acute and their motives so innocent that they didn't know any better.

Apart from our church council, members at the grass roots began to talk. They considered the needs of these refugees and realized that we actually could help here and there. Assignments were made to those with skills that were precisely what the Cambodians sought. Piecemeal became wholehearted and concerted. Before we knew it, more despite ourselves and because of the Holy Spirit, our church became a bustling center for refugee resettlement. And the spontaneous generosity of that congregation mobilized from the grass roots was nothing less than remarkable.

Overcoming the initial rebuff, that church regathered itself and eagerly addressed every dimension of these Cambodians' lives in a new world. They needed help finding apartments? The church found affordable apartments. They needed help with a new language? The church collaborated with the Roman Catholic diocese and formed an English as a Second Language program in our education wing, which went on to help *thousands* of Cubans, Haitians, and Romanians as well. The families needed help with driver's licenses or loans or math tutors or medical care or babysitting for their children? They needed help with the legal and tax implications of creating their own businesses? That church became truly the church of Jesus Christ as it expertly saw to all of this and more.

The age-old American success story unfolded in ways fairly predictable. The Cambodian families were so grateful, determined, industrious, and unified that their fortunes soared. More than one of their children became valedictorian of local graduating high school classes. Many of their businesses or trades quickly carved out niches and flourished. I recall taking my family to a wonderful restaurant founded by a Cambodian family. I was treated royally, like long-lost Prince Sihanouk, simply by virtue of being "the pastor." This despite that I did nothing more than smile in their direction, arriving so late in the process as I did.

119

This success story would be complete, except for one important detail. For we were unable or unwilling to offer even a minimal response in one essential dimension in the lives of this immigrant people. As the Cambodians expressed interest in things spiritual, as they even inquired directly about worshipping the God in Jesus Christ who had led us to engage them so wholeheartedly, we were flummoxed. We were frozen stiff and paralyzed. Here we became lost and useless to them. We experienced a failure of nerve and dithered in addressing the needs of their souls. As a result, they ended up in other churches (best-case scenario) or assimilated into secular America (sad-case scenario).

Our existing Sunday-morning worship was at a level of English discourse still inaccessible to them, couched in a cultivated European musical heritage and shaped by formal Christian liturgy. The Cambodians wanted and tried to attend that traditional service. But they didn't "get it," because in their circumstances they couldn't get it. And it was only a matter of time before their initiative atrophied. They could knock on the door marked "worship" for only so long and find no response to their life situation for only so long before they went elsewhere.

As an alternative, it was suggested that the Cambodians worship with their own native musical forms, their own people elevated into positions of worship leadership, and the distinctive forms of worship that spoke to them. For generations, this is how immigrant populations coming to America have rooted themselves spiritually, first harking back to and reinforcing their immigrant roots as a platform for worshipping God in a new and alien land. Then in the second generation, the desire to worship in more integrated, polyglot, American forms typically takes over.

No, came the answer, when it comes to worship, our church needs to be united—one big happy family. Besides, we said, their Buddhist background should be respected, and we wouldn't want to "force our religion upon them." But we couldn't see what we were really doing by invoking such a "freedom" only around worship. Essentially, we were deciding that worship was the only place in ministering to them that we would not extend ourselves all of the way by reaching deep down into their unusual situation, meeting them entirely on their own terms. This weak response came from us despite that they were begging for our spiritual mentoring no less than for our domestic tutoring.

Imagine this. We were not shy about sharing our native tongue with them. We did not hesitate to initiate them into the mysteries of the American tax code or health care establishment. We gave them a running start in the workings of capitalism and our American public school system. But somehow, even when they asked, matters of the Christian faith—probably seeing them as "private" or a matter of "personal opinion"—were off limits in assimilating these newcomers into our way of life. And this setting was not a PTA, a neighborhood watch, a Masonic temple, or a chamber of commerce, but the church of Jesus Christ.

On balance, most everything in this story was positive, most everything that congregation did for these vulnerable sojourners was in the image of Christ. This last part of our ministry to the Cambodians, the part that had more to do with their soul, however, revealed our own spiritual poverty and disinclination.

This vignette captures the modern church's crisis of authority and identity. We didn't hesitate to promote systems of language, commerce, schooling, transportation, communication, domesticity, and the rest. As the church, we didn't hesitate to advocate the American way of life. But as the church, it was too much to personally share the spiritual mainspring that drove our actions, our common life as followers of Jesus Christ. And this one downtown midwestern church is far from alone; it is in most ways representative of this failure of nerve, at least among established mainline churches.

Church at the Crossroads

What does the church want to be? Relocation specialist? Conduit of social services? Child and youth programmers? Neighborhood glue for urban America? Definitive social justice agency? Or maybe the question at the heart of this is: who does God want and call the church to be? Maybe we have been so busy reinventing ourselves, we have forgotten to ask that one. Maybe we have lost touch with our mission as outposts for the reign of God.

We often behave less and less like churches, that is, places where the *telos* is to praise and proclaim God in Jesus Christ. Somehow many churches have grown awkward or embarrassed about glorifying God and allowing the holy mysteries that God has entrusted to us to do their work. One gets the feeling that for many, celebrating the God of the cross is not enough, that being more immediately practical or creating a buzz like those within popular culture are the measuring sticks. Questions of immediate relevance and sexier social posture take precedence over praising Jesus Christ in all things. Too often we want to be anything and everything but the stewards of sacred mysteries in word and sacrament.

I tell this story about mainline-liberal Protestantism in its well-ordered, broad-minded, sophisticated, latitudinarian fustiness because that is where I am blessed to serve. But we could offer equally biting stories of evangelical-conservative churches losing their way, with their carefully coiffed, "America-first," domestic-family-worshipping ministries that miss entire populations and dodge substantial biblically based issues.

These are churches where focus groups posing as governing boards have removed the cross in favor of a sizzling brunch grill in the church lobby, where our abundant "having" has formed a hard crust of "I've-gotten-mine-why-haven't-you-gotten-yours?" against the have-nots, where protecting the rights of gun owners displaces Jesus's *via dolorosa* through the Jerusalem streets, where reinforcing the supremacy of America's economic imperial reach turns a cold shoulder toward hemispheric neighbors who disagree with our State Department, where legitimate concerns of sexual morality have become the only moral acid test, creating a hubris that would humble the Pharisee antagonists dogging Jesus's every step.

In other words, whether left or right, liberal or conservative, modernist or fundamentalist, progressive or evangelical, no matter how you slice it, the transformative spiritual thrust of the Western Christian church has lost its oomph. Toying with being the church rather than living out our charter as the body of Christ, our mainspring has grown stressed and overheated through misuse and has lost its tensile strength. Our unique story has been usurped and overshadowed by other narratives, many of them having to do with worldly ideological rifts that were traced earlier. Our will has slackened, and we have become hesitant where we might be bold. And we have become bold where that has been very, very stupid.

This recalls the legendary story of the couple touring York, Seville, Milan, and Chartres, to see the magnificent cathedrals, monuments of Christian faith defying the centuries. They were awestruck at how closely the mammoth stones were joined atop precarious perches and altitudes that made their heads swim. All had been constructed in an era with much less technology and wealth, with no diesel or hydraulic power, but with much more sheer determination. Mildly exasperated, one asked, "Why is the church no longer capable of something like this?" The other countered, "Back then, faith was a matter of conviction. Today faith is a matter of opinion. It takes conviction to build cathedrals." Not only does it require conviction to make such a time-and-space-defying witness, it requires convictions in all of the right places.

Our spires have shrunk into the shadows of other, more popular high-rises. Perhaps the trend is most visible among vaunted celebrities who dismiss Christianity with a wave of the hand as if to say, "How could any sentient, educated person take such backward superstition seriously anymore? Is there anybody left who is so silly?" But the dismissive, self-assertive hubris of the stars we emulate has filtered down to ordinary, everyday people. And what was the exception has become the rule. In

California there is an obscure woman who has achieved near-legendary status among those who ponder such matters.

Sociologist Robert Bellah discovered her back in the eighties. Since then much has been written about the young nurse named Sheila Larson. Academics have analyzed and dissected her. She describes her faith as "Sheilaism." "I believe in God," she insists. "I'm not a religious fanatic. I can't remember the last time I went to church. My faith has carried me a long way. It's Sheilaism. Just my own little voice within." Sometimes I would like to find her and ask, "Isn't it a little lonely in there, Sheila? Doesn't God want more for you than being a homeless spiritual vagabond? Will it be enough for you when your whole world comes crashing down, as it eventually must upon all of us?" Sheilaism enervated the otherwise excellent response of that midwestern downtown congregation responding to sojourning refugee Cambodians.

Bellah not only observes this as a phenomenon, he describes where it is taking us.

> If the individual self must be its own source of moral guidance, then each individual must always know what he wants and desires or intuit what he feels. . . . Objectified moral goodness . . . turns into the subjective goodness of getting what you want, and enjoying it. Utility replaces duty; self-expression unseats authority. "Being good" becomes "feeling good."[2]

At first blush the results of letting humankind displace God as the measure for all things might seem as mild and inoffensive as Sheila's harmless theological patter. But who can smile as we see bumper crops of its bitter fruits harvested around us?

Virtue becomes advancing one's own cause. Celebration is the hubris of getting and having our own way. Obligation to each other or anything higher than ourselves is usurped by whatever works to "get ahead" individually. Accountability means rationalizing anything to ourselves to quell any last vestiges of conscience. Life so much resembles the *Jerry Springer Show* that we gawk and stare blankly at the car wreck of humankind until we begin to notice that we are also becoming that.

In this setting, texts like Paul's famous words to the Romans become precisely the cold cup of water we need to have thrown into our face:

> Do not be conformed to this world, but be transformed by the renewing of your minds, so that you may discern what is the will of God—what is good and acceptable and perfect. For by the grace given to me I say to everyone among you not to think of yourself more highly than you ought to think, but to think with sober judgment, each according to the measure of faith that God has assigned. For as in one body we have many members, and

not all the members have the same function, so we, who are many, are one body in Christ, and individually we are members one of another.

(Romans 12:2–5)

The church has not said enough about how Western society's reigning stark consumer acquisitiveness translates into individual narcissism, which gets called discipleship, and corporate commodification of religion, which gets called ministry.

If we would follow Jesus, it is by holding ourselves to a standard from beyond us, it is by taking God more seriously and ourselves less seriously, it is by finding our unique place within God's drama of redemption and offering our gifts for God's reign, but it is also realizing that we cannot do this in isolation, but only in community, as "members of one another."

To correctly perceive the church in the context of contemporary culture and within the mirror of our founding covenants, hear these words with which Roberta Smith closes her *New York Times* article, as a last fling with our chapter opening parable of the art museum:

> Museums abandon art at their own peril. We needn't worry about their lending their vaunted imprimaturs to dubious forms. . . . Any museum that does so often will lose that imprimatur. . . . Buildings don't make museums; art and only art does. It is art, speaking unequivocally for itself, that creates a museum's imprimatur in the first place. The debt of museums to art and artists down through time cannot be overestimated, can never be repaid; it is an obligation that can only be respected, abided by, and learned from. And as we are once again being reminded, it can also be profoundly betrayed.[3]

What the church calls art is God in Jesus Christ, reconciling the world to himself. We heed the warning as we peer into the future.

That May Be All Right for Them, but It Is No Good for Us

Jesus was not crucified for offering conventionally acceptable answers that were commonly heard to the hard questions weighing on the hearts of his contemporaries. Jesus was crucified because not one of the camps of his day—Roman, Sadducee, Pharisee, Essene, or Zealot—could co-opt him to advance the purposes of their agenda. And the new order of God's reign that he came to proclaim cut across what each of these held most dear, demanding that they be taken apart and put together in an entirely new way. In other words, Jesus was crucified because there was hardly a vested interest that was not threatened by his revolutionary message.

That his thinking and message were such a buzz saw is clear, for example, in places like the Sermon on the Mount, where Jesus goes after the human way of being human in favor of God's way of being human, saying, "You have heard it said . . . but I say to you" on everything from relations with Rome to generosity toward others. He cut a wide swath through the social underbrush and forest. And no towering, spreading tree rooted deeply since time immemorial could withstand Jesus's relentless articulation of God's truth, opposing the sanctification of our self-interest and advancing the cause of God's rule over us.

It is much too mild to say that Jesus spoke truth to power. That is what we do as we periodically challenge entrenched pagan interests and then scamper back into safe obscurity. Rather, through the words and deeds of his ministry, Jesus forever bracketed and temporized the pretense of all earthly powers bent upon their own dominion. Then, through his surrender to the Father, out of the yielding weakness of a horrible defeat, Jesus put all of these powers in their place through becoming the singular conquering redeeming power for all time. Our job is to bring this news of his conquest to those powers: locally, regionally, nationally, and globally. For they continue on oblivious, as though Jesus remains dead.

This conquest stands at the crossroads of eternity before which the direction and content of our life will be forever empowered and judged. Nobody could have predicted such an unfolding of God's will through weak, self-emptying, sacrificial triumph. It was and is completely counterintuitive to how power is wielded to establish the reign of any empire, much less that one we call the reign of God. It is completely alien to our imaginations. It is the mark of true spiritual authority.

Correspondingly, one of the earmarks of vitality and authenticity in our discipleship as the church is when we find ourselves saying, "That might be right for other people, but that is not right for us. We are not like them. We are different. For we follow a crucified and risen Messiah." Being followers of Jesus will always make us different, but not because of an inherent contrariness that needs to draw attention to ourselves. Not because we consider ourselves better than others. Not because we are particularly original as human beings. No, we will always be different because, if we are truly following Jesus, we are following One the likes of whom this world has never seen before and will never see again. Our marching orders issue from a story of redemption much larger than ourselves and unlike anything the world could invent or conceive.

People who truly walk in the ways of One so completely different as Jesus, rather than toying with what he represents, will necessarily become different. And this difference is not something we should apologize for or be embarrassed about so much as we glory in (without sneering at anyone else). For as we glory in this difference, we praise God. For these reasons, the pastors I admire most are those who actually look forward to and revel in preaching Jesus's hard sayings, even knowing in advance that that morning's sermon will never be anyone's favorite. Those, and not the huggy-bear and pop-culture-spoofing messages, are the sermons that I am most eager to hear.

Given all of this, it is shocking the extent to which the church has felt the need to lean on the world to form the foundation for its thinking. While it is true that theology happens in the moment, that it emerges from the context amid the struggles where we live, we cannot depend upon media and mood extrinsic to the message to define it. Ultimately, we can only trust the history of the people of Israel and the life, death, and resurrection of Jesus to do that. And we look to these founts of revelation not only for the substance of the message we bring, but also the form in which it presents itself.

The past one hundred years have seen systematic theologies having more to do with Descartes than Dorcas; liberation theologies more driven by Marx than Mark; process theologies bowing down to Hegel and Darwin before Hebrews and Daniel; existential theologies owing more to Sartre than to Samuel; social gospel theologies leaning more toward Ritschl and Harnack than to James and John; feminist theologies that give voice to Steinem at the expense of Miriam; liberal and conservative theologies that call to mind Immanuel Kant and Adam Smith respectively more than the Jewish carpenter from Nazareth whom no worldly power could co-opt.

Our approach to theology has come to resemble the revered modern cathedral of our day—the shopping mall—and our deepest-seated intuitive wisdom whispers from within that this cannot be a good thing. The ordering of our Christian faith as it expresses itself in the life of the church will founder and falter when it has become the theological equivalent of the Book of the Month Club. We are discussing here the unified and coherent vision of God's promised rule in Jesus Christ (or lack thereof) that drives the church.

To be sure, much good has come of these theologies as they contributed from such different places in so many ways. But is it any surprise that such a scattershot approach has left us fragmented and wondering where the center is? Is it any wonder that such a wild cacophony of voices, many of them even alien to the cause of the gospel, has not helped us hear the voice in which God would have us speak today? Is it possible for theology to range as far as these polarities and speak from so many perspectives without first giving so much away in how the questions get posed and how responses are generated?

Perhaps the final word over these fragmenting modern efforts was spoken generations ago by philosopher George Santayana:

> The attempt to speak without speaking any particular language is not more hopeless than the attempt to have a religion that shall be no religion in particular. . . . Thus every living and healthy religion has a marked idiosyncrasy. Its power consists in its special and surprising message and in the bias which that revelation gives to life. The vistas it opens and the mysteries it propounds are another world to live in; and another world to live in—whether we expect ever to pass wholly over into it or no—is what we mean by having a religion.[4]

Our language and its corresponding logic in mounting up the vision for the revolution of grace and good which is God's reign seems so much more terribly important than we have realized. Why are we more enamored of other languages and logics than our own? Why do we so often feel as though the biblical vision must be "spruced up" with Bernie Siegel or Deepak Chopra or Sting's latest lyrics to have relevance and convicting power? How can we take full stock of the power of our inherent forms and substance, lest we overlook our own particular gifts while coveting those of others? What sets us apart? This is worth pausing over.

Looking for Faith in All the Wrong Places

My dear friend, wonderful pastor, and fine writer the Reverend Martin Copenhaver came, as a result of attending a funeral in Boston not so long ago, to describe a woman who understood the church's unique role and power.[5] The service was for Marguerite Cooper McCain. "Nita" as she was called, was mother to Marguerite and mother-in-law to the Reverend Samuel Lloyd, current dean of the National Cathedral in Washington, D.C.

Nita spent much of her life in Okoloma, Mississippi, where she was an active member of Grace Episcopal Church. Her faith profoundly shaped her life until her life deeply shaped those around her. She was a regular at prayer group and Bible studies. Reading spiritually enriching books was another great love.

There in small-town Mississippi was actually a second Episcopal church, St. Bernard's. That perhaps seems unusual, and it may seem more so when we know that the congregation at St. Bernard's was African American and Grace Episcopal Church was Anglo. Back in those days—or maybe still as much today—having two races necessitated two churches. It was certainly just that way back in Mississippi back in those days.

At one point, the Episcopal bishop ordered the two churches to merge into one congregation. They would move into the building of Grace Church, because St. Bernard's didn't own a building. They had always worshipped in borrowed space. And they would call the new congregation St. Bernard's. Two races, one Episcopal Church.

But not so fast—things don't always unfold according to the most sensible patterns and sacred designs. Of course, in the Episcopal polity a bishop has every right to order two congregations to become one. Still again, you cannot alter human hearts by fiat. Nikolai Lenin once observed that refugees vote with their feet.

Many of the members of Grace Church stopped coming in silent protest. Eventually, only one member of Grace Church remained—Nita. She still came to worship every Sunday, the only white person left in the congregation. The character of the service of worship changed, as did the composition of the laity in the pews. But Nita kept coming. It wasn't so much a conscious decision to hang in there as an extension of her lifelong habit. Better said, it was that the idea of leaving her church never occurred to her. Not to mention that the people of St. Bernard's had endeared themselves to her, and they loved Nita as well.

When she died a memorial service was held for her at St. Bernard's in the sanctuary that once housed Grace Church. The service attracted people from both congregations. The ushers of St. Bernard's escorted the former members of Grace Church to their familiar pews, some of whom had not darkened the doorway of their church since the merger. Together they celebrated Nita's life and worshipped the same God. In her quiet, simple, unassuming way, Nita was able to bring about the change that a powerful bishop could not. Everything about her Christian witness was unremarkable except, in retrospect, the example she set and the result brought about. This is what spiritual authority looks like.

Sometimes it is in faithless ways that we imagine the personal change and social transformation that would remake the world in God's image. We look for the massively grand gesture. We aspire after the larger-than-life stage. From the get-go we want dramatic results compounding themselves for good and visible rewards vindicating our lonely stands. But Jesus was not speaking only about money when he said that she who is faithful in little will be found faithful in much (Luke 16:10). Jesus was also speaking about the spiritual capital of how we invest ourselves moment to moment in little things we do on a daily basis. In our mustard-seed faith, they add up to more than we would imagine in the grand scope of things if we can trust that, more often than we suppose, little is enough.

Nita was not a social activist. She didn't set out to stir things up. She just went to church, uttered her prayers, studied the Bible, and praised God with beloved friends. Do we have enough faith to see that matters as mundane as this loom larger than we would suppose in the corridors of eternity? If we do, then we will see that undramatic callings like parenthood, friendship, work, neighborliness, and churchmanship are more fraught with the possibility of Christlike redemptive global transformation than we would allow.

It wasn't so much that Nita had such a strong grip on the church that it was her church and she wasn't going to give it up. It was more that the church as the living body of Christ had a strong grip on her as the spiritual home where she enjoyed refreshment by word and sacrament. It wasn't that the church belonged to Nita so much as she belonged to the church. It held an authority over her that was not domineering or oppressive, but liberating for her and those whom she amazed. The path of Nita's leadership was a path of surrender, and surrender to the true and living God makes all the difference in the world.

With our earlier parable of the art museum, Nita can teach us what it means to be called and grounded as the church of Jesus Christ, to have our identity and purpose in place so that grace can be mediated in the everyday, and greatness can grow from such ordinary events as daily happen upon us.

Where the Rubber Hits the Road

As I tell others how much I adore being a pastor, sometimes I am asked what I find most rewarding or gratifying in my work. My thoughts turn to the many Habitat for Humanity Global Village work trips that I have been blessed to lead over the past seventeen years. The last three churches that I have served have worked with simple peasants (who by far did most of the work!) to build fifty-three homes for the poorest of the poor, mostly in Latin America. As great as that is, building shelter for deserving families worldwide is not even the most gratifying part.

The part in this that excites me and feels like ministry that is mobilizing for the reign of God are the changes that I observe in those who venture forth in these faith adventures and the changes that I observe in myself. Sometimes North Americans say how good and kind we are for undertaking these trips. "Are you kidding?" is my immediate reaction. "I go to Honduras so that I can see the face of Jesus in my neighbor, get my head screwed on right, and rediscover a heart for ministry so I can return here and serve this affluent parish week in and week out." This hope is a spiritual gift that people in the developing world give us, likely even more important than the material homes that result. The peasants experience this hope as well. It is the grace that Jesus offered when he said, "Blessed are the poor." They are generous enough to share their blessing with us.

Conversion is the word that I use to describe what happens. Not that we aren't Christians before going. Not that we aren't practicing our faith to the best of our ability amid our routine. Not that what the church does as a matter of course is without merit. But that by depending on each other as community, breaching the world's implacable barriers, and intensely engaging with God at work in the trenches of the front lines of God's reign, we feel our own lives change in these short days in a way that affects us for the rest of our lives.

Participants smile blandly or look skeptical during the first orientation meeting when I suggest that this pending trip will indeed make a difference for the rest of their lives. But once immersed in the experience, they understand perfectly. Suddenly otherwise obscure and impenetrable words from Jesus's lips—whoever would save his life will lose it, but whoever would lose his life for my sake will save it, for example—become real and living and true. Words like these make no sense to us until we share such intense and godly experiences. For reasons like this, Stanley Hauerwas claims that we shouldn't hand the Bible out for just anyone to read. They must have suitable practices and experiences first if we expect it to make any sense to them.

The point is that ministry is never more powerful than when we experience and engender transformation as disciples of Jesus Christ. These trips are but small capsules of that change. By this I mean not only our transformation as individuals, but with it the transformation of the world around us, the active and palpable sense that God is in Jesus Christ reconciling the world to God's self. Too seldom do we get to taste, touch, and feel this holy and whole-souled change.

For many years it seemed that people came to church to find a sanctuary or escape from change. For them the church needed to accommodate its message to help them fit into and make sense of an increasingly crazy world. It wasn't the world that needed to change, neither was it we ourselves; these were constants. The gospel was supposed to accommodate itself and "make sense" of this. If the church couldn't or didn't make sense of how to prosper in settings that were predicated upon God's absence, how life in Babylon could be easier or less stressful, then that church was dubbed "irrelevant." Rather than a healing balm in Gilead, this gospel has become a stopgap palliative in hospice.

In more recent years, I have noticed a significant shift here. More and more, people who are world-weary come to the church looking precisely for alternatives to the barren and unacceptable options we face during the week. We long to know of and glimpse other realities, and to discover leverage points beyond the usual pick-me-ups. We are hungry for change, and we want to know there is another way.

More and more, what propels people through our front doors is no longer how to be a model American or a good corporate citizen or how to spackle the widening cracks in our way of life. Rather, it is how to deal with daily life, not on its own terms as an unavoidable given, but on other terms more real and true, more enduring and holy. It is about how to not lose our soul as our foundations tremble by anchoring ourselves in an order where God dwells and rules over all.

One pastor who grasps the centrality of human transformation as the power of the gospel and the purpose of the church is the Reverend Tony Robinson of Seattle. As a writer, he insightfully speaks of our natural allies in this quest.

> So far as I can tell, Jesus was not mainly in the business of providing answers, managing and quelling conflict, or reinforcing communal norms. Rather, he drew attention to the gap between present realities and the Kingdom, which is another way of describing an adaptive challenge: it is where there is a gap, a dissonance between the values and ideals we profess and the realities we live. Scripture, too . . . is not a book of moral examples, a sort of really old book of virtues. No, Scripture tells the story of God's intrusions into our settled worlds, of God's determination to turn over the world as it is and to form a people for God's glory. This God is not in the business of keeping things tidy, nailed down, and predictable. Rather this is a God who disturbs the status quo, breaks open the settled worlds, reverses this world order, and raises the dead.[6]

Like Jesus, the church is in the business of making disciples, of forming Christians. If we find ourselves apologizing for that, or trying to describe that in terms that seem more chic, then our authority as the body of Christ is unclear. And we need to get clear on that purpose, beginning with the pastor first, before we do anything else.

Our job is to throw our people into dilemmas where faithfulness to God is absolutely demanded because any other response will seem pale and inadequate. As we do, we comfort our people by walking alongside in this same pilgrimage of faith, scratching our heads and raising our voices and clasping our hands in prayer over the same dilemmas. In other words, as the church we lack nothing so much as to be turned out of our self-absorption and back toward God, to be born from above as part of the ongoing story narrated by scripture, to be altered and changed in the shape of human life as modeled by Jesus, and to be made new by the gospel promises where the end point is God's victory and our own.

For this to happen, where we now have overflowing storehouses of goodwill (people blandly wanting the best for the church), we need superabundant breakthroughs of imagination (people willing to ask questions in new ways in order to break things loose). Imagination—which at once requires childlikeness, courage, boldness, vision, and a very thick skin—is the least appreciated, most downtrodden virtue that our people bring to the church. It is effectively silenced with two phrases. One is "We have never done it that way before." The other is "We tried that and it didn't work." But the power of imagination to capture the wonder of where people might yet see God at work in the world is our greatest untapped resource, if we could let go of ourselves and our fears for a moment.

Think, for example, of how the stories and dramas of the American cowboy on the Western prairies have dominated our consciousness for 150 years. Did you know that at the apex of their numbers, there were never more than 100,000 cowboys at one time in America on the move, driving cattle? Capture people's imagination, and the image of how life might be will stick in ways disproportionate to what we think possible. With millions of professing Christians in the West, we can do better here. Carol Zaleski writes that what is possible for us as Jesus's disciples is directly proportional to what we will imagine:

> Every institution with which we deal—our schools, hospitals, courts, theaters, newspapers, stores, playgrounds, and even our churches—tells us by signs overt or subliminal that the dramatic parts of the Christian story are over, except for some commotion at the end on which it's best not to dwell. We know this can't be right, and yet these blandishments, claiming to be the voice of reason, whisper in our ears so continuously that we begin to suffer imagination fatigue. Imagination fatigue doesn't directly attack the Christian faith: instead, it diminishes the power of the Christian story to quicken culture. "The heart is commonly reached," as John Henry Newman wrote, "not through the reason, but through the imagination, by means of direct impressions, by the testimony of facts and events, by history, by description." But if imagination is fatigued, faith is surely in jeopardy, and even testimony begins to falter.[7]

So what does imagination look like when it strikes our steeples like lightning? Its charge can originate from the least likely places, even out of the dust of our past.

A Final, Bright, Hopeful Note

Nowhere has the church's confusion about the nature of its identity and the power of its authority been more at issue than in youth ministry. So often the poor youth minister is asked to be babysitter, cruise ship activities director, and hall monitor. So often the measure of her success is how well she keeps the kids busy and distracted all the way to Six Flags Over America. But recently I heard about a youth ministry that wreaks havoc with such an exasperatingly reduced vision of this youth minister role.

My friend and colleague the Reverend Skip Masback is senior pastor of a splendid congregation neighboring my own. His was an unusual path to that position; not only is he a former attorney, but he entered the ministry as a youth pastor. He built this youth ministry of the Congregational Church of New Canaan emphasizing Christian community as a refuge where youth can know themselves here and now as beloved children of God, and he persuaded them to trust that this is sufficient in all circumstances. This may sound innocuous enough, but it has resonance in communities like ours, where entirely too much self-worth is predicated on which college accepts you and where that takes you professionally.

Skip built this church's youth ministry through deep biblical reflection and transporting privileged youth outside of their comfort zone into the front lines of human need, working with new friends they had never met before in places far away, and a world apart from New Canaan. Amazing and transformative things result as one slogs through the unglamorous work of laying down such a solid and soul-shaping spiritual foundation. What is this but the work of the Holy Spirit?

Thinking that he was too much pushing the envelope of youth ministry, once Skip went so far as to experiment with contemplative monastic spiritual disciplines originating in the guided meditations of the church father Ignatius. He brought this to a small group one weekday evening, half expecting them to roll their eyes and turn up their noses. Afterward, he moved them on to something else more conventional to their age in a suburban setting. "Can we go back to the prayer disciplines?" came their sweet protestation. "We should be doing more of those, don't you think? And how about all of the time, every week?" They had just returned from one of their mission trips and were aching to fill the spiritual void awakened within them.

Seven years later, this handful of youth has grown into twenty-eight who attend what they call Youth Group Quest every Thursday night for prayerful meditation—this on top of their usual Sunday youth group participation. Not only have these practices shaped the interior of their lives, this group of young people has galvanized into a tightly knit community in good times or in bad, at church or at school.

I am not sure what to call the opposite of the failure of nerve, but this is what it looks like in the church, and it is in short supply. I am not sure what to call the opposite of an identity crisis, but this is what it looks like in the church, and it makes us stand taller. Sometimes as the church recognizes its distinctive charter and acts out of its covenant instead of living out worldlier stories, we rise up in ways we could have never predicted. In these sublime moments, we want nothing more than the chance and blessing of being the resurrected body of Jesus Christ loosed upon and alive in the world. This is how we honor the specialness and mystery of the church and allow it to have full impact upon our lives and the world.

8

THE WORD OF GOD:
IN THE BEGINNING

Often we toss out simple statements about matters of spirit that at face value seem inviting, helpful, and forward-thinking. But upon closer scrutiny, these phrases actually cut the nerve from which the faithful would dare worthy and great things for God. These are not obvious; they are almost invisible.

For example, "It doesn't matter what you believe, so long as you are sincere." Or, similarly, "Any efforts to define who we are and what we stand for make me nervous. That is for each of us to decide!" Or, for the purposes of this chapter, "Sure, the Bible is a good book, but no more so than other good and holy books." At face value, it seems fair-minded and obliging, but it is damning the Bible by faint praise.

Typically, I want to ask such well-meaning people, posturing the grand gesture toward other religions, "Would you be willing to say these things to a deeply faithful Buddhist or Sikh or Muslim, and still expect him to take you seriously as a person of Christian conviction?" Or, more to the point, I might want to ask them, "When you realize how deeply people of other faiths revere their sacred texts, doesn't presenting the Bible so casually and off-handedly sound silly and sophomoric?" Even knowing little about these other faiths, we already know the answer to such questions as these.

As tepid uncertainty becomes ascendant in the name of fair-mindedness, our identity as God's people erodes, our chosenness for a holy purpose muddies, our charter of faith is one more helpful outlook, our covenant of salvation feels like mere self-fulfillment, and the steady forward step of discipleship reduces to the distraction of intermittent wanderings, full of the self and absent of God. Here the word *Christian* becomes bland and amorphous, like another pet nostrum from the grab bag of self-improvement, like being vegetarian. In fact, if such equivocation about the centerpiece of our faith does not sound downright weak in our ears, this reveals more about our modern spiritual failure of nerve as Christians than it shows anything like broad-mindedness.

Not a God Who Would Occur to Us in a Spring Meadow

With the eclipse of authority in things biblical, we do well to underscore a distinction that has been mentioned earlier. Christianity is a revealed faith and not a natural religion. Natural religion ineluctably edges us toward pantheism, where God is no less and no more present in any person, place, thing, or iota of being. In natural religion, God is equally present everywhere, from a tender shoot breaking through the ground to the stars shining in the night sky to the music still hanging in the air at an outdoor concert to the baby born yesterday to the lady down the block. Our egalitarian, democratic instincts gravitate toward such a view of revelation in that we assume it would be how God self-discloses if we were to invent God, even if it is not how God chose to self-disclose.

In a revealed faith such as Christianity, we acknowledge that God chooses to reveal the divine self more in some events, places, lives, stories, and even books than in others. We don't know why God does this—it is part of God's mystery—but we must affirm that this is how God works. As hard as this is on the Western mind, and as unjust as this strikes reasonable, fair-minded adults, we believe that God's self-disclosure is most intense and most illuminating even as it is most particular. For example, "in the sixth month the angel Gabriel was sent by God to a town in Galilee called Nazareth, to a virgin engaged to a man whose name was Joseph" (Luke 1:26–27). We believe that this moment and message says more specific and helpful things about the divine will and purpose across space and time than do the blades of grass that Thoreau plucked and inspected at Walden Pond.

If only those dismayed by the particularity of biblical revelation could take a longer, more dynamic view of its story of redemption instead of evaluating the text as far-off tale about out-of-the-way places and odd people. For as Christians, we believe that God starts in small and specific places and then works outward toward the universal. More to the point, we hold that the will and the ways of the true and living God are everywhere evident in the Hebrew account of the genesis of life, the migrations of the patriarchs, the utterances of the prophets of Israel, and the rise of the kingdoms of Israel and Judah. Moreover, we confess that God is most supremely known in the person and example, the death and resurrection, of Jesus Christ. Finally, we glimpse how we are cast in the finish of this drama at the commissioning of apostles and the all-too-mundane struggles of fledgling congregations in places like Ephesus or Philippi or Corinth.

The Christian claim is that revealed faith is not less universal than natural religion. It only starts in smaller places, asking our trust that God will accomplish God's purposes, needing time and space to reach its destination, just as we do. It holds that the waters of divine disclosure first trickle through rivulets that next become brooks that later become canals that eventually become tributaries that ultimately become mighty rivers before those major waterways unite with oceans, touching the shores of the entire world.

God's revelation progressively reaches out toward the universal through the particular, not by the general broadcast of some cosmic radio wave like the Emergency Broadcast System that periodically beeps upon our radios as a test. This notion is as old as Isaiah declaring the people of Israel to be God's instrument saying, "I will give you as a light to the nations, that my salvation may reach to the end of the earth" (49:6). That light was a ray to a few before it became a beacon to the many.

The stark particularity of our revealed faith and the specificity of our story jar those who prefer the gentle egalitarian generalities of natural religion. It is hard on those who could not understand why God would not bring salvation simply by building upon what we and our human undertakings have already built.

To their point, yes, God *can* be anywhere or in anything making himself known. God could have saved the world through a dead dog by the side of the road if God had so chosen, wrote theologian Karl Barth.[1] But is that indeed what God has done? we ask. *Is* that where God is most known? No, comes the sober answer, when our hypothetical-philosophical head games and imaginary possibility-think are said and done. Natural religion is the religious romanticism that is the dewy-eyed child of the eternal, but it lacks the seriousness of the eternal. For it won't take us back to the God who is both Creator and Redeemer.

Sooner or later real discipleship beckons us to pull back from our self-construed ideals of spiritual possibility to what our forebears have for millennia delivered to us as the divine self-communication, the Word of God. God has been most fully revealed and is knowable to us through the winding narrative of the Bible, through the vicissitudes of the people of Israel, and how their shared winding story recapitulates itself again in the life of one man, Jesus of Nazareth, whom we confess as the Christ.

Here in the Bible as nowhere else it comes to light that our human destiny is a movement from nothingness to being, from oppression to freedom, from despair to hope, from estrangement to reconciliation, from suffering to redemption, from hatred to love, from narcissism to sacrifice, from death to resurrection. Though it may seem arbitrary, there is nothing accidental in these revelations through ordinary people like Amos or Jairus's daughter in ancient backwaters, but everything intentional and calculated in these divine initiatives.

Like any good doctor treating a serious disease—in our case sinfulness—God has spoken to our human condition, telling us what we need to know only as we have needed to know it, taking progressively revealing measures with us called covenants, until our condition called for newer and stronger medicine. And God has expected us to trust him enough to go with him from there. Why this comes as such a shock to so many is frankly hard to understand. For requiring simple trust of us as God's people is, after all, why we call it "faith" and not something else. When all is said and done, faith is this simple, childlike trust that even if we don't understand all of God's many turns, by God's side we shall reach our destination.

At Last, a Place Where It Is No Longer Always about Us!

In an age when narcissism is our defining burden, we do well to remind one another: the Bible is not primarily a book about us, it is first and last a book about God. Failure to realize that is at the root of much frustration and disappointment in reading the Bible. I am always surprised at those who profess interest in "spirituality" but have no patience with the Bible. Most of this "spirituality" has pitifully little interest in God. Has that lost its power to shock us?

But the Bible is not a book about us; it is a book about God. And it is not like any other book—alternately charming and disturbing, captivating and boring—because our God is unlike every other god. Yes, the Bible is a strange new world, to quote Karl Barth, because as high as the heavens are above the earth, God is that much greater than we are. We are like insects trying to read the mind of Einstein.

Just as the Bible tells us about God rather than indulging our own vanities, so also it carries with it the authority that it knows more about God than we do. In our modern arrogance, where we assume that we already know God's being, purposes, and means because we are such genuine, sensitive human beings, we too easily lose track of this. In this, thinking we know all about God simply by being such "good people," when so much of that god is but humankind projected in a loud voice, we owe the Bible more respect than modernity grants.

By the power of the Holy Spirit, even its obscure or puzzling parts, its archaic or obscure verses will yield something about God that we cannot know about God apart from the Bible. How deeply do we really hunger for God? More deeply than the parlor snacks that the bookstore calls "spirituality" will feed us? The reading we give the Bible and the place that we grant it in things most precious to us is the best answer for that question.

The Bible is the story of God's mysterious self-disclosure, how that has changed everything, how that tempers what it means to be partly or fully or even eternally alive. It is in the Bible that we learn that life is pointed toward a joyous end point despite everything that would dispirit and convince us otherwise. It is in the Bible that we are called upon to make decisions with consequences rather than passing through life as though meandering through a nether world of shades of grey. It is the Bible that gets passed down across generations, ensuring that none of this will be lost even if generations along the way are wayward and remiss in imparting God's interventions on our behalf to our children.

The important point here is contained in two simple Latin words, *extra nos*, meaning "beyond us." Revelation by its nature comes not from within us or from among us, but from *beyond us*. It is not a human achievement of our finding, striving, procuring, thinking, or imagining. Revelation is always given us as a gift of God's grace. It is *extra nos*, beyond us. This means that the content of our Christian message doesn't arbitrarily depend upon how we feel or where we look on a given day for inspiration. Our Christian faith has about it a givenness that was here before us and will outlast us once we are gone. Further, as with Moses removing his sandals before the burning bush, this means humility is the most appropriate disposition of those gifted with Biblical revelation. In other words, if the brilliance of God's showing forth in the Bible reveals our neighbor's sinfulness and we still think that we are pretty swell, then we have entirely missed the point.

Still, such age-old truth will not easily quench the querulous spirit asking, Why the Bible (as opposed to Oprah's Book Club) as a guide to the life and light of God? Pastor Tony Robinson speaks with clarity and conviction about the Bible as our distinctive font of revelation, and as the basis of our identity as Christians.

> Why this book indeed? And what role do the scriptures of our faith play in the church? I sometimes draw an analogy to the Constitution of the United States of America. We in the U.S. may find the constitutions of other nations to be interesting and instructive, but they aren't ours. We have a special obligation to our own Constitution. We grant it an authoritative status so that we can remember and know who we are. It is crucial to our identity. In a similar way, while there are undoubtedly many beautiful and inspiring books, the Bible is "our" book in a twofold sense. One, it is the creation of the church, of our forebears in the faith. Two, it reminds the church who and whose it is, and who and whose it isn't.[2]

Robinson further says that the Bible is our personal library, just as universities or law firms have their own personal library, reflective of their origins, character, calling, and destiny. Hesitation or negligence to eagerly tap into the power of our library collection as the most precious message that we could conceivably receive is nothing less than dry rot around the foundation of the temple of God.

In truth, as the church neglects the Bible, as that book gathers dust on shelves rather than shines as our centerpiece, that is exactly when the church is most given to whiny moralizing. The imperative "shoulds" and "oughts" of the left's social-justice rants and the right's shrill lecturing on personal conduct fill the void created by ignoring weighty biblical indicatives like, "So Abram went, as the LORD had told him" (Gen. 12:4), or "And I said, 'Here am I; send me!'" (Isa. 6:8), or "After [Jesus] had said this, he went on ahead, going up to Jerusalem" (Luke 19:28), or "Then I saw the Lamb open one of the seven seals, and I heard one of the four living creatures call out" (Rev. 6:1).

Taking It Personally

Every group has constitutive stories about its leaders that make up its lore and shape its ethos. One such tale about a larger-than-life seminary professor—a man at once difficult, brilliant, and deeply faithful—circulated among his teaching assistants.

The faculty of Yale Divinity School was meeting together in a retreat-type setting, meaning to articulate the essentials of who they were and where they were headed. For focus, they plopped down in their midst a text with which they would all attempt to come to grips. It was the miraculous story of Jesus feeding the five thousand with five barley loaves and two fish. Of course, given the assembly, they had at their disposal a formidable arsenal of academic-based exegetical and hermeneutical skills. No method or angle from this scholarly armory was neglected as the discussion of the Gospel text swirled round. The proponents of text criticism held sway. The advocates of redaction criticism responded. The champions of form criticism could not remain silent.

As the exchange spent itself and new ground was no longer being broken, a professor turned to Paul Holmer, this theology professor without formal credentials in the historical-critical method of biblical scholarship. "You've been silent all of this while," said he. "What would you make of this text, Paul?" With his trademark smirk, Mr. Holmer suggested, "Well, I was just thinking that if Jesus could feed all of those people, perhaps he could also feed me." I imagine a long, pregnant pause following this remark, the long and tangled skein of the preceding conversation eclipsed with one brief phrase.

The point is that unless the biblical narrative becomes personal in the joys and sorrows of our own heartfelt struggles, unless we become vulnerable to the text in the very places where we live, the Word of God will not yield its mysteries. But this strength of personal passion also has a shadowy side of weakness. For we immediately ask, How can the Bible become personal to us without its message becoming esoteric and tendentious along the lines of our pet biases? The key here is Christian community. I can hardly imagine where reading the Bible by oneself is superior to a reading with fellow Christians. Yet so much "inspirational literature" of our personal devotions is geared for reading the Bible alone.

Probably the most visible common point where the people of God engage scripture together is on Sunday morning, as the reading of the Word is the pinnacle of corporate worship. From there the preacher must decide where God's people will travel as a result of the message we have heard. The Sunday sermon is the most familiar and in some ways the most telling statement on the options available to us in hearing and living out the meaning of the sacred text.

We are familiar with the deductive method of proclamation, whereby the preacher begins with abstract principles and builds toward concrete reality. Many of us are of an age where we have heard enough three-point sermons with a poem and a conclusion that we know that exposition of high-flown doctrine does not always land us in the fields where we live, breathe, and strive. And we leave church on Sunday with the message still circling somewhere overhead.

We are also familiar with the inductive method, whereby the preacher starts with familiar stories from everyday reality and then builds toward biblical principles. Back in the seventies Fred Craddock, among others, showed the way here, beginning with where we live and finding where this intersects with scripture, and then moving with us into the larger realms of redemption, salvation, and reconciliation. Still, even this model for responding to the text falls short of the power and presence of living in the Word of God, which Jesus demonstrated.

Formally, we may be less familiar with what Leonard Sweet calls abductive logic (philosopher Charles Sanders Peirce coined this term).[3] Abductive reasoning seizes us by the imagination and transports us from our current world to another world, where human insight and perspective experience something like a quantum leap from the stock ways of construing meaning from a text. The most definitive form of this language and logic is the parable.

Abductive or parabolic logic resists the outlines and subsections that typify both deductive and inductive exposition of scripture. In other words, the message is not built around rational, conventionally structured analysis. Rather, it removes us from the presumptions of our station in life, removes us from the comfort of our prevailing biases, breaking down the walls behind which we feel safe, posing the alternative of God's idea of what it means to be faithful or true as opposed to our ideas of that, and opening to us fields of serving and glorifying God bounded by horizons that we would otherwise never glimpse.

Abductive approaches are less about "making a point" than about summoning the shimmering or enigmatic or confrontational image of where God dwells to throw us into the dilemma of being faithful. The parables invite the unfolding of just such a process. Surprise and unpredictability are key elements here—just as they were in Jesus's parables. So are humor, disorientation, astonishment, dislocation, amazement, inscrutability, and surprise. Like Garrison Keillor taking us to Lake Wobegon, the abduction of the parabolic word is a metaphorical kidnapping that transports us to another place before we return and resume our lives as those forever changed by God's startling and amazing ways.

When Jesus came out of the desert, having outlasted the temptations before beginning his ministry, he immediately lined out the main theme of his ministry: "Repent, for the kingdom of heaven is at hand" (Mark 4:17). By *repent,* Jesus didn't mean that we should put on long, sad faces for having been caught in our sin. He didn't mean that we should remain morosely stuck, lamenting the past. He didn't mean for us to lie down and accept that we are captive to evil. Rather, Jesus meant that we have new hope for the future. He meant that God is turning the world around 180 degrees. He meant that if we let him, God will transform us with a redemption befitting our resurrection destiny that Jesus prefigured. He meant that the news of Jesus's advent and the fulfillment of his earthly mission really is good news.

142

Somewhere we have lost this charge to be changed and to become agents of spiritual metamorphosis. Somewhere this glorious destiny has devolved into patching up a flawed status quo and making the best of human disappointment and misery as it is. As the church slouches into such a posture, it should not surprise us that many consider the religious life a kind of purgatory. For here Jesus's powerful and risky movement is degraded into one more status-quo-reinforcing institution, more wedded to how things are than to how God shall remake them at the day of the Lord.

There is the story of a man who had visited a large church for several weeks. Excited at the newness of the Bible account, he approached one of the ushers after worship. "When do we get to *do* some of these things?" he asked. "Do what things?" the usher responded. "You know," answered the first man, "the healings, the miracles, the showdowns for goodness and mercy and truth that we hear about in the Bible." "Oh, we don't actually *do* those things here," the usher clarified. "We just talk about them." I can almost see that visitor's posture slump.

Jesus's parables remind us that this was not always so. The parables are where Jesus cleverly threw his hearers into the dilemma of being faithful. Reading or hearing a parable, there is no standing on the sidelines. No one reminds us of this better than the wonderfully salty peanut farmer and New Testament Greek scholar, the late Clarence Jordan.[4]

Jesus's parables were never high-flown abstraction uttered for the sake of lofty scholarly speculation, Jordan reminds us. Rather they focused and sharpened the living and breathing issues of our daily lives, insisting that we are spiritual creatures living our lives out before God before we are economic, domestic, political, or sexual beings, at least as the world defines these categories.

The parables make the matter of God's inbreaking among us personal without capitulating to the hearer's bias. They require the hearer to participate in the message rather than to be spoon-fed, because their meaning is not immediately obvious but must be teased out of the story. Typically, before the hearer realizes what Jesus's parables are about and how he or she might be implicated, it is already too late. For the parable has snuck in—a literary Trojan horse, concealing truth to get it behind seemingly impregnable psychological defenses.

The parables were spoken for such a time as ours, when matters of greatest importance have grown at once dangerous, delicate, and deadly dull. The parables added nothing to the dusty theological tomes preceding and following Jesus. Rather they fomented change within and among us, change that pleases God and befits the new social order of God's reign. The parables attract, bait, involve, enlighten, shock, cajole, and—if we

143

let them have their way—transform our stock ways of understanding ourselves living out our lives before God in the world.

The parables address vital situations fraught with potential for conflict that must be addressed but cannot be faced directly. As Jordan describes it, the parables have their way of saying something that badly needs to be said, but in a way where the mouse plays tricks on the cat. The cat suspects something is going on, he can smell it right under his nose, but he cannot quite put his paw on it. If Jesus had not spoken in parables, he would have been murdered in three months rather than after three years of ministry. If we would engage the real work of Christian ministry, telling the whole truth of God's reign and parsing out its implications for God's people, we would do well to sit up and take notice here.

Of the many forms Jesus employed in launching his message that the reign of God was at hand—miracles, prayer, teaching, symbolic actions, quoting the Septuagint, healings—the only form explicitly and repeatedly discussed in some detail within the Gospels was his use of parables. Luke (8:9–10) records:

> Then his disciples asked him what this parable meant. He said, "To you it has been given to know the secrets of the kingdom of God; but to others I speak in parables, so that 'looking they may not perceive, and listening they may not understand.'"

Moreover, we also read in Matthew (13:34) that "without a parable he told them nothing."

Parables and Things Parabolic

Why are the parables definitive in understanding the special place of the Bible among us and its authority over us? The same Paul Holmer mentioned earlier was fond of saying that if the mood and method of what is being said do not match its content and substance, then the message will be corrupted and betrayed. By their nature, the parables, as Jesus's most typical form of address, reveal so much about the nature of his message, even the point of his ministry, that we must sit up and take notice.

The parables were as powerful as dynamite charges strategically placed in cherished personal strongholds, and as puzzling as the inscrutable God who would generously choose to die at the hands of sinners to be vindicated by rising again rather than wiping out the whole lot of us. Keeping the parables and what they represent front and center is a key to coming under the authority of the Word of God and also recovering our essential calling as the church of Jesus Christ. If we could learn to read the entire Bible not precisely in the same way, but with certainly the same mind-set as the parables invite, we would do very well.

For the parables are not just about the few dozen enigmatic little stories that Jesus told. The parables permeate everything biblical. The parables are paradigmatic. Parabolic thinking is required to understand why the prophet Hosea would marry a harlot, why the virgin birth is something that we would have to invent if it did not exist, what transpired between Jesus and the devil in his wilderness temptation, and the meaning of Jesus turning water into wine at a wedding in Cana of Galilee. Why such a lengthy stop at the parables of Jesus?

Many people today are stuck in a literal versus figurative approach to scripture that covertly reinforces the useless, unhelpful ideological differences that the world calls the right and the left. If we want to get unstuck here and move forward, it will be Jesus's artful, evocative, and provocative sense of the parabolic that can help us sort through the morass of the modern mind-set.

For example, let us consider how a parabolic reading of a text might take us beyond the wooden exchanges of the figurative left and literalist right, and grant us instead a vision of our transformation in Christ's image. Because this book doesn't dodge challenge and provocation, we consider a matter as volatile as same-sex relationships and whether they should be consecrated and blessed.

In Acts chapters 10 and 11 God is at work through the faithful Gentile Christian Cornelius and the Rock, the apostle Peter. Of course, Paul was an early advocate of admitting the Gentiles into the church, and Peter was slow to accept the uncircumcised. But after God points Cornelius toward Peter, and Peter has a vision about all manner of things that he had always considered unclean and reprehensible as now favored and blessed by God, he grants Cornelius an audience. Not only this, Peter next comes around to a living faith: "I truly understand that God shows no partiality, but in every nation anyone who fears him and does what is right is acceptable to him" (Acts 10:34–35).

Peter takes this revelation to the Jerusalem Council gathered to deliberate over this issue. "If then God gave them the same gift that he gave us when we believed in the Lord Jesus Christ, who was I that I could hinder God?" he testifies (Acts 11:17). As the last and most vocal stronghold resisting the unclean Gentile Christian outsiders was removed, they gained full standing in the church of Jesus Christ. Surely this text remains important for Jewish-Christian relations.

But read parabolically, the text also holds promise for our deliberations around the divisive issue of consecrating same-sex relationships. Are new visions today being granted the church over the past twenty years after talking about this subject almost not at all for centuries? Are these visions of God? Have upstanding, faithful followers of Jesus—gay equivalents of Cornelius—emerged from a group always previously considered unclean to break down old dividing walls of hostility? Are we being called to reconsider those scripture has always held to be unclean in light of the visions? Or, some might argue, is this parallel specious and without merit, given biblical revelation as traditionally construed and the nature of human sexuality? Such a conversation among Christians would be a breath of fresh air in the currently polarized church environment around this issue.

The figurative reading that liberals give texts like Sodom and Gomorrah, Leviticus, and Romans chapter one is so loosey-goosey as to say that the Bible doesn't really say what it really says. This is unhelpful and unbiblical. The literal reading that the conservatives give the same biblical readings on homosexuality and lesbianism is so narrowly focused they cannot see that in adjoining Old Testament texts we are prohibited from touching menstruating women or eating lobster, and that in the New Testament the apostle Paul enjoins slaves to be obedient to their masters, directives that we no longer regard as binding. This is unhelpful and unbiblical. A parabolic reading of other texts that we didn't see bearing on the issue—like Acts 10 and 11—might break this logjam and give us forward movement as the people of God where there is now only distrust and even loathing. Breakthrough could await us here, but only if we can read such texts as Acts 10–11 as evocatively and imaginatively as Jesus's parables.

The parables embody a method, a logic, and an essential purpose that have gotten lost along our way. The circuitous parabola-shaped method is as clever as serpents and as innocent as doves. The abductive logic diverges from the conventional deduction and induction in which we trade as if they were stocks and bonds, clearing a path where there was none and announcing a message unlike any other. The purpose is not merely more information or more interesting parlor chatter, but transformation along the lines of Jesus's theme declaration: "Turn your lives around, the rule of God has arrived!"

But what might such "turned-around," metamorphosed lives look like? Sometimes the most powerful parables are about real people in everyday situations. Their story takes on a resonance that unexpectedly creates traffic in the tremulous but promising no-man's land between ourselves and God, where we seldom travel and don't entirely know which way to turn when we find ourselves there. Sometimes the parables show us composite fictional people in whom we can see little or much of ourselves, both in our most resistant and unredeemed foot-dragging and in our most obedient and glorious liberation by God.

To lift up the parables as a key and a core form of biblical literature is to say that imagination and courage, vulnerability and honesty are as important in letting the Bible grasp us where we live as the inconclusive vagaries of historical-criticism that liberals fearfully cling to or the bedrock of moral certitude that conservatives have presumed that the Bible must be about.

When it comes to the Bible, both liberal and conservative ideological camps are too much blinded by science. The liberals think that the buried treasure of the Gospels will be dug out by the scientific approach called the historical-critical method. Carried to the extreme, the results are unfaithful and unfruitful. If the Bible is finally a love letter from God, how much will we miss by squeezing the Bible through such an alien mind-set, like deep-frying a long-stemmed rose. Would someone please tell the Jesus Seminar how silly they are, voting with their colored beads on the veracity of Jesus's words?

The conservatives treat the Bible as a Time-Life book on the facts of God to retool the house they have already built, complete with steps one through ten on how to be saved, valid only in the order that they have enumerated. Carried to the extreme, the results are unfaithful and unfruitful. Would someone tell the Illinois church trustee how little he witnessed to good news in Christ when he entered my study, one month into my ordained ministry, shaking his Bible and pounding on my desk like Krushchev at the United Nations, bellowing, "Ya gotta be fundamental!" Who would think to wave a love letter in the face of another person and say, "Submit to the literal word!" It would betray not only the text but a massive ignorance on the part of the speaker. What a suspicious and untrusting impoverishment of imagination!

As Frederick Buechner has pointed out, what is the "literal" truth of the Bible when John the Baptizer beholds Jesus and announces, "Behold the Lamb of God, who takes away the sins of the world" (John 1:29 NASB)? Does that mean we should shear Jesus and give him some good pasture?

We could not do better than to heed Clarence Jordan's plea to read the Bible parabolically. This doesn't mean blindly reading the Bible as though it were composed of only one type of literature. It means reading the events and stories of the Bible as the events and stories of our own lives, the struggle and hope of our own souls, instead of getting hung up on their facticity. It means loosening up a little and letting the Bible have its way with us where perhaps we are clinging too tightly (our quest for control again!).

Think of it like this: when we see a Broadway play, do we ask for our money back because we suspect that a window or a door in the set might not be "real" but a mere stage prop? What does *real* mean in the unfolding of a play? Do we walk out in a huff because the actors cast as librarians and traveling salesmen might not be "real" librarians and traveling salesmen outside the play?

Reading the Bible parabolically means interacting with biblical characters as living, breathing people instead of as phantom myths. Would somebody tell the liberals that "myth" has little to do with the Bible (apart from brief sections in Genesis and Job) and that the meanings they construe as "figurative" are misplaced?

Myth (as in ancient Greece) is the attempt to explain apart from God how the world fits together and must always be the way it is, but with humans projected large on the screen of storytelling as gods. Parables are the opposite of myth: they explode the world as we thought it must be when we imagined that we were in control. And from the rubble and ruin of that old order rises a new world where God rules. As is most obvious with the parables, so it goes with all of God's Word.

Reading the Bible parabolically means refusing the hero worship of biblical figures and stories that would install them like marble statues in our lives' courtyard to show our friends how spiritual we are. Would someone tell the conservatives that God can speak afresh through the Bible, and that reading it as no more than rules and maxims is to put it a straitjacket? Reducing the people and events of the Bible to spiritual monads used as touchstones to see whether something is or isn't of God is rooted in the scientific desire to see life as a variety of chemical solutions for which we alone have been given litmus paper.

Biblical truth is simply more deeply paradoxical than that, it is more shot through with the tragic than that, and it means to transport us to loftier places than that. If we are unwilling to live in the high-ceilinged spiritual universe where the holy mystery of God's will is more deeply enigmatic than the rings of Saturn, and the destructive mystery of evil dwells more within our own proud desire to fix everyone and everything around us than in the vices that we eagerly condemn in others, then our God has become too small, God's salvation has become a truth greatly reduced, and we have not yet truly heard the first word of the Bible.

Reading the Bible parabolically means yielding everything we thought we knew about power and discovering it anew through Jesus's weakness on the cross. It means reading with our faith-filled imaginations as we see brothers and sisters in Christ around us. It means an honest reading of the Bible still has the power to throw us into a panic, even if we were elected Layperson of the Year. It means hearing all of the voices of the biblical witness held in tension rather than hearing only the voice most like our own and then remaking others in our own image.

How the Bible Reads Us

Notice that in essence I describe "letting the Bible grasp us" rather than grasping it. This is the first problem and the nature of the earlier allusion and plea for humility in approaching the text. It is not so much that we need to do something with the Bible as that we need to allow the Bible to do something with us. We should never forget that. The Bible is not the problem; we are. And if we were not the problem, the Bible would have never been written in the first place.

Whether owing to the left or the right, our interpretative apparatuses often become thick layers of insulation ironically preventing precisely this breakthrough of a personal engagement. What C. S. Lewis said of the Gospels, he could have said of the whole Bible, when he urged that rather than defend the Gospels, we would do better to turn them loose, like a lion. We can trust the Bible to devour the world where we rule. And we can further trust it to build a whole new world in which we were destined to serve, a world where God rules.

Back in 1936, Dietrich Bonhoeffer gave a famous lecture to Germany's Confessing Church, a small and fragile body of Christians seeking to resist Nazism. Instead of questioning the Bible from their own personal orientation, Bonhoeffer urged them to let the Bible challenge all that they took for granted as a given. He wanted this discipline to become as transformational for the church as it had become for him. In his own time and place, Bonhoeffer discovered a pivotal spiritual reality that had been blocked in his German Christian upbringing: the deep significance of the Old Testament and the people Israel. Scripture called him and the people of Nazi Germany on the carpet for their scapegoating of the Jews. It completely changed the course of his life. He wrote, "only he who cries out for the Jews may sing Gregorian chants."

L. Gregory Jones of Duke University writes about what this means to him:

> The challenge to "allow scripture to question us" is also important for our own day—I have noticed how regularly I read scripture with my own interests in mind. At times this is rather prosaic, as when I simply read with the interests of writing a sermon or preparing a lecture or getting ready for a Bible study. But at other times it is more perverse. For example . . . I [don't] read in a way that opens me to the vulnerability and surprise, that would put me and my assumptions in question. We all face this temptation of being so preoccupied with our own interests that we find it difficult to open ourselves to how God might question us.[5]

Certainly, it matters how we understand the Bible, but something else matters more. Can we first be still to allow the Bible to have its way with us long enough to reveal how it understands us? Do we have that much respect for the Bible and for Jesus when he told us that to enter the kingdom of God, we must become like children? Asking such questions is why the considerable erudition of the professors of Yale Divinity School was hushed as Paul Holmer turned a silly, arcane conversation around toward the very transformation that God's reign invites.

What does it mean to allow the Bible "to have its way with us"? Let someone as imaginative and candidly vulnerable as Barbara Brown Taylor comment here. This is a living, breathing sense of the authority of scripture.

> I love the Bible. I encounter God in it reliably enough to commit myself on a daily basis to practicing the core teachings of both testaments. When I do this, however, a peculiar thing happens. As I practice what I learn in the Bible, the Bible turns its back on me. Like some parent intent on my getting my own place, the Bible won't let me set up house in its pages. It gives me a kiss and boots me into the world, promising me that I have everything I need to find God not only on the page but also in the flesh. Whether I am reading Torah or the Gospels, the written word keeps evicting me to go and embody the word.[6]

The best way to understand the Bible is also the best way to grant it authority over us: stand under the Bible. Attempt to live out scripture's ongoing narrative of redemption. Grant the Bible a place in our lives such that it narrates our days. Do we imagine it an accident that Jesus left unfinished parables like that of the prodigal son?

Stanley Hauerwas goes so far as to insist that without active and vibrant discipleship, the Bible itself is insufficient. Do we recall that it was only after a lengthy walk and in the breaking of the bread that the fullness of Jesus's resurrection was revealed to Cleopas and his friend after endless disputations on the road to Emmaus? Only then were the Law and the Prophets fully disclosed. So it is no less for us today.

The daily attempt to live out God's Word in priorities, habits, and practices as simple as welcoming a stranger and breaking bread trumps abstract, "scientific" speculation and self-advancing ideological axe-grinding. Our personal striving to live the Bible's humbling message exposes its richness in such a way that the text comes alive to us. Here it springs from its drab familiarity and funereal leather cover to shock and surprise, instead of reinforcing our ossified prejudices.

Congregationalism and Biblical Authority

Neophytes to revealed faith in general and serious Christian discipleship in particular harbor deep fears about the possible abuse of spiritual authority in ways that destroy other human beings and serve evil instead of good. These fears are sometimes exaggerated, but they are never entirely misplaced, because authority in spiritual matters can be turned toward what is godly or toward the demonic. One hears this all of the time, in the form of trembling at the thought of Jim Jones actually hearing God calling him to make that vat of Kool-Aid or the abusive priests believing they had God's permission to exploit vulnerable children or Osama bin Laden claiming that it was Allah who led him to explode airplanes into inhabited buildings.

Facing these concerns, the plodding, awkward, and seemingly arbitrary polity of the Congregational churches I have served suddenly turns and becomes a source of great comfort. For every significant revelation given to individuals must be tested out by a discerning community. Jill believes that God is calling her to parish ministry. Can the rest of us see that? A member of our mission board believes that God is leading us to be alongside and work with the incarcerated. Do others feel this impulse of the Holy Spirit? Our new student intern believes that God wants us to give half of our endowment to build homes for the homeless. Is she loopy or right on? we search our hearts. This was what Paul meant when he wrote Philippi (Phil. 2:12), "Work out your own salvation with fear and trembling."

Something like this must occur in reading the Bible to grant it rightful authority while protecting those beneath it from abuse. The collective power of Christian community—superficially ungainly and seemingly a bother, but way down deep wise—must have time and room to hold us in its sway. I speak not only of the contemporary Christian community but also of the ancient ones who left us their written revelatory record. The same process that we observe today within the discernments of the church for the rightful exercise of spiritual authority also inheres within the Bible. Let me explain.

Like the authority of the church, even when the authority of scripture seems univocal, it is always multivocal. The truth arises not so much out of one witness as multiple witnesses—a variegated community of faith—balancing and correcting and amplifying one another. So much abuse of biblical authority happens when this is no longer kept directly in front of us as a people, hearing one voice rather than the chorus of witnesses, in the text as well as in our lives. In other words, the Bible is not so much a book as it is a library, and all of the authors need to be heard.

For example, as we quote Jesus as though we can perceive those around us who will get to heaven and who will not, we do well to hold complementary voices, verses, and versions in tension. So we quote him saying not only, "I am the way, and the truth, and the life. No one comes to the Father except through me" (John 14:6). We also quote the same Jesus in John's Gospel saying, "I do not judge anyone who hears my words and does not keep them, for I came not to judge the world, but to save the world" (John 12:47).

Our posture must include the Jesus who said, "Enter through the narrow gate; for the gate is wide and the road is easy that leads to destruction, and there are many who take it. For the gate is narrow and the road is hard that leads to life, and there are few who find it" (Matt. 7:13–14). But we also include the Jesus who said to the criminal upon the cross next to him, whom he had just met moments before, "Truly I tell you, today you will be with me in Paradise" (Luke 23:43). The final truth of God that we construe from the Bible must accommodate all of these voices and moments, and the truth they represent, or it is an evasion.

Which Is the Most Trustworthy Account of Life?

The Bible asks us: are we willing to trust that its story of God for us and with us says more about our human destiny than even our own little autobiographies? Once we trust what the Bible tells us about God, and our lives lived out before God, even more than what is revealed in our personal history and experience, we hold ourselves accountable to the text in a way that is holy and authoritative. The vast, sweeping story of the Bible brings the good news that our own little stories are not the final story. The outcome of the great and final story is already known, even if the ending has not yet been acted out on the stage of the eternal.

9

THE SACRAMENTS:
WORD AND DEED SEAMLESSLY ONE

Having paused over God's self-disclosure in the Word, we now move toward the sacraments, the other principal arm of Christian worship. Here we begin with the pregnant-with-meaning prologue (1:1–5) to the Gospel of John:

> In the beginning was the Word, and the Word was with God, and the Word was God. He was in the beginning with God. All things came into being through him, and without him not one thing came into being. What has come into being in him was life, and the life was the light of all people. The light shines in the darkness, and the darkness did not overcome it.

John the Evangelist opens with this self-conscious hearkening to the Genesis account of how things were and how things with God shall always be. Here Jesus is the preexisting core of God's purposefulness in whom all things cohere and make sense. John invites us to grasp the story of life backward and forward through Jesus. Not only is God in Christ, reconciling the world to himself (2 Cor. 5:19), but the incarnation reveals the essential nature and direction of God's designs. These designs stretch back to Genesis, with their outlines eminently discernible even then.

Most noteworthy in the pristine harmony of the primeval design of Genesis, there is no gap between word and deed. The two are one and indistinguishable. In Genesis, God speaks and creation ineluctably springs from God's uttered Word. The inherent force of divine speech sinuously flows into the creative transformation of nothingness into somethingness, from void to foundation. And the result is good.

Witness this essential unity in the testimony of Genesis's creation narrative: "Then God said, 'Let there be light'; and there was light" (Gen. 1:3). The light was good, separate from the darkness. "And God said, 'Let the waters under the sky be gathered together into one place, and let the dry land appear'" (Gen. 1:9). And it was immediately so as shores of the continents withdrew and stretched back apart from the primeval waters where life first sprang. This also was good.

"And God said, "Let the waters bring forth swarms of living creatures, and let birds fly above the earth across the dome of the sky'" (Gen. 1:20). The monsters of the deep and the winged animals above appeared and flourished. "And God said, 'Let the earth bring forth living creatures of every kind: cattle and creeping things and wild animals of the earth of every kind'" (Gen. 1:24). And it instantly happened, just as God spoke. "Then God said, 'Let us make humankind in our image, according to our likeness. . . . So God created humankind in his image, in the image of God he created them; male and female he created them'" (Gen. 1:26–27). No sooner did God utter these words than human life appeared. We get the picture: the sheer repetition emphasizes a seamless unity of thought and action.

In Genesis, the essential unity of speech and action is certainly the earliest and perhaps the most defining characteristic of what it means for God to be God.[1] In that seamless congruity of word and deed, it becomes immediately apparent that God is essentially different from how we are. This unity that we lack defines the Creator over against the creatures. For on our side, at every turn large troubling gaps appear between what we say and what we do. As Eden has become a distant memory, we notice that these gaps do not disappear but only widen and deepen.

In Hebrew, the word for say or speak is *dabar*. It is also the same Hebrew word for "to do" or "to act." Imagine one word in English encompassing these two vastly different meanings! Without God, our language and thinking presume a choice between word and deed. We have stretched this breach into an irreconcilable polarity of the ideal and the actual. But for the God of Hebrew cosmogyny, to say is to do and to speak is to act. No dichotomy exists between articulation and fulfillment, between pure ideals and compromised actuality. In the primordial prehistory of Genesis, there is no gap between word and deed.

As the Word became flesh to dwell among us, full of grace and truth, the pristine harmony of our essential origins is reasserted in such a way as to recall our origins and also to define our spiritual destiny. Jesus's glory is full of grace and truth because there is no gap between what he says and what he does, what he teaches and who he finally is (John 1:14ff). Jesus doesn't only show the way, teach the truth, and give the life. Jesus *is* the way, the truth, and the life (John 14:6). Meaning and being fuse as one. This is where life comes from; this is where God would take us, worshipping God in word and sacrament, if we would allow God.

Jesus is like us in every way except for flaws like this cavity between what truth is and how we truly live. No such gap exists for Jesus. Herein resides his authority to bridge heaven and earth. Here is his warrant to carry us aloft to God under the weight of the cross. From the fullness of Jesus's fully congruent purposes and manifestations, he creates new traffic between heaven and earth, recalling the dawning light of prehistory as God summoned creation into being, grace upon grace.

The Word was prior to all things known, Genesis teaches and John the Evangelist reminds. But as God thought and spoke the universe into being, there was no hesitation. There was no stumble. There was no breach between ideal and real. It was a flawless surge of Life into life. This Life was the light of all nations and people. And the seamless unity of word and deed between the Father and the Son (which mimics the primeval unity of the Creator to the creation) is indestructible and shall flourish for all time. It stands not just as a promise beyond, but as real promise here and now, to be fully consummated at Jesus's return. The drama embedded within the sacraments tangibly symbolizes, reenacts, celebrates, and anticipates this in ways which the word alone cannot.

The same animating Spirit that swooped down upon the waters at the dawn of creation today moves upon the sacraments of Holy Communion and holy baptism. Jesus bequeathed these gifts of the Holy Spirit to recall and recreate the sacred creative place and moment where message and being are one. Whether the faithful can articulate it or not, whether non-Christians can recognize it or not, all of creation yearns for this reunion, and the scandal of its absence haunts us. The sacraments signal the restoration of that essential unity that human disobedience has put asunder. What was good in Genesis, God deemed no less good in sending Jesus and remains our hope for the future.

Narrowing the Gaps between Heaven and Earth

So why does any of this matter in our grinding routines, where a cynical world watches as we strive to live out our faith in God's supreme adequacy? Here is why. Detractors perhaps most commonly preempt our witness by complaining, "All of your talk on Sunday mornings is well and good. But what happens during the rest of the week?" Or perhaps, "I could listen to the message of your Gospels, but does it make any difference in the world? I don't see it." Or even the tiresome, "When you learn to practice what you preach, then find me and talk to me about your Jesus." It is the charge of hypocrisy in espousing grand truth claims that are only partially realized in the world around us. God seems missing in action to jaded eyes of wan faith. The gap between God's promises and the reality of how things are makes eyes roll and shoulders shrug.

We could answer these familiar bromides by acknowledging the Gospels' loftiness and our own feet of clay. We could point to heaven's perfection and its poor approximation on earth below. We could plead that we must inevitably fall short of such lofty standards. But this line of approach is finally always a mistake. Besides capitulating to a Platonic universe of pure ideals and fallen materiality, which Judeo-Christianity refuses to admit as a description of the universe, all of this is weak backpedaling anyway. It is a rear-guard action unbefitting our universal message of salvation. It is apologetics in the worst sense of the word.

If we expect the world to sit up and take notice of the Gospels' incredible truth claims, the authority of our witness is here at stake—*does* the Gospels' message make any difference in the world? Is it truly alive on the other side of the empty tomb, or did it die upon the cross? The sacraments are our opportunity to dramatize that God's promises in Jesus Christ are real and ongoing today.

But we can reenact this proclamation with credibility in the sacraments only if in fact we are congregations living out the truth of the resurrected Christ in the vital issues of today's alleys and byways of life. If we have hid the light of the Gospels under a bushel by remaining safely within our own walls and not engaging the poor, the broken, the forgotten, the attacked, the imprisoned, the abused, and the discarded, then perhaps we should consider calling a moratorium on celebrating the sacraments until such time as we are willing to get out and take these risks.

The sacraments describe and elevate the primal unity of creation emerging from the ideals of the Creator. The sacraments retain this essential primeval unity without the disturbing impasse that we trip over. As the sacraments reassure the reunion of divine promise above with human fulfillment below, they tangibly anticipate it. But celebrating the sacraments has authority only as they point to our active participation in God's victory by entering the trenches of need and squalor, and asserting that victory with Jesus's same sacrificial love.

Only then will the sacraments take on resonance and celebrate God's presence here and now as a foretaste of heaven. Only then will they recall what once was in Eden and infuse everything with the hope that God's purposes cannot be thwarted. The sacraments are the moment in the church's life when we sing with Eliza Doolittle of *My Fair Lady*, "Don't talk of love, *show me!*"

From this vantage point, we creatively respond to our disparagers' surface reading of things, whose herdlike despair is predicated upon a human-centered universe, cold and empty, without any master plan. With sighs wrapped around heavenly dreams grander than any human imagination, the sacraments remind us that all hope is caught up in the story of Jesus Christ, located eternally before time, yet also within time as we know it.

How can this play out in our ministry? The best answer to cynics who throw "hypocrisy" in our faces is to urge them to continue questioning us in ways that keep us accountable. Honest doubt can sanctify and redeem. Are we living in ways that are acting out of the promise of God's reign or hiding within the walls of the church and settling with merely becoming less miserable? This is a constant temptation.

But after we thank our critics for giving us a gift, we might also challenge them to receive one. Is their asking wrongly grounded in human delusions of grandeur that have necessarily gone bad? Is it the sour grapes that would deride any lofty hope as unrealistic because they ask in the shadow of our ultimate human impotence?

Jesus said, "Apart from me, you can do nothing" (John 15:5). John Calvin added, "All thought about God which does not proceed from the fact of Christ is a fathomless abyss."[2] To be serious, the questing probe of the gap between what is ideal and what is real needs the broader context of where God dwells and reigns. Otherwise, all is lost, this seeking is but idle wandering, and it might have been better never to ask at all.

As seekers ask hard questions, let them also simultaneously put on and try out the claims of faith. For their asking, if it is earnest, cannot happen from outside looking in, but only from the inside. Are they toying with these questions, using our human corruptibility as an excuse to distance themselves from God and the claims of the cross? Are they dilettantes dabbling in the divine, or is eternity something they sincerely wish to try on for size? If they are honest about seeking to participate in the life of God in this badly broken world, it will always be a matter of their faith seeking understanding, not understanding seeking faith.

Like Jesus confronting the rich young ruler, we need to call their bluff so they themselves can evaluate how serious their search is. Today, people imagine themselves deeply spiritual for merely being stubborn, defiant, and individualistic. Modernity does not know the difference between understanding seeking faith and faith seeking understanding. The Enlightenment has blurred the former as the "factual" basis of truth and all but denied the latter as a valid way of knowing.

More specifically, how can we make such questioning accountable? A covenant clarifying expectations all around would be a good place to start. If they haven't been baptized, perhaps they should be. If they have been baptized, that baptism must be actively called to remembrance by rehearsing and reinterpreting its claims. If they aren't taking communion, they need to be receiving from the bread and cup regularly. And they should formally unite with the members of a faith community where working out our salvation in fear and trembling is a way of life. We grow in faith only by making holy vows and then growing into them.

How long should this regimen continue? At least for one year, long enough to run up against these gaps inside-looking-out, to see God at work in ways that CNN never reports. To adapt Gil Scott-Heron, the revolution of God's reign will not be televised. To see the difference God has made, it must be glimpsed from within, or it will remain elusive and invisible. If after a year, they still cannot embrace God because of these gaps, rather than finding themselves called into these gaps to narrow them—like Jesus before us—they can renounce their baptism, eschew the table of the Lord, and revoke their church membership.

Is This So Completely Unrealistic?

I can practically hear the hue and cry against such a proposal set up from the very quarters that we wish to address. "How could you suggest such a thing? I could never partake in the rituals of a religion to which I don't fully ascribe. Such a thing would be terribly false. It would distort my objectivity." Of course, all of this is lies. Ask the same person to solve a math problem or test a scientific theorem and they will accept and operate under enough presuppositions to make their heads spin; they will gladly take on those "trial baptisms" to test the veracity of that truth system. Why should things be any different in matter of spiritual truth?

I can also hear protest from the Christian side against such a proposal. "How could you suggest such a thing? It would debase our sacraments. It would be terribly false. It would distort the purity of what we share among ourselves as sacred." Of course, all of this is wrong. *If the Word is discipleship proclaimed, then the sacraments are discipleship enacted.* And Jesus never hesitated to invite any to follow in his way, whether fishermen or Roman soldiers or tax collectors or rich young rulers. Jesus welcomed them all, if they came earnestly seeking rather than

158

merely dabbling. For spiritual transformation happens not as we think ourselves into new ways of being, but as we act ourselves into new ways of thinking, especially as we are held accountable to our vows before the community of faith.

So much of Paul's letters was imploring the people on the verge of heeding his call to "put on" the faith and live it out before actually ever completely "getting it": putting on the light in Jesus Christ (Rom. 13:12–14), putting on the armor of God (Eph. 6:11–15), and putting on faith and love (1 Thess. 5:8). Before we can cloak ourselves in the garments of God's righteousness in Jesus Christ, we are like children in the attic going through the trunks bequeathed us from the past. We pull the clothes out, try them on, ask others how we look, and ask ourselves whether we can see ourselves going around like this. All of us who now consider ourselves within the mainstream of discipleship have done this. Participating in the sacraments is where Christianity comes down from abstraction into the nitty-gritty of living and doing and dressing up for the part.

The sacraments of the Lord's Supper and baptism close the troubling gaps between the Creator and creation by recalling the bridge of redemption that Jesus has built. We see how Jesus willingly built these bridges and closed these gaps as we see that he allowed himself to be baptized, even though he had no need. John the Baptizer would have prevented Jesus, acknowledging that their roles should be reversed (Matt. 3:14). But Jesus knew there was no other way if he would fulfill for us a righteousness that we could not fulfill for ourselves.

We also note God's forgiving, redeeming grace in how Jesus offered the food and drink of his body and blood in that First Supper which was also a Last Supper. He freely offered himself to Judas, who betrayed him, to Peter who denied him, and to the other disciples who abandoned him. He washed all of their feet. Nowhere are we more vividly reminded that Jesus lived to fill the painful gaps between what should be and what is than in the sacraments. Here we recall once that no one is good enough to deserve these gifts, and no one who seeks them in earnest is bad enough to be denied them.

Not Idle Spectators, but Active Participants

The story still circulates about a survivor from the Holocaust's systematic murder of Jews by the Nazis before and during World War II.[2] This survivor was obsessed with returning to the small village in Hungary where he grew up. It was the same village where, at age fourteen, he was herded, along with other area Jews, into the village square, then into boxcars for the horrifying trip to the concentration camp. The survivor doesn't know why he feels compelled to return, only that he must.

When at last he stands again in that village square, he suddenly realizes why he had to come back. On that morning, so long ago, he had glanced up and seen a face in the window. It was an impassive face, devoid of affect, flat, impassive, and noncommittal, even as the persecuted people of a chosen race were marched off to doom. As the survivor stands looking at the same window, flooded with bitter and incomprehensible memories, the face is still there, cutting into his mind's eye like acid etching into glass. He will never forget that face. He will recognize it in all of the faces like it that he will yet see. It was the face of the spectator upon life, the one who observes but does not participate in the drama of redemption, which the Hebrew Bible and the Christian Testament have laid out in front of us. The story begs us to ask what the world sees in our faces.

How do we become spectators upon life rather than participants in and even instruments of the life of God's reign? What is it about our response to the gospel that makes us like little diplomats quibbling with God? We accept the gospel in principle and then qualify it in a hundred different ways with our objections and reservations and hesitations. "I can't right now," we weakly protest. "Someone else will take care of that," we rationalize. "It would just cost too much," we hedge. And the mighty oaken staff that is the gospel of Jesus Christ, having been relentlessly whittled down day in and day out, becomes shavings in the evening dust, to be swept up and thrown away.

We are all tempted to remain spectators on life like the man in the window. Doubtless he thought of himself as a good and godly man, as we all do. Probably he would have identified himself as a "Christian" in that impersonal sense of cultural Christianity so popular in Europe for decades, and now on the rise in the United States. But the connection between God's saving promises and our response is necessary and essential. Without accountability here, we confuse things primary with things secondary, and we worship ourselves by burrowing more deeply into the status quo rather than anticipating and living into existence the order of heaven that God shall bring to pass for all people and places and times. Without actively putting them to use, we fail to receive them as our gifts.

Has the vastness of the claim of being a Christian ever overwhelmed you in a goodly and compelling way when you received the bread and cup? Sometimes the ritual can be rote, but other times it can pick us up by the scruff of the neck and make us see things differently. The moment can make our faith real instead of a collection of abstract ideals. The sacraments have a gravitas that, when heeded, will not allow us to remain disinterested spectators on the incomplete drama of redemption, the closing of those disturbing gaps. Gaps between holiness and profanity, gaps between treating some like human beings and others like animals, gaps between opportunity and dead ends, gaps between the spirit of charity and hardness of heart. The sacraments are sacred space where the divine will is recalled and celebrated in heaven above, but no less where they are recalled and celebrated and mobilized here on earth below.

Every time we see a baptism and remember the waters three times on our head, every time we taste of the substance and life of Jesus on our tongue, we are asked about our own participation with Christ in closing the gaps between heaven and earth. We may have grown deaf to the asking of this question for our lack of a good answer. But God ever asks it of us for those with ears to hear.

Walking the Talk

The most sacramental churches are not necessarily the most liturgical ones. The truly sacramental churches are the ones most wholly impassioned after the cause of the broken, the discarded, the exploited, the forgotten, the poor, the diminished, the discriminated, and the depersonalized. And they are also the ones with the good theological instincts to connect this with what happens at the font and the table, and to unfailingly celebrate the seamless Lord God whose word and deed are one, the timeless God who entered time in Jesus Christ.

Sacramental churches have a low tolerance of alarming gaps that most churches have learned to take for granted through hardness of heart and lack of imagination. "The poor you will always have with you," we quote Jesus, as though he were giving a mandate rather than making a plaintive cry, as though he were relaxing the demands of the cross and reducing resurrection hope, rather than lifting up the invisible and ignored precious in God's sight (Mark 14:7 NIV).

When our church groups travel on Global Village work camps to Latin America to build houses with the poor through Habitat for Humanity, an eagerly anticipated highlight is celebrating the Lord's Supper at the trip's close. It is amazing how what is so perfunctory in the familiarity of home can become a breathless, living participation in the fulfillment of God's promises for all as we are led out of our comfort zones. It is disembodied faith becoming the embodied faith that John described in writing, "the Word became flesh and lived among us . . . full of grace and truth . . . from his fullness we have all received, grace upon grace." (John 1:14, 16) It is a capstone for the experience, and if we didn't put that last keystroke in place, the experience would not hold together with the transforming power it brings every time.

In 2001, we were ending our stay with the people of Santa Elena in central Honduras. Three hard-earned foundations had emerged from steep hills on which walls and roofs would quickly rise. Although the Hondurans did most of the work, we were completely exhausted, as we always are. The batches of concrete we had mixed and carried by hand, buckets mounting up toward tonnage, numbered many dozens. Mercifully, Habitat mandates Sabbath rest at the end of every trip. So we made our way to the scruffy Caribbean beach of La Ceiba for recovery, repose, and reflection.

As we departed La Ceiba to fly home, our van broke down. We found ourselves roadside at the edge of a royal palm oil plantation where the canopy of massive tropical trees stretched geometrically in diagonals as far as the eye could see. One hour delay became several hours. Edginess rose within us. How long would we wait? Would anyone come for us? What would become of us? Rather than wait for later at the hotel to celebrate Holy Communion, as was our custom, we decided that this royal palm roadside was a God-given sacramental moment.

We fifteen gathered as a worshipping body along that roadside with drivers along that busy highway honking at us. We were not distracted. We were called to worship. We invoked God's presence. We confessed our sins. We heard and then interpreted God's Word. It came alive for us in that moment and setting in a way that renewed us as though we had never heard such a thing before. And then we turned to the altar of the Lord, a beverage cooler, before which I knelt. Our half bottle of red wine was brought from the States, but we were without bread. Sugarless windmill cookies were pressed into service as the body of Jesus Christ to the smirking amusement and theological enlargement of all present. Our spirits were badly in need of refreshment, and refreshed we were.

We talked about the yawning chasms God had filled in the course of the planning and the unfolding of our work trip. Before leaving they always seem impossibly wide. We were to venture out and across the steep worldly divides of race, culture, language, religion, geography, class, generation, and religion? And something wonderfully mysterious and holy of God would result? There are never any guarantees. Some quite awful things regularly happen in those same gaps.

But if by the grace of God we make it across these spaces, we agreed during orientation before departure, we will be changed for the rest of our lives. The Holy Spirit will be loosed in ways that we cannot ordinarily access and enjoy. At the table of the Lord, we harked back to that brash claim of months before. And we suggested that it was being fulfilled not just in an incredible exchange between different peoples, not just in the miracle of those with almost nothing watching a strong, secure home rise from the ground, not just in all of this being as much fun as we would ever have rather than being a march of grim obligation.

All of this was now fulfilled at the Lord's Table because in both instances we were being honored with a foretaste of God's heavenly banquet, the closing of the infernal gaps between God's promises and the world's realities. It is not by accident that the New Testament Greek word for "worship"—*leitourgia*—is the same word for "work." *Connecting these two—Christlike worship and Christlike work—is true sacramentality.* In both cases, the Word becomes flesh and dwells among us. This message would have never sealed itself upon our hearts in the way it did without wine and windmill cookies, speaking more deeply than any words that I could summon, tangibly reasserting the persistence of God's intentions at work in this world of dark cynicism, through Jesus's loving sacrifice.

It got a bit scary there on the side of the highway sharing the Lord's Supper. Earlier, on the way into La Ceiba, a police pickup truck cut through a jammed line of traffic immediately before us with sirens blaring and guns drawn. In the bed of the pickup a man was shot—a would-be car thief, we heard later—and bleeding to death. Much of the crime in that part of the world happens on the open road. As the hours passed, with no relief in sight and the sun dropping in the sky, we began to wonder about ourselves. Just as the darkness set in and our anxiety level peaked, the substitute van appeared from San Pedro Sula.

The Lord's Supper helped us keep the faith as well as our composure in the face of adversity. God does not call us outside ourselves and send us into the gaps between the high purposes of heaven and hard realities of earth to abandon us. We closed out our visit feeling like our brokenness as the church of Jesus Christ sent out into the world was but an extension of the brokenness of the bread that is the body of Christ. We are fully broken but not forgotten. We know fear but are vindicated by the One beyond ourselves. In the years since that late afternoon, many of the fifteen have told me that after the arduous and satisfying work we shared in Santa Elena, that simple, improvised heavenly feast on the highway outside La Ceiba was the deepest communion they have experienced with God and with others around the body and blood of Jesus Christ.

The Word proclaims, but the sacraments enact, pointing at once toward our restoration in Genesis and our fulfillment in Revelation. Proclamation without enactment sounds tinny in the ears of today's world. Enactment completes proclamation by recalling the unity of the divine not just in a world preexisting this one or the world to come, but in the here and now of where we live.

163

A Question of Balance

We Protestants often assail as superstitious the Roman Catholic doctrine of transubstantiation, which claims that the elements of bread and cup actually and truly and physically become Jesus's body and blood at the moment of consecration. Rather than be so dismissive, we would do better to ponder, pray, and reinterpret these matters. I, for one, have come to a place where I believe in transubstantiation, that the bread and wine actually and truly and physically become Jesus's body and blood. Except I don't believe that happens as we clergy magically consecrate them. I believe it happens as the emblems mysteriously consecrate us as we serve our neighbor, as we enter with God into breaches that haunt the grandest designs of heaven and aching heartaches on earth below.

We are accustomed to speak of baptism as having claims upon us. The claims are the formation of Christians through practices of faith like prayer, Bible reading, worship, Sabbath-keeping, tithing, and all of the rest. Perhaps we should be no less willing to speak of Holy Communion as having claims upon us. Its first claim is being aware of other Christians around us with their hurts and needs, burdens and hungers. Its next claim is venturing beyond the immediate faith community of our local church into gaps where we take up the cause of strangers beloved in God's heart: the broken, the exhausted, the lost, the exploited, the mourning, the poor, and all the rest who populate the Beatitudes. Strangers to us, they are precious to and beloved of God. Such a church who goes to these places will not fail to have a ring of authority that even the most acidic and hardened disbeliever cannot deny. Their most constant complaint toward the good news we bring is answered even before we open our mouths.

Having said this, we remember that worship is never a means to an end, but always an end in itself. It bears reminding that this is no less true of the sacraments. The sacraments take us places where we need to go—like outside of ourselves—but not unless we are fully present in the moment of baptism and in receiving the sacred emblems of Jesus's death and resurrection for us. Baptism and the Lord's Supper by their very nature demand a more central and exalted place in our common life than they have enjoyed in most Protestant churches.

It is said not without warrant about the churches at our end of the Reformation—United Church of Christ, Presbyterian, Baptist, for example—that in worship we are too much Christians from the neck up. That means we are overbalanced toward thinking and talking and underbalanced toward acting and embodying. The balance that we seek is to become churches of Word and sacrament. This means that if our communion liturgies are lacking, we should write livelier ones, employing multiple unique orders of worship for high holy days as well as simple evening prayers. This means that celebrating Holy Communion four times a year or even once a month is not enough. The goal is to find a way toward weekly celebration of the Lord's Supper, at least in some church setting.

Becoming churches of Word and sacrament means that baptisms should occupy a special place in our common life and that the liturgy should be celebrated with special care. It means that we need to take the time to interpret both for the biological family of the one being baptized as well as for the spiritual body of the church, the vastness and richness of the claim of God on us that we celebrate.

Rites and Rituals Rule, but Sacraments Pale

Consider the social and religious context within which we operate as described by Cardinal Godfried Daneels, Archbishop of Mechelen-Brussels:

> The Western churches of established Christianity are passing through a profound crisis in their perception of sacramentality. It is as though the Western person has a blind spot. The liturgy risks being dominated by an excess of words or of being merely a way to recharge one's batteries for [service] and social action. The church seems to be nothing more than a place where one speaks and one places oneself at the center of the world. The sacramental life is shifting from the center of the church to its periphery.[3]

Daneels believes that our perception of sacramental reality is feeble, that we are in love with rites and ritualization, but essentially allergic to the Christian sacraments. Whether it is the winter solstice or the ceremonies opening and closing the Olympics or the pageantry and festivals surrounding a presidential inauguration, popular rituals are ironically vested with power in a day when Christian sacraments are increasingly ignored, neglected, and unappreciated.

Daneels says of secular rites, "They sprout like the luxuriant of a tropical forest. One invents—and markets—secular and cosmic rites or rites linked to natural religion for all of the great passages of human life: birth, puberty, marriage, and death. . . . These rites are not able to provide conversion of heart; rather, they promise only therapeutic illusions and/or the self-redemption of man or woman."[4]

I know whereof the archbishop speaks. In the first half of this book, we discovered the personal price to be paid and the lessons to be learned from the vows of marriage when we challenge how any real Christian content of those vows is all but absent. I now recount a similar story that threw my deacons and me into a parallel dilemma around the sacrament of baptism, another setting where sacred vows were uttered with no real or serious intention of keeping them.

As I began my ministry, baptism meant coming to the font as a "means of grace." I wasn't paying enough attention to the vows that the families, sponsors, and congregation were making. If couples expressed even the vaguest interest in baptizing their child, I agreed to do the baptism. The problem is that as a domestic rite of passage, when it means no more than baby's first bath, baby's first haircut, or baby's first vaccination, Christian baptism is so diminished that it might as well not exist.

Regrettably, baptism often has no more spiritual content than these rites of passage for young families making their way in the world. As a young pastor, I was unprepared for how many phone calls I would get telling me the Sunday their baby must be baptized (the brunch was already planned and extended family invited) and asking me to "do" their boy or girl. In many cases, I wouldn't see the family again until years later, when another child had been born and another baptismal Sunday was chosen for me to work around.

After a few years, I realized where we were going wrong. Much as with the Ken-and-Barbie weddings, the families were expecting grandiose promises from the church and were getting them. We were expecting nothing of the families and were getting just that. Sacraments lose their redeeming power within such a disequilibrium of commitment, with such yawning gaps between what the church is saying and what the family is doing.

We were doing a grave disservice to these people, not to mention participating in an ugly lie. The lie was that they were doing all that was necessary to spiritually care for their children. This lie hurt all who participated in it—as every lie does—but it damaged none more than the little ones over whose advent God's grace was being celebrated. Rather than allowing the church to become the picturesque backdrop for the baby's first coming-out party, and allowing myself to become the smiling game show host in the photo snapped afterward, I decided it was time to give the holy vows some content.

Like the marriage vows, the baptismal vows at every point assumed they would be lived out in Christian community. I decided to extend baptism only to families who were already united with a Christian church (and might need baptism in our locality because the family was there) or couples in the process of joining a church. It did not have to be our church (wanting to avoid religious imperialism). But they had to indicate to the pastor of the new church their intentions to unite. This guarded the church and kept me from feeling like a cult prostitute. I even-handedly applied the policy, even for children raised in our church living elsewhere.

Talk about a formula for trouble! Much of the pushback came from older generations, from grandparents whose feelings were deeply stirred by the arrival of the little ones, but who were unwilling to consider in hard terms the costly implications of keeping or not keeping promises. One such grandfather was a full professor at the local university. He was so angry at me for troubling his son with the demands of baptism that he asked for time on the agenda at the next deacon meeting. He came to the meeting smiling the deceptively affable smile of civilized polite society. But having felt stung, he meant to sting, and he did not disappoint.

The deacons were shocked to find an agenda item where something vital was on the line, as opposed to our dress code for Sunday morning or what size to cut the communion bread. I explained my experience with baptism over the years, my call to leadership as pastor, and my attempts to dignify baptism as a sacrament. I shared that as a baby boomer I had grown up as a know-it-all teen assailing the church in the sixties for its half-truths about struggles like Vietnam, civil rights, and poverty. Now the tables were turned. Now circumstances demanded that we check ourselves on this same score. If we didn't really mean it, then we shouldn't say it.

The professor explained that his son and daughter-in-law were both rising professionals. They had long commutes in a congested metropolis every weekday. The baby was making unexpected demands. They were tired every weekend and needed Sunday to sleep late. Besides, they would likely move in a year or two. It was clearly irrational to expect them to get up on Sunday and unite with a church.

I expressed empathy with how difficult their lives must be. Balancing burgeoning careers and children is tough. Expecting young children to abide by a schedule that will approximate our lives before they arrived teaches a real life lesson. My wife (a practicing clinical psychologist and college professor) and I had daughters who were three and one at the time. Like this young couple, we were scrambling big-time. But that was all the more reason to be in Christian community, where not all of the child-rearing would fall upon us alone. Because I intimately knew their struggle (although he perceived their lives as infinitely more difficult, for they had *real* jobs), I felt that the parallels of my station in life with theirs fairly demanded that I challenge my own generation's Yuppie sense of entitlement.

Why not wait for baptism until they moved, at such time that they could unite with a church? Then instead of mouthing promises we didn't really yet mean, the words would have real content. God would look more kindly on their waiting than on making promises that we knowingly had no immediate plans to keep. Because I married this couple, I had grave reservations about their intentions to raise the child in the church but said nothing of this. But if I as pastor did nothing and mouthed these vows, what would that mean? The Bible tells of people who, whereupon breaking holy vows, were turned into things like pillars of salt.

"There is nothing holy about the church," the professor scowled to the now shocked deacons, his disdain unconcealed. "It is no more than one more institution rendering a service. It is just one more social group." He actually said that! I so recoiled with anger and disgust that my good friend and wise adviser the senior deacon kicked me hard beneath the table. She was protecting me from answering his proud, dismissive evil with my own self-righteous brand. She had deliberately seated herself next to me before the meeting to deliver the much needed blow.

The words the professor blurted out were a turning point in our deliberations. Frankly, he is to be commended for his honesty in saying what so many think but dare not utter. Until then, many deacons only dimly understood what I was going after by raising the standards instead of simply getting along by going along. I was trying to alter the playing field where the sacrament was acted out, expecting minimal standards of these holy vows. Some perceived me as unfairly making a young couple's life more difficult. After all, if the point is getting ahead, then life is all about convenience. Suddenly, shaken at this brusque disrespect, they realized that something bigger was at stake. One woman wept afterward to hear the church assailed by a man of distinction in the community, himself a former deacon, to boot.

Birth and Rebirth, It All Begins with Baptism

Contrast the foregoing with the centrality and honor that baptism once held within the Christian church. Those who are familiar with Florence, Italy, look to the *duomo,* or principal cathedral, as the most familiar landmark, rising above the terrazzo roofs. The dome of Brunelleschi is the center from which the Florentines take their bearings, in every sense of the word. But a smaller building in front of and preceding the imposing *duomo* is the true center of this remarkable and storied city. It is the Baptistery of San Giovanni.

Legend has it that a Roman temple to Mars at this site was converted to a baptistery in the fourth or fifth century. The current eight-sided structure from the medieval era sheaths brilliant white, green, and rose marble into geometric patterns. The octagonal shape hints at the eighth

168

day of creation beyond Genesis, the day without sunset, the perfect day of resurrection. It reminds us that baptism is not only about God's claim upon us as we emerge from birth, but about how we are destined for rebirth as well.

Since time immemorial, disciples would enter this building only one time in their lives: for baptism. Here held in such high regard, the singular experience of baptism was mystical, occurring in the most remarkable building in the city. A 1960s archeological discovery yielded findings that a graveyard surrounds the baptistery. This means that the candidates walked through a cemetery to arrive, further dramatizing their spiritual pilgrimage from death to life. Upon entering, they saw the most incredible sight in the city: glittering candlelit marble mosaics of Jesus as Christus Victor, triumphant above.

Having come back from death, Jesus directly eyes the onlooker below, the nail marks in his hands and feet clearly evident. In the supporting mosaics, the graves of his own are opened at Jesus's feet, conqueror of death who has made it his doormat. After years of preparation, first learning the practices of faith, and at this crowning place and moment, the baptized underwent a truly once-in-a-lifetime experience. There they passed from death caused by sin to new life in Christ and knew rebirth.

Again, as people think of Florence, in their mind's eye they see the *duomo*. As the locals are away too long and grow nostalgic for home, they speak of *duomo*-sickness. But it was only after the completion of the current baptistery that the citizenry decided to "resuscitate" the old *duomo* of Santa Reparata, which next to the baptistery had come to seem small and very crude in design. This gave birth to the idea of and commitment to the current *duomo*, Santa Maria del Fiore. Notice what is happening here: the baptistery drove the ministry of the church, not the other way around.

In the sixteenth century, Giorgio Vasari wrote that in a sense the Renaissance stems from this one octagonal building. If the city of Florence represents rebirth, the baptistery even more than the vaunted *duomo* launched this resurgence: a pagan past reborn in Christian worship, human believers rising to new life beyond, a city whose creative energies flowed from this place and rose up to change the world in art, science, and engineering.

How would the contemporary church be reborn if we took baptism this seriously, made it this central, and experienced its claims so deeply and completely? One can only hope, dream, and pray. In the beginning was the Word, but the sacraments are not far behind if the message of salvation will find traction among us that God is not lost and gone, but alive and at work in the world.

10

Parish Ministry: Losing Our Voice, Then Finding It Again

I t is sad how we pastors can fall all over ourselves seeking self-respect and credibility by associating ourselves with sexier lines of work essentially unrelated to ministry. This spinning of our vocational life begins early, even during seminary days. "I attend a graduate and professional divinity school," Professor William Muehl paraphrased us as bamboozling friends back home after our first Christmas break. He knew we would try to make ministry sound way cool. "There I engage in interdisciplinary studies around cross-cultural perceptions of the Infinite, how they impinge on the human condition, and their shared commentary upon contemporary society as a numinous meta-narrative." Blah, blah, blah. Blah, blah, blah.

In one's twenties, such pretexts sound more impressive to one's peers than admitting, "I went to seminary and will likely end up a pastor because I couldn't get into University of Michigan Law School, local churches sorely need pastors, and right now I can't think of what else to do with my life." It is as though we fail to realize that everyone somehow got into what they are doing through a combination of closed doors and open doors, through self-serving and honorable motives, through sheer opportunity and accident (or perhaps providence) of being in a certain place at a certain time. Or as Clarence Jordan summed up this state of affairs, "A hot sun and a slow mule called more than one man to the pulpit."[1]

It is beyond me how Mr. Muehl knew of our dissimulation in familiar haunts when reunited with old friends. "So what happened to you, anyway?" incredulous others would inquire into our new track. Then we would spew our theological razzle-dazzle. In that first sermon after Christmas break, Muehl pulled us back toward more mundane realities of Christian service (nevertheless infused with eternity to those who see with eyes of faith). He refused to let us indulge in the smallest delusions of grandeur (even if there is real glory to walk in the steps of the adventure that Jesus Christ walked before us). He meant to pluck from the freshly turned soil of our lives all noxious and foreign forms of pastoral authority so that the real seed of the gospel might be planted within us, take root, and flourish over time.

A Stumbling Block to Jews, a Scandal to Gentiles, an Embarrassment to Clergy

It is one thing to spin our call in our callow youth because of embarrassment. It is something else entirely when this doesn't change over whole decades for clergy. Too many of us hang out around the church for a job and pick up a check as a pastor but look elsewhere for credibility and authority. I am talking about the earnestly sensitive ministers who happen to serve local churches under the guise of pastoral counseling, the more-relevant-than-thou ministers wrapped up in flaming social activism, the self-styled au courant, cutting-edge ministers hiding out as spiritual directors, and other wannabe clergy who primarily see themselves as writer, educator, social worker, artist, therapist, or ever-present enabler of self-fulfillment.

I am talking about the legions of will-you-respect-me-in-the-morning pastors who rationalize their calling as a "helping profession" with the vaguest of religious tinctures and then cut out of ministry after a while because such dizzying horizons without any theologically informed boundaries cannot help but make one crazy over time. I am talking about those empire-building pastors who first see themselves as CEOs, megamanagers, or captains of spiritual industry, who then reflexively move up some Fortune 500 careerist ladder to more lucrative and prestigious parishes.

A pastoral predecessor in a church I served envisioned becoming President of the United States as the fulfillment of his calling. He inquired of a leading layman, a top-tier IBM executive, as to how to achieve this last leg in his personal quest. "You can't get there from here," the executive shook his head, with no little sadness at what he heard. More than anything, the church that sets us apart for leadership needs to fill its clergy with a sense of honor and nobility, conviction and passion for our calling such that we will perceive becoming president as a step down. We may be well on the road to that, but it is more owing to how the presidency is slipping than to how the pastoral ministry has been elevated.

Of course, there is nothing wrong per se with these other lines of work. What is painful is our refusal to acknowledge and grasp what will always be front and center to our calling: that the church ordains us, the gospel authorizes us, and Jesus Christ's Great Compassion (Matt. 25:31–46) and Great Commission (Matt. 28:19–20) send us. And that this is more than enough. At such crucial life junctures, the Evil One always laughs hungrily as we neglect things of first and essential importance and then substitute what is merely secondary. For that desperate ploy, usually rooted in our pride, always makes his work so much easier.

What is the basis of our authority as pastors? Søren Kierkegaard explores this in his essay entitled, "On the Difference between a Genius and an Apostle."[2] Genius is based on exercising our own expertise. A genius is someone born with an outsized natural talent that often gets exercised way before its time. Thus, a genius will bring something entirely new to his field. A genius is appreciated on the basis of the content he brings to his area. How momentous is this new insight? How deep does it go? How far does it advance our civilization? How well has it been articulated? What earth-shattering thing that a genius says or does could just as easily have been said by anyone else, if the other had gotten there first? What is key to genius is personal expertise. But apostleship is very different.

An apostle (that's us) does not so much mean to say something original, new, and clever. Rather, we speak the truth that our forebears delivered to us, truth that has been uttered many times before us, and we mean to say it over and over again until the world sits up and takes notice. When an apostle speaks, the point is not how well she or he phrases the message. But it matters immensely *who* delivers the message. And what matters most about who delivers the message is whether she or he has truly been called and sent by God. What matters most is that the message is spoken out of the divine authority of being an apostle of Jesus Christ.

In other words, we do not bow to the writings of Paul the apostle because he was clever, wrote well, and was in effect the first Christian theologian. We bow to his message because he has the stamp of God as being of God. The genius must establish his own authority by the quality of the message. For the apostle, this is impossible, as both our message and its authority come from far beyond us.

The heralded and sacred uniqueness of parish ministry has never been better described and celebrated than by Stanley Hauerwas and William Willimon in their watershed 1989 work *Resident Aliens* (subtitled "a Provocative Christian Assessment of Culture and Ministry for People Who Know That Something Is Wrong"), a work which at every point informs the direction and logic of my own considerations in these pages:

> The pastoral ministry is too adventuresome and demanding to be sustained by trivial, psychological self-improvement advice. What pastors, as well as the laity they serve, need is a theological rationale for ministry which is so cosmic, so eschatological and therefore countercultural, that they are enabled to keep at Christian ministry in a world determined to live as though God were dead. Anything less misreads the scandal of the gospel and the corruption of our culture.[3]

Too many of us never settle in, get the hang of it, and fall under the spell of the ministry's unique logic, a logic of God and not of limited human contrivance. Too many of us over the past two millennia have never understood that what we do as pastors is noble, momentous, and fraught with possibility for transformation (theirs and ours) on a grand scale in a way that the end of history will vindicate beyond our imagining, provided that we are faithful in the smallest things and in the most remote places. Too many of us fail to grasp that long after information technicians and software analysts, public relations officers and policy specialists cease to exist as job titles, women and men will continue to be called into leading the people of God in following Jesus Christ toward this cosmic destiny in backwaters like Bonesteel, South Dakota, or Bad Axe, Michigan, or Stab, Kentucky.

Dr. Charles Copenhaver, my mentor in ministry, would refer in passing to what we pastors do as a "strangely satisfying profession." This slant on our vocation can be parsed in many different directions. Think about that over time and roll it across your tongue. You will find that our work is indeed all of that and more.

Too many pastors want to blend in with the world until ministry is a conventionally satisfying profession. Too many clergy wear the "strange" part as epithet and burden, failing to celebrate that our peculiarity radically cuts against the grain of a grim popular culture that universally accepts grinding, abject misery with a happy face as the status quo. Too many clergy fail to experience how grand this strangeness is against the backdrop of generations significantly shaped for good into more than they could ever have been alone, and certainly into something much closer to what their Creator intended in making them.

Yes, some disparage and mock us as oddities. But have you ever looked closely at a room full of clergy? Frankly, we *are* odd in many ways. And I am not even talking about our fashion sense, goofy laughs, bumper stickers, quirks, and tics. Still, it might surprise us that many people—perhaps the laity more than the clergy—find hope in that we pastors are so completely different from other people. They may chide us about being weird, in both good-natured and mean-spirited ways. But when it comes down to it, when their mother is dying and they want us to pray at her bedside, they do not want or need another affable insurance salesman.

You Will Know the Truth, and It Will Make You Odd

For years I served on the bio-ethics advisory board of a Colorado hospital. From day one I disciplined myself that rather than parrot the best available judgments of health care experts, I would bring something different to these three dozen surgeons, administrators, nurses, social workers, radiologists, general practitioners, ethicists, teachers, and former patients already serving on the board.

I wanted to bring the view of the gospel, how it defines human life, how it configures healing, how it construes suffering, how it demands truthfulness, how it puts no price on the right kind of sacrifice. Let's face it, when we pastors are honest, when we are faithful, and when we think imaginatively, the logic of the gospel is utterly unlike the usual answers that get rounded up and trotted out. Articulating that off-the-beaten-path logic before this bright and diverse group, and injecting into these discussions the rumor of the Holy Spirit as Great and Ultimate Healer (who would otherwise go without any mention in that setting) was my calling.

Things went poorly at first. As new kid on the block, my decidedly offbeat remarks were met with awkward silence until the philosophy professor who chaired us would benignly clear his throat, smile, nod, and gently nudge us forward. He was kind to save face for me. One intensive-care nurse, a strong presence in the best possible sense, would cast a lingering glare in my direction after I spoke, when the rest of the group had already moved on. I became rather used to that glare. I took it personally, because I know that I am inadequate as an exponent of the majestic and ineffable gospel of Jesus Christ, crucified and risen. I am keenly aware of that every day. But I also suffer from a disorder that my mother diagnosed when I was a boy: "He doesn't know enough to go away and shut up when he needs to." (They thought that I might become an attorney.) And so, effectively, I couldn't *not* speak.

Over time, they grew accustomed to my deviations and slowly began to extend me the grace to welcome them. "What will he say this time? This should be good at least for a break in our boredom," was their sense. Over time, they were not laughing but even listening. Over time, my persistence in this perspective with its peculiar logic had created room and a context for hearing subsequent remarks. It often goes like that, asking great perseverance and patience of us pastors, whether it is being heard as a Christian in an overwhelmingly secular environment or bringing a country-club church back into the fold of Christianity, a whole other story unto itself.

When I served on this panel, it was the heyday of Jack Kevorkian before his imprisonment. Inevitably, this issue of mercy killing was considered by the hospital bio-ethics board. This was an issue about which I have spoken loudly and strongly without holding back, denouncing the self-interested slippery slope that euthanasia creates for all ages, while affirming that we have allowed medical technology to put us into positions where euthanasia could seem like a feasible and attractive option.

Anyway, I patiently listened to the many arguments for why euthanasia was beneficent and progressive, how much it would save us in health care and all the suffering that people would be spared. After hearing this out, I was shocked at how easily this conversation turned completely around. And all I really did was warm up the principal theme of chapter 3.

"All of your points are certainly well considered," I offered, "and I would likely agree with you, except that we Christians don't believe that our lives belong to us. We believe that our lives belong to God. We believe life is a gift from God, and to always treat it as such, even to the bitterest end, is better than throwing it back in God's face. Besides that, we also believe that suffering is not the worst thing that can happen to us. We believe that not telling the truth about life being a gift from God—and treating it as such no matter how much it costs us—is something worse." You could have heard a pin drop, but it was a pregnant silence of bright, good people who were thinking very hard. It took years to work up to that moment.

When the time came for me to move to my current church in New England, I bid the group farewell and thanked them. Afterward, the intensive-care nurse made a point of finding me in the hall on my way out, taking my elbow, and saying with something like astonishment and grudging respect, "Half the time I have no idea what you are talking about. Where do you get these things, anyway? I can't believe what comes out of your mouth." It may not sound like much, but I took it

175

as a victory. For any whiff of vindication in our work is fleeting, sweet, and worth receiving as such.

I said nothing at all original and then again nothing else particularly well. But given half a chance, we can count on the gospel not only to make enemies such as have been described in previous chapters, but also to make friends, and often in surprising places. This story is not about being a pastor-hero; I am not one. It is rather about learning to enjoy our oddness rather than apologizing for it. The story is not about needing to be different to draw attention to ourselves in order to stand out as colorful characters. It is about letting the gospel make us different, because it always will if we retain its sharp edges rather than dulling them until the gospel sounds like what everyone else has already said much better elsewhere.

This story is about putting truth before sentimentality by sticking to God's account of truth rather than humankind's, which is too much informed by situation comedies, where conflict is tidily resolved and everyone falls into each other's arms in the last thirty seconds of a half-hour program. It is about how others truly do expect something different from pastors, because deep down they revel in the possibility that God still might touch some in order that these few might touch others in ways that are not of this earth.

The Second Naïveté

As the familiar story has it, at the University of Chicago, after a lengthy conference on his magnificent *Church Dogmatics*, theologian Karl Barth was asked if he could summarize in a simple phrase what the magnum opus of those eleven volumes amounted to. "Jesus loves me, this I know; for the Bible tells me so," came his wry reply. Barth disarmed that august academic assemblage in the same way Mr. Rogers (a Presbyterian minister) once disarmed the urbane Dick Cavett (who was mocking Rogers on his show) by singing to him one of his inanely simple and caring ditties that he would sing to children, a song about their radical acceptability. It melted Cavett's devastating irony, in which no one and nothing were ever quite acceptable.

Compare these responses with our sophomoric attempts to persuade cultured despisers of religion that we may be clergy, but we are pretty much nothing much different from a college professor or a spiritually inclined aromatherapist. And allow yourself the inward refreshment and bracing renewal of feeling a few moments of genuine shame for trading our pastoral birthright for a mess of pottage.

When we clergy are as comfortable as Barth speaking in such transparent and childlike ways about our calling, in a manner laid completely bare, when we are less neurotic about "fitting in," the authority of the pastoral office will be restored. Frankly, I like to think that Barth was able to say such a remarkable thing because he spent early formative years as a local church pastor in Switzerland doing the same things that continue to humble and enlighten, frustrate and challenge me as a local church pastor after serving for twenty-five years.

Historian Martin Marty insists it is no coincidence that the five theologians he considers the greatest in American history—Jonathan Edwards, Horace Bushnell, Walter Rauschenbusch, Reinhold Niebuhr, and Martin Luther King Jr.—all served for a time as pastors. While copious honorary degrees were conferred upon him, Karl Barth never earned the equivalent of a PhD as a graduate student, as incredible and even scandalous as that may sound. (Realizing this inspired me to be bold enough to attempt a book such as this.) Yes, Barth wrote out of prolonged and intense study as well as deep and whole-souled reflection. But the mainspring of his piercing, revolutionary work was participating in Europe's deep crisis of faith after World War I *as a rural pastor* in the Alps. That experience was what finally drove the *Church Dogmatics*.

Many pastors who outlast the rigors of ministry are those for whom these theological dimensions never stop informing everything else that they do. We need more "pastor-theologians" in this sense as opposed to technicians, Rotarians, managers, huggy-bears, and game show hosts. Our calling is not to put a Christian tint on the world's ways of salvation or to trumpet the good life of affluence while protecting our feeble share in it. Our calling is to proclaim and interpret how in Jesus's death and resurrection God has already saved us and now frees us and the world to live in light of God's saving acts. One must be a theologian of this ilk in some way, shape, or form to stay on the right track, avoid blind alleys of secular distraction, and not go mad at the impossible challenges over decades of ministry.

Church consultant and maven Lyle Schaller claims that in the past forty to fifty years the parish ministry has gone from a low-stress and high-status occupation to a high-stress and low-status occupation. For millennia, it has never been easy work, although the popular image persists of the pastor as someone who merely stands up and speaks for an hour or so on Sunday.

Stanley Hauerwas claims that we pastors, like school principals, have the most difficult political challenge of anyone around. After all, apart from election years, senators and representatives rarely see their constituencies. They are whisked about in black limousines. But our people gather weekly and are directly in our face about the most significant and probing questions, the most personal and volatile issues imaginable. Recently, I sat with a leading parishioner who moved back to town, Lee McMaster, recently retired from Dow Chemical after masterfully presiding over its merger with Union Carbide. He told me, with more appreciation and respect than I deserve, "You have a much harder job than I do."

Someone said that parish ministry is at once the most glorious calling and the worst possible job. That sounds damning in the ears of some, but in fact it would put us within a stone's throw of Jesus's life and ministry, which is just where we want to be.

Ours certainly is a life where we must continually find ourselves grounded anew after lofty highs and allow God to pick us up again from devastating lows. We are like Elijah, in one moment defeating the prophets of Baal and then in the next huddled and hidden in a cave (1 Kings 19), feeling sorry for ourselves, wanting to die. My, but we do have a flair for the dramatic, accustomed as we are to constantly being out in front of others! Seeing us in those caves of self-indulgence, the question upon God's lips is "What are you doing in there?"

God's asking this of us will not knock us over like a two-by-four across the back of the head. Rather, God's still, small voice gently beckons us back to our feet to engage anew the fray. God will not force us, but God will persistently beckon us back to the front lines where we are needed. Sadly, today many pastors remain within that cave of introspection and won't come out. They are burned out. They have had enough. They have given up. They are as angry and resentful as Elijah tucked away in that mountain, over having such an exacting calling and impossible duty, over feeling abandoned by God. This book and this chapter are for you. For I know just how you feel, except for the part about giving up on the pastoral ministry.

Even more sadly, today many don't even know of the exciting adventure that awaits us outside of remaining huddled within our personal goals and struggles. For droves of highly gifted young people who once would have considered seminary now opt for becoming investment bankers or fund managers. They must have gotten some wind of what Schaller meant by the reversal of our status and stress. My denomination of over 5,000 churches boasts of only 207 clergy younger than age thirty-five. Hearing Dean Attridge talk about Yale Divinity School, I learned that only 16 percent of last year's graduating class is pointed toward the parish. These alarming trends are not unusual for mainstream churches. Concerted efforts are now being made through seminaries, paraseminary agencies, and denominations to reintroduce a lost generation to the parish ministry as an option for serving God instead of self. This book and this chapter are for such as these as well. For I was pretty much the last person my peers thought would ever become a pastor, and some still openly question whether it was a good idea.

It is true, the church is blessed by many wonderful second-career people who, ironically enough, might have once graduated from the University of Michigan Law School. But parish ministry no longer even appears on the radar of more and more young people. To a sad extent, the dreams of God's reign that the ministry represents are not their dreams anymore. And this trend will reverse itself only as we who are religious for a living reclaim and reassert this dream of God's agency for history being worked out through the church by word and sacrament. We are called to enjoy what we do, and to do it with humor, composure, and courage.

God calls us to dignify what we do by projecting pastor not only as humble servant leader, but also as bold steward of holy mysteries that God deigns to reveal. These sacred mysteries of mercy and grace, reconciliation and redemption, death and resurrection are lifted up and heard nowhere else in our so-called open society. We must mobilize and take action. As Eleanor Roosevelt said, "No one can make you feel inferior without your consent."

Think of all that pivots upon the ministry of the church and its pastoral leadership: what if the world never hears this saving message? Where would we look for hope? What reason would there be to live? Such are the stakes of our vocation, and the grandeur of our striving, and the special place that we occupy in God's heart for what we have willingly taken on. These are no small potatoes. Do not be deceived by the mundane routines that we clergy keep. Something much bigger beneath the surface of things is going on, something that does not fully meet the eye. Eye has not seen, nor ear heard, nor human imagination envisioned what God might be up to through the likes of people and parsons as ordinary as we are.

Reduced in One Small Stroke

So how has one of the most prominent and vocal and universal callings over the past few centuries been effectively muted in recent generations? That could be a book in itself. At least in America, this impulse originates in the inflection of a few simple dismissive words directed at our pastoral posture and our proclamations as preachers: "That is just one more opinion. Your point of view isn't necessarily any better than anyone else's. Tell me, who are you to say such a thing?" In essence, we have returned to where this book began.

179

Of course, if we clergy are simply regurgitating editorial columns of the *National Review* or the *New York Times* from the pulpit, without any transcendent reference point rooted in the will and ways of God in Jesus Christ, this point might be well taken. Or if our covenant with our congregation is strictly social, that is, if we promise to mingle with the membership during the week so that they let us spout for twenty minutes on Sunday, again, we might actually need to hear such an objection.

Still, most have not lost their nerve in lifting up the gospel and no less. There is a bigger picture worth talking about in the struggle over what is godly and what is not. For in modernity, whenever our human preferences clash with the application of the divine will, and a preacher has the nerve to point that out, the disaffected reach first and often for precisely this objection: "That is just your opinion. Who are you to say?"

Clearly, something like this was going on in the case discussed in the last chapter involving the professor and the baptism of his grandchild. In his own way of seeing things, he had as much say as any deacon or pastor about when and under what conditions his grandchild might be baptized. He was a bona fide spiritual consumer, he had his rights, and by golly, he was going to assert them. It is interesting what happens when basic institutions as foundational as the sacraments are no longer so much rites as rights, to be shaped according to personal liking and convenience.

As the saying goes, opinions are like noses, everybody has one. And it is not just those from outside who have become bolder and bolder in reminding us of this as they would narrow and reduce to mere opinion the gospel we attempt to expand and grant dominion over all things in heaven and on earth. And that is why we must make certain to do more than recycle mere opinion in what we proclaim and then make sure that we educate the congregation in who we are and what we are about. Really, it's not our message that we convey; we are but the messengers.

Our authority as pastors is not derived from some special, unique, indescribable spiritual quality that we possess apart from the laity, which is initially exposed like water with divining rods by bishops or ordination committees. Our authority for ministry, like that of the laity, is rooted in our baptism. Have you ever noticed how much an ordination, with its laying on of hands, resembles a baptism? This is no accident. Our ordination is but an extension of the same baptism that all Christians share, with baptism remaining the primary and most essential ordination to Christian ministry, and ordination a secondary, specialized subspecies within baptism.

In other words, what makes us special as pastors is not some remarkable hallowed difference found deep within our souls. It is some remark-

180

able difference that can be made and has been made across the centuries deep within the life of the church in its ministry to the world.

Our authority resides in that the church needs leadership, and God mysteriously taps some on the shoulder (and not others) as witnesses to articulate what God has been up to in the world for the past millennia. This word *witness* is very important in maintaining the balance of who we are and who we are not, in helping us find our voice, and answering objections like "That is just your opinion."

Read about the emergence of Christian preaching as the apostles rise from the ashes of self-doubt, where Peter and John must tell of what God has done despite the threat of imprisonment (Acts 2:14–4:37), and the overwhelming image that emerges is pastor and preacher as witness. God calls us clergy as witnesses who cannot and will not remain silent about the miracle of new life we have beheld in Jesus Christ. Someone has to speak the truth more important than any other truth, and God has chosen us, wonder of wonders. Anything else can happen to us, but we cannot keep quiet about that. With his last words to us before ascending into heaven, Jesus described our essential mission: "You will be my witnesses in Jerusalem, in all Judea and Samaria, and to the ends of the earth" (Acts 1:8).

The purpose of a witness, say, in a courtroom, is not to be original, but to be truthful. The purpose of a witness is not to be amusing, but to make certain the whole story is told, and not only the engaging parts. The purpose of a witness is not to put oneself at the center of the action. Rather it is to allow one's own life, presence, and participation in the story to be the occasion for the telling of a much larger, more pressing story, the consequences of which affect not only the speaker, but everyone imaginable. The witness speaks knowing that upon his or her testimony the freedom or bondage of many could hang in the balance, knowing that the ruling on that testimony will become a benchmark and a precedent for generations to come.

So we speak with great seriousness, clarity and urgency, but not as though everything is up to us. After all, we are but witnesses to the principal actor in the story, who is the God of Israel, whom we take to be the same God in Jesus Christ. We have something to say about speaking the truth, the whole truth, and nothing but the truth. But we have no control over verdicts. In the face of pressure to be successful at the expense of being faithful, keeping God somewhere other than at the center of our testimony is a great temptation and test of our ministries, given our proclivity for substituting our own outsized personalities, the conventional answers to human problems, or "the next big thing," whatever that happens to be at the moment.

And so, if we are faithful witnesses to the gospel, and our people have a problem with how hard or unexpected or strange the message is, we need to point the people back to the source with their disputations rather than abusing our likes. Alas, Jesus promised us our own fair share of this abuse, no matter how much we point back to God as the source of our storytelling and truth-telling. To better understand this, let us consider a recent example of what this might look like.

In the spring of 2003, an unusual number of clergy spoke out on the war against Iraq. Of course, some pastors thought it was wonderful to go after the Islamic infidels. But a remarkable consensus of Christian churches condemned the preemptive attack on Iraq. As this word got out through the pulpits and classes and newsletters, one common response from those in the pews who disagreed was, "Who are you to speak on this? You soft-headed pastors clearly don't know what you are talking about. Better leave tough matters of national security to the experts!"

Others otherwise undermined our word of protest: "How can Christian clergy call into question the policies of our clearly committed Christian president? How can you *not* support him?" Perhaps more interesting than this shallow ploy was that still others assumed that our resistance must necessarily be a matter of political partisanship rather than the witness of following Jesus Christ. Sadly, we have too much brought this last charge on ourselves by indulging in ideological politics of the left and right, imagining that true relevance lies here, rather than sticking to the theological politics of Jesus as revealed in, say, the Sermon on the Mount.

Of course, we later learned it was our government who didn't know what it was talking about in the so-called threat to our national security posed by Iraq *not* having weapons of mass destruction or demonstrable ties to Al Qaeda. We have learned that the most common objection from the houses of worship—our arrogant, headlong rush to war signaled national hubris—was not at all misplaced, as the Iraqi prison abuse scandal at Abu Ghraib sadly and vividly illustrates. The so-called governmental experts who have thrown up their hands before Senate investigative panels, and the clergy who had the temerity to speak out against the war back then, have since reversed roles in terms of "being in the know," at least in the minds of many.

Much has changed in the tone and tenor of our national conversation about this war since those days when U.S. forces first invaded Iraq. Recently, a member of my church had the temerity to stand up during worship and ask why we clergy have remained so *silent* on the war. Did that ever feel like an about-face! The worship setting permitted little room for an immediate exchange with him, but I did call on the man later that afternoon. Thinking that he was going to tell me that he roomed with Dick Cheney in college, and that the church should be selling war bonds during coffee hour, I drove by his house a few times to screw up my courage before walking up the flagstones to knock upon his door.

They welcomed me in, and he patiently explained that during the Vietnam War, the clergy finally did speak up, but it was too late to do any good. What was I waiting for? Why wasn't I saying more? His goading pricked my conscience. Since that first weekend when the war was launched, I had said pitifully little. "Why aren't you doing your job? Why do you think God called you as pastor? Why are you wasting my time? Where is the church in this—missing in action?"

The point is that our prophetic office of ministry is seldom popular, and filling out the authority of those charged with telling the truth in a world of lies will always arouse controversy. But that is who we are. That is what we are asked to do. That is the place God has given us in the larger scheme of things. And until we accept it and make peace with it, our people surely cannot.

Fall down before the One You Serve, You're Going to Get What You Deserve

Another point worth making here is the extent to which the church gets the ministers it deserves based upon its willingness to grant authority to the pastoral office. Those who come to church thinking they are only going to hear one more opinion cannot possibly come away from worship with anything more robust than that. They have sentenced themselves to a flattened, two-dimensional existence. They should not complain when they are bored, because they are the ones who have removed God from the equation. As my friend Martin Copenhaver observes, having the church without God or Jesus must surely be the worst of all possible worlds.

Those who insist and demand that the church speak the whole truth in a self-interested world of lies can expect a different result. It will be something much more dynamic, even if the preacher they passionately agree with one Sunday might be goring their sacred ox the next week. Here God is set loose among us to have God's way with us, to range around our expectations and defy them. Here there is a sense of adventure and the excitement of being on the front lines in a righteous campaign. Here Jesus frees us to realize how much better it is to struggle, suffer, and even die for the sake of the gospel than to submit to more glamorous and popular idols who would string us along benignly to kill for them without a peep.

Carefully read the story of Jesus coming home to his synagogue in Nazareth and preaching to his neighbors (Luke 4:16–28). The people opened the scroll of the prophet Isaiah and gave it to him to read and interpret. He gladly did so, and they got exactly what they asked for, which ended up being much more than they bargained for. Jesus announced the radical good news brought by the Spirit of the Lord, a blanket of grace enfolding not only insiders like his hearers, but even favor for outsiders like the *goyim* they despised. Let the pews be forewarned: never give the Word of God to a prophet of God and expect nothing to happen! Smiles at the first mellifluous words of Joseph's carpenter son over how nice it was to be together soon became scowls as an angry mob chased Jesus to the edge of a cliff, where they would have heaved him had he not beaten a hasty retreat.

As Will Willimon points out, the church will hear God's word authoritatively preached by men and women of God in proportion to their willingness to allow us to unwrap the scroll, and not killing us for reading and interpreting what it actually says. This transcends opinion and personal point of view. As God's people allow us less room, they can expect a correspondingly reduced ministry. It is that simple. No record exists that this Nazareth synagogue any longer benefited from the ministry of the Son of God, who also happened to be their favorite son. Despite how terribly crestfallen Jesus likely felt, whose loss was that ultimately?

They could well have thought that Jesus's message was particular to him, that is, his own opinion, because those who filled that Nazareth pulpit before him dared not actually say all of what Isaiah really said. But there is no mistaking the text. It is still there before us. And they were, after all, the ones who picked the scroll and gave him the text for explication! This is the best possible response to those who would accuse us of merely bringing opinion when in fact we seek to faithfully proclaim the Word and the will of God. The story of God at work among his people for the past thousands of years is bigger than we are. And if the shoe fits, somebody must wear it.

This story that we are handed is not one that we are capable of making up. It is beyond human scale. It has been stewed over and passed down across generations of striving faithful before it was ever put in our hands. Maintaining the authority of the pulpit means having a healthy respect for this story, and respecting this story means letting the story renarrate our lives even before we consider how the presuppositions and biases of our own personal story interpret the scriptural story. We grant the story of God with us a primacy over every other story, even before our own autobigraphical story. As we pastors observe this discipline, what we say will transcend mere "opinion," and it cannot be dismissed as such. We are part of a continuous line of revelation and interpretation that stretches back thousands of years. All of this is swept aside by the undermining remark, "But that is just your point of view."

Of course, all of these considerations are qualified by the simple fact that some people shall find themselves able at life's end to stand before the judgment throne of God. And upon hearing God's verdict upon their lives, they shall say to their Maker, "Well . . . that's just your opinion." What I am most curious about is what God will say or do after that.

Pastoral Authority as Conferred, Granted, and Earned

Martin Copenhaver reminds me that pastoral authority is essentially threefold in nature. It is at once conferred, granted, and earned.[4] Pastoral ministry is a gift simultaneously given by God, received by the people of God, and lived out by the pastors who serve God.

It is conferred in the sense that once we are ordained, we stand in a long line of men and women set apart for service, specially designated by God as his witnesses across the ages. That is nothing small or insignificant. It is true that our vocation is essentially rooted in the same baptism that all Christians share. But as we regularly fill a pulpit or stand behind a communion table or reach into a baptismal font, we become identified with a line of messengers and intercessors stretching deep into the past and far into the future. That pastoral ministry is conferred on us reminds us that it is a gift of the Holy Spirit to the church across the ages. This conferring is God's doing. And we clergy are called to maintain and exemplify that this is a cherished gift to us, no less than to the church, no matter how difficult our service is.

Pastoral ministry is also granted us as we enter the life of a local church. The people of God whom we serve and admonish look to us with expectation as we come to them out of that long line of prophets, apostles, and teachers. When we are new in a local church, we do not have to carve a role out for ourselves from scratch. Pastors have (usually) served in that local congregation before. And just as those pastors were granted a place of honor and influence within individual families as well as in the gathered community, so we newly arrived are granted this running start. Before the people of God know much about us or have any other reason to listen to us or heed us, our ministry is received as a gift as we are granted a unique place in the common life of the church.

Pastoral ministry is also earned, as pastors do not take for granted what God has created in our pastoral office and what God's people grant us but respond to this generosity from above and from below in ways befitting our vocation. In some ways we shall inevitably disappoint expectations, and in other ways we shall perhaps exceed them. Our strengths and weaknesses become so visibly exposed over a relatively short time that we quickly become a mixed report—neither saviors nor villains—in the mind of most people. But the rise and fall of our best and worst does not necessarily carry the day with the final word on this. For as long as we remain clearly convicted by the gospel and deeply concerned for our people's well-being, we attend to the essentials of establishing a basis for pastoral leadership across time. And this nearly universally makes an impression upon local churches, apart from the full-of-themselves Corinthian churches or the asleep-at-the-wheel Laodicean churches.

Personally, I have found that shepherding people through the stress and exhilaration of life's shared transitions looms particularly large here. How do we respond to settings where there is birth and death, marriage and divorce, baptism and confirmation? How do we speak for God and stand by our people through the testing of natural disasters, wars, economic depressions, and terrorist attacks? How do we act as stewards of the Christian seasons and high holy days, including Christmas, Easter, and Pentecost? The answers will go a long way in determining what authority we shall earn on top of what God confers and the people grant us.

Of course, this means that it truly takes years to earn our pastoral authority. For the unfolding of life like this is slow and requires patience, slogging through both the good and bad, becoming a reliable and trustworthy constant as the mouthpiece of God and advocate for the people, like Moses leading Israel through forty years of wilderness wandering. If we are overeager soon to become the "beloved pastor," we will likely be disappointed. For as we truly confront people with the cosmic and countercultural gospel entrusted us, and as we speak out of the sacred mysteries of which we are stewards, ever speaking the truth in love, "beloved pastor" will not come soon, and we shouldn't worry about it too much. Frankly, "beloved pastor" is usually how the church in retrospect views former pastors who acted in their best interests even as they could not notice it at the time.

The Pastors We Need

Søren Kierkegaard summarized the foregoing in these words on the pastors we need:

[P]astors who are able to split up "the crowd" and turn it into individuals; pastors who would not set up too great study-requirements and would want nothing less than to dominate; pastors who, if possible, are powerfully eloquent but are no less eloquent in keeping silent and enduring without complaining; pastors who, if possible, know the human heart but are no less learned in refraining from judging and denouncing; pastors who know how to use authority through the art of making sacrifices; pastors who are disciplined and educated and are prepared to obey and to suffer so they would be able to mitigate, admonish, build up, move, but able to constrain—not with force, anything but, no, constrain by their own obedience, and above all patiently, to suffer all the rudeness of the sick without being disturbed, no more than the physician is disturbed by the patient's abusive language and kicks during the operation.[5]

So what does this look like in action? Any pastor who regularly scolds a church will never attain much authority. (Joseph Campbell: "Preachers make a mistake . . . when they try to talk people into belief; better they reveal the radiance of their own discovery."[6]) Any pastor who seeks to simplify the gospel by reducing it to terms that are already within people's spiritual, emotional, and intellectual repertoire will lose authority as he or she distorts, reduces, and falsifies the faith. (Johnston McKay: ". . . religion is not about things that are natural, clear, simple and unambiguous."[7])

Any pastor who keeps first external rewards in the form of creating a sensation by filling a market niche will lack stature. (Eugene Peterson: "We're not selling anything, and we're not providing goods and services. If a pastor is not discerning and discriminating . . . then the demands or the desires of the congregation can dominate . . . and that creates the conditions for nonpastoral work."[8]) Any pastor who never takes the risk of actively challenging a congregation and stretching the borders of their faith will command limited respect. (Dr. Martin Luther King Jr.: "Ultimately a genuine leader is not a searcher of consensus but a molder of consensus."[9])

A story is told of Samuel Wells, the vicar of a small Anglican church in a marginal neighborhood. One Sunday, as the Eucharist was being celebrated, a gang of surly adolescents burst into the church. While the congregation looked on in horror, the youths stood before the altar and their leader demanded, "Are you going to give us some of that?"

"If you look behind you," Wells responded, "you will see a small group of people who are here to do the most important thing in their lives. I don't think this is the most important thing in your life. I hope it may become so one day. But for now, I suggest that you wait outside until we've finished, and then we'll have a chat about what things are really important and how we learn how to do them." Amazingly, the rowdy boys complied and took up the vicar on his invitation, staying for that chat.[10]

That is pastoral authority. If we do this, we will not only recover our voice just when the world most needs what we have to say, but we will also live and prosper in the favor of God, and so will the Church of Jesus Christ.

NOTES

Chapter 1

1. Adam Liptak, Courts Weighing Rights of States to Curb Aid for Religion Majors, *New York Times*, August 10, 2003, 1.

2. Brian D. McLaren, *A New Kind of Christian: A Tale of Two Friends on a Spiritual Journey* (San Francisco: Jossey-Bass, 2001), 17.

3. Chris Hedges, *Harvard Divinity School Bulletin*, Fall/Winter, 2003.

4. *The Vision of Piers Plowman*, ed. Rev. Walter W. Skeat (Oxford: Oxford University Press, 1969), passus XV, line 519.

5. Dr. Martin Luther King Jr., "Letter from Birmingham Jail," in *A Testament of Hope: The Essential Writings of Martin Luther King, Jr.*, edited by James Melvin Washington (San Francisco: Harper and Row, 1986), 300.

6. C. S. Lewis, *Mere Christianity* (New York: Macmillan, 1972), 63.

7. *The Journals of Søren Kierkegaard*, trans. Alexander Dru (San Francisco: Harper and Row, 1959), 192.

8. Søren Kierkegaard, *Journal*, as quoted in *Works of Love*, translated by Howard and Edna Hong (New York: Harper & Row, 1962) translators' introduction, 11.

9. Karl Barth, *Dogmatics in Outline*, trans. G. T. Thompson (New York: Harper, 1959), 83.

10. Ibid., 87.

11. Millard Fuller, personal communication, October 1982.

Chapter 2

1. Robert Clyde Johnson, *The Meaning of Christ* (Philadelphia: Westminster, 1975), 37.

2. Allen R. Hilton, "Bridge-Building: An Ordination Paper," unpublished, March 2005, 3–4.

3. Quoted by Miroslav Volf in "Dancing for God," *Christian Century,* September 6, 2003, 35.

4. Transcript of "Now: Bill Moyers Interviews Julie Taymor," (October 25, 2002), www.pbs.org.

5. Personal communication from the Reverend John McFadden, Senior Minister, First Congregational Church, Appleton, WI. Italics mine.

6. G. F. Handel, *Messiah* (vocal score).

Chapter 3

1. *City Slickers,* directed by Ron Underwood (1991; Hollywood: Columbia Pictures).

2. Søren Kierkegaard, "On the Difference Between a Genius and an Apostle," in *The*

189

Present Age (San Francisco: Harper and Row, 1962), 106.

3. Susan Miller, quoted in "Century-marks," *Christian Century*, August 9, 2003, 6.

4. P. T. Forsyth, *Positive Preaching and the Modern Mind* (1907).

5. Hymn as printed in the Order of Worship, Family Service, October 2000, St. Peter's Church, Ipsley, Redditch, England.

6. Portions of this story are told in Charles Colson's *The Body: Being Light in Darkness* (Dallas: Word, 1992), and also at Acts International, "The Light of Christmas," http://actsweb.org/christmas/light1.htm.

Chapter 4

1. G. K. Chesterton, *The Brave New Family* (San Francisco: Ignatius Press, 1990), 24.

2. Oswald Chambers, *My Utmost for His Highest* (Oswald Chambers Publication Association, 1992), entry for November 1.

Chapter 5

1. L. Gregory Jones, "Tale of Two T-shirts,"*Christian Century*, September 7, 2004, 47.

2. John Buchanan, "Authority Figures," *Christian Century*, August 16–23, 2000, 821.

3. Henri Nouwen, *The Wounded Healer* (Garden City, NY: Image Books, 1979), 41–42.

4. Mark R. Schwehn, "Christianity and Postmodernism: Uneasy Allies," quoted in Marva J. Dawn, "Pop Spirituality or Genuine Story?: The Church's Gifts for Postmodern Times, *Theology Matters* 6 (September–October 2000): 6–16.

5. Douglas John Hall, "Disciplines and Ministry," *Journal for Preachers*, Lent 2000, 14.

6. Miroslav Volf, "Rules, Rules, and More Rules," *Christian Century*, February 28, 2001, 26.

7. Ibid.

8. John McFadden, personal communication, June 12, 2001.

9. Alice Camille, "Long Live the King," *US Catholic*, November 2000, 24.

10. Donald W. McCullough, *The Trivialization of God: The Dangerous Illusion of a Manageable Deity* (Colorado Springs: Navpress, 1995), 256.

Chapter 6

1. Eberhard Jungel, "Toward the Heart of the Matter," trans. Paul E. Capetz, *Christian Century*, February 27, 1991, 228.

2. Douglas John Hall, "Discipline and Ministry," *Journal for Preachers*, Lent 2000, 14.

3. Eugene H. Peterson, "Transparent Lives," *Christian Century*, November 29, 2003, 24.

4. Trans. J. E. Crawford Flitch (New York: Dover, 1954).

5. Alan Wolfe, *The Transformation of American Religion: How We Actually Live Our Faith* (New York: Free Press, 2003).

6. Alan Wolfe interview, *Homiletics*, March–April, 2004.

7. C. S. Lewis, *The Screwtape Letters* (New York: Macmillan, 1961), 9.

8. R. Scott Appleby, "When They Say Jesus, Which Jesus Do They Mean?" Review of Stephen Prothero, *American Jesus* (New York: Farrar, Straus and Giroux, 2003), *New York Times*, January 8, 2004.

9. T. S. Eliot, *Poems* (1919).

10. Alice Camille, "Long Live the King," *US Catholic*, November 2000, 34.

11. Quoted in Donald W. McCullough, *The Trivialization of God: The Dangerous Illusion of a Manageable Deity* (Colorado Springs: Navpress, 1995), 151.

Chapter 7

1. Roberta Smith, "Memo to the Art Museums: Don't Give Up on Art," *New York Times*, December 3, 2000, sec. 2.

2. Robert Bellah, *Habits of the Heart* (Berkeley: University of California Press, 1985), 77.

3. Smith, "Memo."

4. George Santayana, *Reason and Religion* (New York: Collier Books, 1962), 10–11.

5. Martin Copenhaver, *The Village Spire* (newsletter of the Wellesley Congregational Church) Wellesley, MA, vol. 8, no. 11, February 9–23, 2003.

6. Anthony B. Robinson, *Transforming Congregational Culture* (Grand Rapids: Eerdmans, 2003), 23.

7. Carol Zaleski, "Faith Matters, Habits of Hobbits," *Christian Century*, June 14, 2003, 37.

Chapter 8

1. Karl Barth, *Church Dogmatics*, I.1, 60.

2. Anthony B. Robinson, "Back to Basics: Rx for Congregational Health," *Christian Century*, July 26, 2003, 25.

3. Leonard Sweet, *A Is for Abductive* (Grand Rapids: Zondervan, 2003), 31.

4. Clarence Jordan, *Power from Parables*, audiotape series, Koinonia Partners.

5. L. Gregory Jones, "Welcome Interruption," *Christian Century*, June 1, 2004, 31.

6. Barbara Brown Taylor, "Stand and Deliver," *Christian Century*, October 18, 2003, 28.

Chapter 9

1. Bonnie Kittel, oral communication, January 13, 1977.

2. Quoted in Robert Clyde Johnson, *The Meaning of Christ* (Philadelphia: Westminster, 1958), 11.

3. Godfried Daneels, as quoted in *Context*, Martin E. Marty, ed., November 15, 2001, 6.

4. Ibid.

Chapter 10

1. Clarence Jordan, *Power from Parables*, audiotape series, Koinonia Partners.

2. Søren Kierkegaard, *The Present Age and Of the Difference between a Genius and an Apostle*, trans. Alexander Dru (San Francisco: Harper and Row, 1962).

3. Stanley Hauerwas and William Willimon, *Resident Aliens: Life in the Christian Colony* (Nashville: Abingdon Press, 1989), 145.

4. Martin Copenhaver, oral communication, August 10, 2004.

5. *Søren Kierkegaard's Journals and Papers*, Vol. 6, Autobiographical, part 2, 1848–1855, ed. and trans. Howard V. Hong and Edna H. Hong, assist. Gregor Malantshuk (Bloomington and London: Indiana University Press, 1978), 60–61.

6. Bill Moyers, quoting Joseph Campbell, "Centurymarks," *Christian Century*, July 13, 2004, 7.

7. Johnston McKay, quoted in "Centurymarks," *Christian Century*, July 26, 2003, 6.

8. David Wood, "Eugene Peterson on Pastoral Ministry," *Christian Century*, March 13–20, 2002, 18–25.

9. Martin Luther King Jr., *A Testament of Hope: The Essential Writings of Martin Luther King, Jr.,* ed. James Melvin Washington (San Francisco: Harper and Row, 1986), 276.

10. Samuel Wells, quoted in "Centurymarks," *Christian Century*, July 13, 2004, 6.

191

Acknowledgments

I was able to pursue and complete this writing project due to the generous financial support and encouragement of the Louisville Institute. Their ongoing Pastors' Sabbatical Grant Program allowed me freedom to gather my thoughts and writings on this theme, now published by Brazos Press decades after the initial few ideas were first rubbed together, and four years now after my sabbatical. Rodney Clapp of Brazos Press has been exceptional at each step of the process.

Also, I lift up the Ekklesia Project, a movement of church leaders and Christian Scholars who published my booklet, "Authority, Freedom, and the Dreams that We Are Made Of," containing many seminal ideas for this book. Parts of other chapters originate in a paper, "Who Are You to Say?" presented in 1992 at the Craigville Colloquy of the United Church of Christ, Craigville, Massachusetts.

Most especially, I wish to thank the members of the First Congregational Church, United Church of Christ, Ridgefield, Connecticut, for the sabbatical leave, the continuing education, and the vacation time when I wrote this book. It is written by, for, and out of the loving hearts, thoughtful minds, and faithful disciples of this New England church where God has called and abundantly blessed me to lead.

Finally, as I escaped to seize those moments of sabbatical, continuing education, and vacation, friends and loved ones offered quiet settings for my writing. For opening their homes and offering gifts of glad hospitality, I heartily thank all who took me in: Walter and Margaret Romanow for their Homosassa, Florida, tropical bungalow, complete with surrounding nature refuge; the Reverend Martin and Karen Copenhaver for their charming Yankee retreat home gazing down on Woodstock, Vermont, as well as their sabbatical Tuscan villa overlooking renaissance embers glowing below at night in Florence; Garth and Marcela Rosenberger for their open-air condo ajoining the egret and coyote marches of Huntington Beach, California; Ray and Marcia Freeman for their civilized Cape Cod idyll in the heart of Chatham, Massachusetts; Dr. Lewis and pam Trusheim for their warm, woodsy moose house rising among the White Mountain foothills of Intervale, New Hampshire; Alesix Peter and Timothy Hastings for generous hospitality when it mattered most right close to home in Ridgefield, Connecticut. If nothing else, it's a well-traveled book, owing to the kindness of beloved friends.